品牌联名战略

PINPAI LIANMING ZHANLÜE

对消费者影响的实证研究

DUI XIAOFEIZHE YINGXIANG DE SHIZHENG YANJIU

张 可 ◎ 著

上海大学出版社

·上海·

图书在版编目(CIP)数据

品牌联名战略对消费者影响的实证研究／张可著. ——上海：上海大学出版社,2021.11
ISBN 978-7-5671-4378-4

Ⅰ.①品… Ⅱ.①张… Ⅲ.①品牌战略—影响—消费者—研究 Ⅳ.①F273.2②F036.3

中国版本图书馆 CIP 数据核字(2021)第 223085 号

责任编辑　刘　强
封面设计　柯国富
技术编辑　金　鑫　钱宇坤

品牌联名战略对消费者影响的实证研究

张　可　著

上海大学出版社出版发行
(上海市上大路 99 号　邮政编码 200444)
(http://www.shupress.cn　发行热线 021-66135112)
出版人　戴骏豪

*

南京展望文化发展有限公司排版
上海颛辉印刷厂有限公司印刷　各地新华书店经销
开本 890mm×1240mm　1/32　印张 10.25　字数 239 千字
2021 年 11 月第 1 版　2021 年 11 月第 1 次印刷
ISBN 978-7-5671-4378-4/F·219　定价　75.00 元

版权所有　侵权必究
如发现本书有印装质量问题请与印刷厂质量科联系
联系电话：021-57602918

前　言

笔者在北京大学求学期间师从甘怡群教授,攻读积极心理学和统计学。因缘际会之下在光华管理学院徐菁教授课题组从事助研工作,从而接触到了消费者行为这一学科。这段助研的经历也让笔者萌生了从行为科学角度研究营销乃至更广义的经济管理问题的想法。后来在香港大学跟随博士生导师万雯教授和 Sara Kim 副教授学习的过程,也让笔者愈发坚定自己的选择。

身处香港这样一座融合中西文化、商业气氛浓厚的城市,笔者开始留心观察身边的营销现象。其中最吸引笔者的问题便来自消费者的品牌感知与品牌选择。经历了四十多年的改革开放,今天的中国营销从业者正在逐渐强化品牌意识,努力打造属于中国人自己的国货品牌。而在这个过程中,他们既经历过风光无限的时刻,也遭遇过迷茫乃至挫败。这也对今天的中国营销学者提出了要求:我们需要在学术研究上为中国的品牌战略和品牌实践提供理论依据,从而更好地让中国人的品牌"强起来,走出去"。这也构成了笔者在品牌战略领域进行研究的原动力。

在对国内外多种品牌战略和数十万字的商务调研报告进行分析后,笔者把目光投向了品牌联名(Co-branding)这一领域。品牌联名,顾名思义,是指两个或多个品牌之间的合作和联盟(Cunha, Forehand, and Angle 2015; Simonin and Ruth 1998)。在过去的三十年中,它已逐渐成为国际上一种广泛流行的品牌战略。当共同创建新产品或提供新服务时,品牌联名可以使合作品牌实现品牌资产(Brand equity)的共享和品牌资源的互补,从而达到双赢的效果。目前营销学界对于品牌联名的研究主要集中在两个方面:第一,基于品牌方本身的研究主要探讨品牌间合作的选择和产品/服务开发策略(Van der Lans, Van den Bergh, and Dieleman 2014);第二,从消费者视角的品牌联名研究则主要集中于该战略对于消费者品牌态度的影响(Monga and Lau-Gesk 2007)。

然而,越来越多基于心理学和认知神经科学的研究指出,品牌战略对于消费者判断的影响并不局限于对品牌的整体态度,还可以影响到其他的层面。例如有研究相继探讨了品牌战略如何影响消费者对品牌人格(Brand personality)的感知(Aaker, Vohs, and Mogilner 2010),以及消费者对产品的感官体验(McClure, Li, Tomlin, Cypert, Montague, and Montague 2004)。这也意味着品牌联名对于消费者判断的影响研究还存在巨大的延伸空间。基于此,本书从消费者行为的视角入手,运用行为科学中的实验法,结合心理学中的推断形成(Inference-making)理论,系统探索了品牌联名如何影响消费者对品牌与产品的判断。笔者相信,本书有助于厘清品牌联名战略在微观(消费者个体)层面上的影响和作用,而本研究的发现对于品牌从业者和品牌理论相关的研究者也具有一定的理论和实践意义。

本书致力于为品牌联名相关的消费者行为研究提供一个相对全面的总结和归纳,写作逻辑也遵循笔者从问题提出、理论构建到实证检验的完整路径。具体来说,本书的第一章介绍了品牌联名的概念发展、经典理论、研究范式和研究结论。在此基础上,笔者提出可以从消费者推论这一新视角进行品牌联名的相关研究。在

第二章中,笔者系统整理和总结了过往文献中消费者推论的相关理论和研究发现,并指出了当前消费者推论领域的部分研究空白。第三章则梳理了品牌相关信息如何影响消费者对品牌和产品属性的推论,并提出研究品牌联名对品牌/产品推论影响的新思路。这三章在概念形成和理论框架上互为补充,从而帮助我们建立起探讨品牌联名战略(自变量)、消费者推论(中介变量),以及品牌与产品属性判断(因变量)的完整理论框架。接下来,在本书的第四章和第五章中,笔者则通过多个基于行为实验法的实证研究,探讨了品牌联名如何影响消费者对品牌和产品的判断。第四章通过行为实验研究探讨了品牌联名对象传递的价值观如何影响到消费者对联名产品感官属性(例如重量、容量、卡路里含量)的判断。本研究指出,个体在进行感官判断时会调用自己的机体反应(具身模拟理论)作为推论的依据。基于这一理论,该研究揭示了品牌联名影响消费者对联名产品判断的全新作用机制,从而在品牌联名、消费者推论与感官营销这三个研究领域之间架起了桥梁。第五章则通过行为实验的方法探讨了与知名品牌联名这一近年来广受欢迎的品牌联名战略如何影响消费者对初创品牌的判断。基于消费者推论与品牌人格的相关理论,该研究发现与知名品牌进行联名会影响消费者对初创品牌不同人格维度(温暖 vs.能力)的判断。在当前创新创业的时代背景下,这一研究的发现对于初创品牌的品牌定位和品牌战略选择具有很强的实践意义。最后,在本书的第六章,笔者对本书第四章和第五章所提及的研究内容进行了拓展,并提出了从消费者个人因素、消费者与品牌关系因素、文化因素这三个角度研究品牌联名作用与效果的新思路和新框架。笔者期待这种理论综述与实证研究结合的写作形式,能够做到深入浅出,为读者提供相对愉悦的阅读体验。本书的理论研讨部分收集并整理了大量文献资料,而实证研究部分则通过行为实验手段收集了大量的数据,这些研究受到了国家自然科学基金面上项目、上海市浦江人才计划项目、上海市晨光人才计划项目的资助,在此特别鸣谢:

(1) 上海市浦江人才计划项目,18PJC063,品牌联合战略对新生公司的影响:基于消费者信息加工模式的探究;

(2) 国家自然科学基金面上项目,72172087,旅游直播如何助推目的地旅游:基于代言人类型的说服力模型;

(3) 上海市晨光人才计划项目,18CG45,零售场景中的拥挤环境对消费者产品偏好的影响研究。

本书稿的想法也起源于笔者在攻读博士学位期间开展的消费者行为研究,在此衷心感谢在笔者的博士学习阶段给予诸多指导的万雯教授、Sara Kim副教授、贾轼副教授和贾鹤副教授。他们的言传身教让笔者受益良多。同时也特别感谢在写作本书过程中给予宝贵建议和帮助的许销冰教授、才源源副教授和吕斐斐副教授。笔者希望本书能抛砖引玉,为品牌管理领域的从业者和研究者提供些许助益。随着营销科学的发展,书中的理论与研究也会在新时代拥有全新的解读和完善的空间。在此,笔者也希望广大读者和同仁能不吝赐教,这也将是笔者人生道路上的重要财富。

张　可

上海大学悉尼工商学院　讲师

2021年3月于上海嘉定

目录 Contents

第一章 品牌联名背后的心理学理论 ………1
第一节 品牌联名相关概念和对应的心理学理论 ………4
第二节 品牌联名的营销学研究 ………15

第二章 消费者推论：推论类型与推论目标 ………19
第一节 同化推论与补偿推论 ………24
第二节 对于感官信息的推论 ………28

第三章 品牌相关信息如何影响消费者推论 ………35
第一节 品牌相关信息如何影响消费者对品牌的推断 ………37
第二节 品牌相关信息如何影响消费者对产品属性的推断 ………39

第四章 从感知重要性到物理重量判断：品牌联名如何改变消费者对产品的重量感知 ………45
第一节 研究背景 ………48
第二节 文献综述 ………56

第三节　实证研究部分 67
第四节　关于本章实证研究的综合讨论 99

第五章　与知名品牌联名会帮助还是损害初创品牌？ 113
第一节　研究背景 115
第二节　文献综述 120
第三节　实证研究部分 128
第四节　关于本章实证研究的综合讨论 150

第六章　全书总结与未来研究方向 159
第一节　从消费者推论角度探讨未来可能的研究方向 164
第二节　从品牌联名角度探讨未来可能的研究方向 172

参考文献 210

第一章

品牌联名背后的心理学理论

在已经过去的十年,我们很容易发现一个现象:越来越多的新产品和新服务的广告上开始同时出现两个不同的品牌的名字。例如在 2020 年,国际知名奢侈品牌 Dior 和运动品牌 Air Jordan 进行跨界合作,共同推出了特别款球鞋。有趣的是,这种多品牌联合打造产品的风潮也已席卷了国货界。于是我们看到了喜茶,这款热度极高的中国茶饮品牌,在过去的三年中与多达 50 多个品牌进行合作促销和推广。这其中,既有喜茶和 M&M 巧克力豆合作推出新饮品,也有喜茶与 QQ 音乐合作推出绿钻卡。根据相关学术文献,这种两个甚至更多品牌进行合作从而共同生产、促销新产品和新服务的模式,可以称之为品牌联名(Cunha, Forehand, and Angle 2015)。

最早的关于品牌联名的记载可以追溯到 1937 年。当时,时尚设计师 Elsa Schiaparelli 将画家 Salvador Dalí 绘制的龙虾图案融入自己的服装中,创造出了一款全新的时尚服装"龙虾装"(Lobster Dress),大受好评。这种"时尚品牌×艺术家"的合作模式也为后来的时尚业人士提供了借鉴。时至今日,品牌联名早已超出了这一范畴,拥有了更多不同的形式。这些品牌联名既可能存在于两个相似行业的品牌之间(例如联名推出冰激凌的喜茶与和路雪均从事食品行业),也可能横跨了两个听上去风马牛不相及的行业(例如前文提到的化妆品品牌与运动鞋品牌的组合);既可以是品牌与真实人物的联动(例如电影《捉妖记》中的动画角色与真人明星),也可以是品牌与影视中的虚拟人物形象的结合(例如泸州老窖和动画电影《姜子牙》中的卡通人物的组合)。可以说,品牌联名战略正处于自诞生以来最红火的阶段。

为什么品牌联名战略会在今天如此受追捧?做出联名决策的背后存在着企业和品牌的何种考量?品牌联名战略又将如何在心理上影响消费者的判断与决策?本章通过对品牌联名相关概念、理论以及研究内容的梳理,展现这一品牌战略的动因和框架。

第一节 品牌联名相关概念和对应的心理学理论

一、基于顾客的品牌资产

品牌(Brand)可以说是市场营销中最重要的概念之一。在各种经典的市场营销学教材和文献中,品牌被定义为一种可以用来标识当前卖方产品或服务的工具。它囊括了一个产品或服务的名称、术语、符号、设计,以及其他特征,从而使得该产品或服务与其他卖家的竞品区别开来(Kotler 1991)。Keller(2020)指出,品牌的诞生本质上是基于差异化的需求。树立良好的品牌有助于让一家公司得到更多关注度、增加商业价值、产生新顾客、增加员工自豪感和满足感、在市场中受到信任,并更好地支持广告促销。因此,品牌不仅仅是一个用于增加企业利润的工具,本身也具有资产属性。

品牌研究者试图从企业(组织)层面和消费者(个体)层面来定义与测量品牌资产。从企业层面定义品牌资产的研究者主要将品牌看作一种无形资产,主张品牌资产应该通过品牌对企业经济利润的贡献度来进行衡量(Simon and Sullivan 1993)。与之不同的是,从消费者层面定义品牌资产的研究者则从心理学角度出发,认为品牌资产来源于消费者对品牌属性和关联信息的感知与态度,因此将消费者层面的品牌资产称为基于顾客的品牌资产(Customer-based brand equity)(Keller 1993)。

Keller(1993)认为,基于顾客的品牌资产出现的前提条件是:顾客对品牌存在一定熟悉度,并且对品牌存在积极、强烈和独特的关联记忆。这一概念也和营销学中的另一个经典概念——定位(Positioning),存在异曲同工之妙。因为本质上,这两个概念都基于认知心理学中的学习和记忆(Learning and memory)理论。

记忆的关联网络模型(Associative network memory model)认为人们对事物的记忆和知识是通过节点(Nodes)和节点之间的链接(Links)组织起来的(Anderson 1983;Srull and Wyer 1989)。其中,节点是一个一个抽象的知识和概念(例如事物的类别),而节点之间的链接的强弱则反映了这两个概念在人的记忆网络中关联的紧密程度。持有这一观点的研究者(Collins and Loftus 1975;Raaijmakers and Shiffrin 1981;Ratcliff and McKoon 1988)认为,人类的记忆提取过程遵循"激活扩散"(Spreading activation)的原则:一旦一个节点被激活(通过外部刺激唤起,或者通过自己的刻意回忆),那么相邻的节点也会被激活。以品牌为例,一旦消费者想起可口可乐这一品牌,那么可口可乐的品牌名本身就是一个节点,而与之相连的节点包括消费者关于可乐的知识和判断,以及他们关于该品牌可乐的体验和回忆,譬如可乐的颜色、口感,甚至是他们曾经消费的场景。

基于这一理论,Keller(2003)指出,基于顾客的品牌资产主要来自两个大类:品牌觉知(Brand awareness)和品牌形象(Brand image)。其中,品牌觉知关系到该品牌是否在消费者记忆中存储并能及时被消费者回忆和提取,而品牌形象则取决于该品牌在消费者记忆网络中的延伸和关联评价。

Chandon(2003)指出,品牌觉知和品牌形象拥有不同的量化方法。具体而言,品牌觉知可以通过消费者对品牌的回忆(Recall)与再认(Recognition)来衡量。例如,市场调查人员可以让消费者列举出自己喝过的饮料的品牌名称(回忆),或者给消费者呈现一系列的饮料品牌来询问他们是否对该品牌有印象(再认)。而近年来,随着计算机技术的发展,眼动仪等设备也可以捕捉消费者对品牌的注意力分配,从而提供了另一种意义上的品牌觉知测量方式。

而在品牌形象上,研究者则从社会知觉的角度开发了不同的测量指标。例如,Aaker(1997)认为品牌也和人类一样,具有人格特征。基于此提出的品牌人格理论(Brand personality theory)用五个不同的人格维度来量化品牌形象,包括真诚(Sincerity)、刺激(Excitement)、能力(Competence)、精细(Sophistication)、粗犷(Ruggedness)。在每一个人格维度上,均开发了一系列形容词来进行描述,从而形成了一个包含42个指标的品牌人格量表(Brand personality scale,BPS)。其他研究者(Fournier and Alvarez 2012)则指出,品牌形象中最重要的两个维度是温暖(Warmth)和能力(Competence),其中他们对能力的定义几乎等同于Aaker(1997)的五维度理论中的能力维度,而他们对温暖维度的定义则表明该维度接近于Aaker(1997)理论中的真诚维度。

研究者指出,基于顾客的品牌资产的建立,其实涵盖了从增强品牌感知到建立品牌依恋的全过程(Chandon 2003;Keller 2003)。具体而言,消费者需要先对品牌产生感知(成功回忆和再认品

第一章 品牌联名背后的心理学理论

牌),进而在记忆网络中构建该品牌形象(功能性的属性和体验性的属性),然后才能逐步发展到对该品牌的理性和感性评价,并最终基于这些评价产生对品牌的忠诚度。这一过程也被称为品牌知识的金字塔模型(The brand knowledge pyramid)(图1-1)。

图1-1 品牌知识的金字塔模型

为了增强品牌资产,企业往往会采用一系列的品牌战略。而其中最被广泛采用的方法包含品牌代言、品牌延伸、品牌联名。其中品牌延伸是从公司内部进行潜力挖掘,而品牌代言和品牌联名则借助于外来的资源和力量。下面,笔者从品牌延伸开始逐一对这三种经典品牌战略进行介绍。

二、品牌延伸

品牌延伸被定义为业已成熟的品牌在现有品牌名的基础上开发其他产品(Völckner and Sattler 2006)。这种品牌延伸既可以是在原有产品范畴内的开发(也被称为近品牌延伸,Near brand extension),也可以是在原有范畴之外的拓展(也被称为远品牌延伸,Far brand extension)。很多营销从业者认为,无论是近品牌延伸还是远品牌延伸,都能给原有母品牌带来积极的作用。因为借助现有品牌推广新产品,意味着在营销成本上的降低(不需要另起炉灶重新打造一个品牌),同时也会反向促进母品牌自身品牌资产的增长(例如品牌延伸意味着向消费者表明自身覆盖了更多的品类,从而可以吸引到更多潜在消费者)。

然而在现实的商业世界中,品牌延伸的失败率却远远超过了百分之五十(Marketing 2003)。这也使得很多研究者开始探讨哪些因素可能会影响到品牌延伸的效果。一系列研究从母品牌自身特征、母品牌和延伸品牌之间的关系、消费者的个体差异因素等方面进行了探讨。

从母品牌自身特征方面进行的探讨：一系列研究指出，母品牌自身的质量和性能(Quality and strength)(Smith and Park 1992)以及所包含的产品生产线数量(Number of products affiliated with a brand)(Dacin and Smith 1994)都和品牌延伸是否成功息息相关。例如，当母品牌含有越多的产品生产线(也意味着更多元化的产品品类)时，消费者越容易对其品牌延伸抱有信心。这都是基于消费者对品牌自身能力和专业程度的考量的结果。

从母品牌和延伸品牌之间的关系方面进行的探讨：Aaker和Keller(1990)指出，延伸品牌和母品牌之间的匹配性(Extension fit)会显著影响品牌延伸的效果。他们指出，消费者往往会基于延伸品牌和母品牌产品之间的互补性(与现有产品在功能上互相补充)、替代性(可以替代现有产品)、可转换性(与现有产品共享制造过程)来判断延伸品牌的匹配性。当延伸品牌和母品牌之间匹配程度较低时，消费者会面临信息加工困难(例如难以想象母品牌如何将自身的技能和专业应用于延伸出来的新产品)，从而降低对品牌延伸的信心。

从消费者的个体差异因素方面进行的探讨：Yorkston等人(2010)发现，消费者对延伸品牌的接受度，一定程度上取决于他们自己对品牌人格的信念。具体而言，当消费者认为品牌人格本身是具有可塑性(Malleable)而不是一成不变(Fixed)时，他们更能接受母品牌进行远品牌延伸。Su、Monga和Jiang(2021)则发现，消费者的自我概念模糊性(Self-concept ambiguity)越高，他们越倾向于使用辩证思维（Dialetical thinking）来合理化延伸品牌和母品牌之间的关联，从而增加他们对远品牌延伸的接受度。这些研究的出发点均是消费者自身信息加工模式可能会增加他们对远品牌延伸的合理化认知，从而为支持远品牌延伸找到了更多的理由。

延伸品牌往往会反过来对母品牌产生反馈效应（Feedback effect）（Dwivedi, Merrilees, and Sweeney 2010）。其中，品牌延伸的成功（vs.失败）会使消费者将对延伸品牌的正面态度（vs.负面态度）转嫁到母品牌上，从而出现正向（vs.负向）的反馈效应。然而有趣的是，即便品牌延伸成功，也有可能对母品牌造成负面影响。其中，品牌稀释现象（Brand dilution）受到了广泛的关注（John, Loken, and Joiner 1998; Pullig, Simmons, and Netemeyer 2006）。这一现象显示，品牌延伸过多过杂，会导致人们认为这个品牌的资源过于分散，无法保证旗下每个产品线的质量（Loken and John 1993; Gürhan-Canli and Maheswaran 1998）。而何时会出现积极或者消极的反馈效应，至今依然是吸引很多品牌研究者着手研究的问题。总体来说，品牌延伸更近似于一种内部挖掘潜力的方法，通过拓展不同的产品线和业务线来为自己的品牌添加更多的产品品类、打造多元的品牌形象、吸引更多的目标客户。而与之不同的是，品牌代言和品牌联名则更多是借助他山之石来为自己的品牌增添品牌价值。

三、品牌代言

过往的营销和传播研究认为，代言策略的产生是因为商家希望消费者将代言人（例如名人）的一些积极特征迁移到被代言的产品或者服务上（Wong, Fock, and Ho 2020）。通过这样的手段，品牌可以直接借用这些代言人的相关资产壮大自己的品牌价值。

这些研究提供了几种经典模型来解释这种迁移过程：情绪迁移模型（Affect-transfer model）、意义迁移模型（Meaning-transfer model）、来源可信度模型（Source-credibility model）、加工迁移模型（Process-transfer model）。

情绪迁移模型认为，消费者对代言人的积极情绪能够被转移到被代言的产品上。通俗地说，观众若喜欢这个代言人，就更容易喜欢这位代言人推荐的产品，也就是俗语中的"爱屋及乌"（Eisend and Langner 2010；Wong, Fock, and Ho 2020）。这一模型指出，观众对代言人在情感上的整体积极反应源自代言人的容貌、吸引力、熟悉度等因素（McCracken 1989；Shang, Reed, and Croson 2008；Weisbuch and Mackie 2009）。由于代言人和其代言的产品会在消费者的记忆网络中形成关联结构，因此消费者对代言人的积极情绪反应会更容易扩散到被代言的产品上，从而也对该产品形成积极的态度（Chaiken 1979；Wong, Fock, and Ho 2020）。

而意义迁移模型指出，代言人所具有的象征意义（例如明星象征的性格与精神）能被迁移到其代言的产品上，从而使得这个产品被消费者感知为也拥有了相应的意义和特征（McCracken 1989）。代言人（尤其是明星代言人）往往会通过作品或者生活事迹在大众中树立自己的特有形象，这也使得他们自身具有了相应的象征意义。例如吴京和施瓦辛格，他们被大众认为代表了"坚强""果敢"与"男子汉气概"。广告商也希望借由代言人的象征意义来强调自身营销产品的形象（Schimmelpfennig and Hunt 2020）。而对于消费者来说，消费由这些名人代言的产品，不仅是因为产品自身的功能属性或者对代言人的喜欢和崇拜，也因为他们希望通过购买该产品来获取这些象征意义，从而树立自我形象和建立身份认同（Choi and Rifon 2012）。

来源可信度模型指出,代言人本身的专业程度和可信任程度也能改变消费者对其代言产品的态度(Amos, Holmes, and Strutton 2008; Pornpitakpan 2004)。其中,感知专业程度(例如让医生打扮的代言人出现在牙膏广告中)指的是观众是否认为代言人具备相应的专业知识(Chaiken and Maheswaran 1994; Erdogan 1999)。而可信任程度则是代言人本身让观众感知到的诚信和正直程度(Schouten, Janssen, and Verspaget 2020)。来源可信度模型认为,消费者感知的代言人专业度/可信任度会迁移到他们对代言人传播信息的感知上。例如医生作为代言人推荐牙膏时,他们的推荐语会更容易被观众认为专业可信,并进而影响观众对牙膏的态度(Bergkvist and Zhou 2016; Priester and Petty 2003)。

加工迁移模型则和上述强调正面属性(喜爱度、可信度、象征意义)迁移的模型不同(Wong, Fock, and Ho 2020)。这一模型认为,消费者对代言人进行信息加工的模式也会迁移到对被代言产品的评价上。例如当消费者在评价代言人时以代言人的来源国和过去成就作为主要评判标准,那么在评价该代言人代言的产品时,他们也更倾向于采用产品的来源国和过去成就作为评判产品性能的主要标准。这一模型也解释了为什么在有些情况下即便代言人和代言产品并不匹配,或者代言人本身并不具备较高的喜爱度时也能实现成功的代言。

不难看出,采用名人或者专业人士代言,既能增强品牌感知度,又能丰富品牌形象。例如,选择明星作为代言人,更容易吸引到明星粉丝的关注与支持。而另一方面,类似于前文提到过的记忆的关联网络模型,这些代言策略本质上是希望通过外来资源丰富和完善品牌形象(例如增加品牌在消费者记忆网络中的关联属性)来增加品牌被消费者选择的概率。接下来讨论的品牌联名兼具品牌延伸和品牌代言的特征。

四、品牌联名

狭义的品牌联名是指两个或多个现有品牌合作推出新产品或新服务,并在广告宣传中同时采用这些品牌名作为新产品或新服务的品牌名,或者采用一个全新的品牌名,但是在制造商信息上强调联名品牌的参与(Park, Jun, and Shocker 1996)。广义的品牌联名除合作推出新产品或新服务之外,还包含了联合促销(Joint sales promotion)、捆绑销售(Bundling)、要素品牌(Ingredient branding)、双重品牌(Dual branding)等形式。关于这几种广义品牌联名的定义如下所示:

联合促销:两个以上的品牌合作开展促销活动。这种品牌战略的最大好处是可以使参与合作的各成员品牌以较少成本进行宣传,但是同时又使得联合促销的参与品牌都以最大限度增加曝光度(Varadarajan 1986)。与此同时,参与联合促销的品牌不需要延伸自己的生产线,也不需要开发新产品,在合作上既可以短期也可以长期,因此使得这一品牌策略更加灵活。

捆绑销售:在一个套餐中以单一的优惠价格推广两个或多个产品/服务(Guiltinan 1987; Stremersch and Tellis 2002; Yadav and Monroe 1993)。套餐中的每一个单独产品,既可以是针对不同的消费市场,也可以是彼此互补的消费产品。

要素品牌:一个品牌的核心要素被另一个品牌引入作为其成分。例如,联想电脑使用Intel的处理器就是一个典型的要素品牌例子(Desai and Keller 2002)。

双重品牌:两个品牌(通常是餐饮业品牌)共享场地和设备来为消费者提供服务,从而使得消费者可以选择其中一种或者两种品牌进行消费。例如在北京,吉野家和冰雪皇后(DQ)冰激凌经常毗邻(Levin and Levin 2000)。

狭义层面的品牌联名主要包含两个特征:其一,类似于品牌代言,品牌联名也是通过寻求外界资源来丰富自身品牌的手段;其二,类似于品牌延伸,品牌联名也涉及生成新的产品或者服务(Cunha, Forehand, and Angle 2015)。兼顾这两个特征也使得品牌联名成为一种性价比较高的品牌战略。

知名品牌之间进行联名往往是为了资源整合的需要(Chang 2009; Oeppen and Jamal 2014)。近年来兴起的"跨界营销"案例中的大部分,本质上就是品牌联名。表面上看,很多跨界营销似乎发生在两个风马牛不相及的品牌之间。然而事实上,成功的跨界营销往往暗含着一个逻辑,即两个品牌的消费者之间存在着某些共性和联系。例如,喜茶和腾讯音乐的跨界联名,本质上是因为两个品牌的核心消费群体都具备年轻化、时尚化的特点,在偏好和个体特征上具有相似之处。而另一方面,相比于采用品牌延伸的策略,跨界品牌联名有三个巨大优势。第一,品牌延伸相关研究已经指出,消费者往往会因为母品牌和延伸品牌之间的低匹配性而对延伸品牌产生负面评价(Spiggle, Nguyen, and Caravella 2012)。然而品牌联名则可以打消消费者的这一顾虑,因为品牌联名往往是将不同品牌的优势和特色进行整合,而不是像品牌延伸需要母品牌独立去开拓新领域。第二,相比于品牌延伸甚至并购,品牌联名涉及的经济和管理成本更小(Blackett and Russel 1999)。这是因为品牌联名不需要联名的任一品牌再单独投入更多资源和建立独立生产线,而合作成功后的收益则是各方共享。第三,品牌联名既可以是长期的,也可以是短期的,并且一个品牌可以选择同时跟多个品牌进行联名(Chang 2009)。这也意味着无论在资源整合方面还是产品/服务创新开发方面,品牌联名比品牌延伸更灵活也更有效率。

当品牌联名涉及初创品牌与成熟知名品牌之间的合作时,这种品牌战略也具有其独到的优势(Leuthesser, Kohil, and Suri 2003)。其一,对于初创品牌而言,其关心的重点是如何以相对较小的经济代价与其他竞争品牌进行差异化竞争。而与知名品牌的联名则可以通过引入和融合知名品牌的品牌形象帮助初创品牌实现这些目标。其二,与知名品牌的联名有助于增加初创品牌在消费者中的品牌觉知度,也有助于向外界展示自身的资源厚度(Cunha, Forehand, and Angle 2015)。而知名品牌也往往需要通过与初创品牌的合作来拓展其产品线。与初创品牌的联名还意味着该知名品牌可以用较小的成本、较快的速度进行迭代与试错(Freeman and Engel 2007)。因此无论参与联名的品牌的规模和性质如何变化,品牌联名都能从一定程度上帮助参与品牌达到多赢的效果。

学者们也总结了一系列关于品牌联名的特点(Leuthesser, Kohil, and Suri 2003):

(1)品牌联名的产物(联名开发的新产品或新服务)能够被消费者知觉为吸收了参与联名品牌各自的显著特性。尤其是当这几个参与品牌各自特性彼此互补时,品牌联名会带来更积极的效果。

(2)品牌联名的产品会反向影响到这几个联名品牌,而其中知名度相对较小、品牌资产相对较少的品牌会受到更大影响。

(3)知名的/高端的品牌与不知名的/低端的品牌的联名并不如外界想象的那样一定会对前者造成负面效果,甚至在很多情况下,这种合作模式会为知名的/高端的品牌带来意想不到的效益。

(4)品牌联名有助于合作品牌之间共享目标消费者,最终促成彼此目标客户群基数增大、范围变广。

总体而言,品牌联名作为一种热门的品牌战略,结合了品牌代言和品牌延伸的特点,不管对学术界还是企业界都有极强的研究价值。下一部分,笔者重点介绍在营销学领域,尤其是在消费行为学领域的品牌联名研究。

第二节 品牌联名的营销学研究

目前关于品牌联名的市场营销学研究主要围绕以下几个主题展开:

(1)品牌联名对于合作推出的产品/服务的影响(Evaluation of cobraned prducts/services)。这是过往品牌联名研究中最受关注的主题。而在这一研究领域,学者最为关注的是两个可能影响合作结果的变量:参与联名品牌自身的特性;联名品牌之间的关系以及联名成果之间的关系。相关研究发现如表1-1所示。

表1-1 品牌联名何时会正面影响消费者对合作产品/服务的评价

参与联名品牌自身的特性	联名品牌之间的关系以及与联名成果之间的关系
① 当品牌产品被知觉为具有高性能和高质量(McCarthy and Norris 1999; Park, Jun, and Shocker 1996; Rao, Qu, and Ruekert 1999) ② 品牌自身在消费者中的正面口碑(Janiszewski and van Osselar 2000; Simonin and Ruth 1998; Baumgarth 2004) ③ 品牌自身具有较多品牌资产和较高品牌觉知度(Desai and Keller 2002; Washburn, Till, and Priluck 2000)	① 品牌之间具有较高的互补性(Park, Jun, and Shocker 1996) ② 品牌涉及的品类之间具有较高的匹配性(Simonin and Ruth 1998; Baumgarth 2004) ③ 参与联名的品牌与最终生产的产品之间具有较高的匹配性(Hadjicharalambous 2013)

基于以上因素,Helmig 等人(2007)建立了一个包含品牌、产品与消费者因素的完整模型并对这些因素进行了统一的分析和比较。他们的研究发现,参与联名的品牌产品之间的匹配度相较于品牌自身特性具有更强的预测作用。此外,他们还发现,消费者在个体特质(卷入度、多元化寻求倾向、品牌意识)上的正向表现也会增强他们对品牌联名的好感。

(2)品牌联名的搭档选择(Partner selection)。在品牌联名的搭档选择上,Park 等人(1996)指出,属性互补(Attribute-complementary)的品牌联名(例如 Godiva 和 Slimfast 这两个品牌一个强调美味,一个强调健康),相比于属性类似(Attribute-similar)的品牌联名(例如 Godiva 和 Haagen-Dazs,两个均是强调美味),会更容易增加消费者的好感。然而 Swaminathan 等人(2015)则提出了不同的观点。他们指出消费者对互补型联名与相似型联名的态度取决于消费者在评价品牌联名时所采用的信息加工模式。具体而言,采用属性映射(Property mapping)的信息加工模式会使消费者更容易接受互补型联名,而采用关系思维(Relational thinking)的信息加工模式会使消费者更容易接受相似型联名。Van der Lans 等人(2014)则探索了品牌人格的作用。他们发现,如果要提升消费者对品牌联名的评价,两个合作品牌应该在精细(Sophistication)和粗犷(Ruggedness)这两个品牌人格维度上相似,而在真诚(Sincerity)和能力(Competence)这两个维度上则应该适度体现差异化。这些研究表明,品牌联名对象的选择依然还存在深挖的空间。

(3)品牌联名如何影响参与联名的品牌。进入 21 世纪以来,一部分研究开始探讨品牌联名对于参与品牌的反馈作用。Washburn 等人(2000)指出,和知名品牌的联名一旦成功,会对品牌资产较少的品牌产生积极作用,而知名品牌则相对较少被品牌联名的结果影响。Cunha 等人(2015)则发现与知名品牌联名既可能有益于,也可能有损于相对不知名品牌。而决定这一影响方向的关键在于消费者采取的信息加工方式如何影响他们对不知名品牌在联名中的贡献比重的判断。

总体而言,目前对于品牌联名的研究已经产生了一系列富有意义的结果,这对品牌理论与实践具有极大的借鉴意义。当然,尽管品牌联名的研究已经取得了一些进展,但是在这一领域依然存在着研究空白。

其一,当前的品牌联名研究的主要研究框架依然承袭自品牌延伸和品牌代言理论。例如,很多品牌联名研究是基于品牌代言理论中的情绪迁移模型和意义迁移模型的,并且和品牌延伸研究一样看重匹配度这一因素的作用。但是站在消费者视角分析他们如何感知和理解品牌联名的研究,依然处于起步阶段。例如,消费者可能具有不同的信念(Lay belief)、情绪(Emotion)、思维模式(Mindset)、动机(Motivation),这就意味着即便面对同样的品牌联名信息,消费者也可能做出不同的解读。因此,未来的研究应该着眼于探讨消费者个体因素的作用。

其二,当前关于消费者对品牌联名(品牌、产品、联名活动本身)评价的研究主要集中在整体性的态度判断上(Overall attitudes),而鲜有深入探讨品牌联名如何影响消费者对品牌或者产品具体属性(Specific attributes)的评价。例如,前人研究探讨了品牌人格在品牌心理学中的重要作用,有待追问的是:包括品牌联名活动在内的诸多品牌战略本身是否会影响到消费者对品牌人格的判断?与此同时,大部分研究涉及的对品牌和产品的判断更多是语义(Semantic)和概念(Conceptual)上的(例如对品牌战略的态度是积极或是消极,评判产品质量是高或是低,感知到的品牌形象是奢侈的还是亲民的),而鲜有探讨品牌联名如何影响消费者在感官上对产品的体验与感受。显然,上述问题也是值得研究者进一步探索的。

  为了填补这两个研究空白,笔者提出了一个基于消费者推论(Consumer inference-making)的理论框架来探究消费者对品牌联名的信息加工过程。此外,本书着重探讨品牌联名如何影响消费者对参与联名的品牌、品牌各自的产品,以及品牌联名成果(例如共同开发的产品)的属性判断。在本书的第二章,笔者将基于已往研究文献回顾和总结消费者推论的产生与作用机制。

第二章

消费者推论：
推论类型与推论目标

在做出消费决策之前,消费者需要考虑与目标产品或品牌有关的各种信息。促使消费者进行决策和判断的最理想情景,莫过于让消费者掌握所有的信息,然后再通过深思熟虑形成最后的决断。然而这样的理想状况在现实生活中很少存在,这主要是因为市场中的每一个参与者几乎都面临信息不对称的困境。例如,产品信息的二手来源(广告、促销或口碑传播)通常会提供有关某些产品属性的信息和特征,但这些产品信息的来源材料并不会包含对所有属性和特征的描述(Kardes, Posavac, and Cronley 2004; Kruglanski and Webster 1996)。即便都提供描述,这些信息也会由于写作者或者传播者的缘故存在各种偏差(Kardes, Posavac, and Cronley 2004)。即便商家竭尽全力提供足够的关于产品的细节并减少可能的描述偏差,消费者在真正购买和消费产品之前也很少能未卜先知他们实际的消费体验(Gunasti and Ross 2009; Kardes, Posavac, and Cronley 2004)。这就意味着依然有很多产品和服务的属性未被呈现,消费者只能自己做出推断(Bruner 1957; Lynch and Srull 1982)。基于以上讨论,消费者推论通常被定义为消费者根据有限或不完整的信息(例如各种线索和背景知识),通过分析和推理来判断未知的信息并进而做出最终决策与判断的过程(Broniarczyk and Alba 1994; Kardes, Posavac, Cronley, and Herr 2008)。为了努力形成正确的推论,消费者需要整合所有与判断目标相关联的信息,然后通过一系列认知工具(例如环境线索、启发式、论点、背景知识)建立已知信息和未知信息之间的主观逻辑链接(出现 A 条件,则出现 B 结果),从而得出最后的结论(Kardes

1993；Yan and Sengupta 2011）。这些作为推断依据的信息，既可以是定量信息（Quantitative information）（Yan and Sengupta 2011），也可以是质性信息（Qualitative information）（Gilovich, Griffin, and Kahneman 2002；Thompson and Ince 2013）。例如，Yan 和 Sengupta（2011）探究了消费者如何用产品价格作为线索进行产品质量的推断；Thompson 和 Ince（2013）则指出个体会通过自己的元认知体验（Meta-cognitive experience），如感知到的信息加工困难，来推断商家、产品以及广告对自身的吸引力。

消费者推论可以发生在很多领域。消费者可以对缺失的产品属性进行推论（Pocheptsova, Labroo, and Dhar 2010；Ross and Creyer 1992；Yan and Sengupta 2011），可以对自己的消费体验进行推论（Maimaran and Fishbach 2014；Kim, Chen, and Zhang 2016），甚至可以对购买相同产品的其他消费者进行推论（He and Bond 2015；Naylor, Lamberton, and Norton 2011）。

从本质上而言，对目标（例如缺失信息）的推论是基于消费者对已有信息和缺失信息之间关系的感知。例如在推论中最经典的因果关系推论（Causal inference）探讨的其实是两个信息之间彼此的影响和作用（基于三个原则：时间序列上是否有先后；两者是否存在相关关系；是否存在第三因素同时影响这两个信息）。然而在大多数情况下，消费者进行的其实是相关（Correlational）推断而非因果（Causal）推断。在相关推断的情况下，消费者对缺失信息进行推断就会被简化为考察已有信息与缺失信息是正向相关关系、负向相关关系，还是彼此独立不存在关联。

要确立两个信息或者属性之间的关系方向（正向、负向、独立），消费者通常会使用内隐理论（Implicit theory，即消费者关于人、事、物之间彼此关系的先验信念）抑或是启发式（Heuristics，一种自动化的快速化的推理思维）将已知信息与未知信息联系起来（Kardes, Posavac, and Cronley 2004; Spiller and Belogolova 2017; Wyer 2006）。内隐理论和启发式都是在帮助消费者快速地形成前文中提及的主观逻辑链接。例如很多消费者相信苦口的药更像良药，便宜的货不是好货（Kardes, Cronley, Kellaris, and Posavac 2004）。这些现象既被过往研究称为内隐理论（或者先天信念），也被看作一种快速决策的启发式。

正如前文所述，消费者在做判断时往往会混淆因果关系和相关关系（Blanco 2017; White 2009），这也就意味着一旦两个属性或者信息在消费者脑海中形成了关联，这种关联很可能是双向的，而不是单向的。具体而言，如果消费者认为苦的药更加有效，那么他们也容易认为有效的药在口感上会更苦（Wyer and Srull, 2014）。同样的道理，当消费者认为一个产品价格越贵代表其质量越好的时候，他们反过来也会认为质量越好的产品价格应当越高（Kardes, Posavac, Cronley, and Herr 2008）。如果消费者认为真实可靠的事物理应让自己感到更熟悉，那么一旦他们觉得某个事物很熟悉，他们也更容易相信这个事物是真实可靠的（Banović, Fontes, Barreira, and Grunert 2012; Fang, Singh, and Ahluwalia 2007）。

尽管目前在消费者推论这一研究领域已经有一定的科学突破与发现，但这一领域依然存在可以拓展和挖掘的空间。其一，现有的关于消费者推论的研究大都是基于内隐理论或启发式的思路来进行的。这样的研究思路的重点在于探索消费者何时以及如何将可用信息与目标产品、品牌和人员的缺失属性联系起来（Spiller and Belogolova 2017; Wu, Han, and Kardes 2020）。但是，这些推论过程（Gneezy, Gneezy, and Lauga 2014; Huang, Lim, Lin, and

Han 2019)目前关注更多的是推论目标为语义或者抽象概念时的情景,例如利用价格(数字信息)推断质量(语义概念),或者通过产品摆放(视觉信息)推断店面的档次(语义概念)。而推断对象为感官体验(Sensory experience,例如味觉、触觉等)的研究相对较少,且背后的理论机制依然缺乏系统梳理。其二,前人的研究通常着重于对产品或品牌的单一维度的推论(Gunasti and Ross 2009; Kim, Barasz, and John 2019; Spiller and Belogolova 2017)。但是,品牌和产品本身具有多种判断维度和属性,这也就提出了一个新的问题:当呈现同样的推论线索时,消费者是否可能对品牌或产品的不同维度做出具有差异化甚至截然相反的推断?为了解答该问题,笔者将在本章接下来的部分就消费者推论的方向性,以及消费者对感官信息的推论这两大问题进行文献综述与理论分析。

第一节　同化推论与补偿推论

消费者行为学研究中涉及最广泛的推论是基于相关的推论(Kardes 2006)。消费者的决策往往受到内隐理论的引导。基于这种先验信念,一个属性的信息就足以使消费者得出关于另一个属性情况的推论(Broniarczyk and Alba 1994a, 1994b; Kardes, Cronley, Kellaris, and Posavac 2004)。许多研究表明,这种内隐理论或者先验信念对于消费者决策产生的影响甚至强于直接呈现属性间的相关数据(Cronley, Posavac, Meyer, Kardes, and Kellaris 2005)。例如,Broniarczyk 和 Alba(1994b)在实验中向被试呈现了

25个品牌的立体声扬声器的价格、质量和广告支出信息。接下来,被试需要判断价格和质量之间的相关程度,以及判断广告支出和质量之间的相关程度。有趣的是,即便呈现给被试的价格和质量数据并不存在显著相关性,即便呈现的广告支出和质量存在显著相关性,被试依然倾向于高估价格和质量的关系,而低估广告支出和质量的关系。这也说明了消费者自身的内隐理论或者先验信念会影响和扭曲他们进行推论的过程。

如上文所述,消费者的推论往往是在探索已有信息和缺失信息之间的相关关系。例如,消费者会被内隐理论驱使,认为产品质量与价格促销、材料选择、保险方案以及品牌定位等线索密切相关。然而这些相关关系却可能呈现不同的方向。在统计学上,显著的相关关系分为正相关和负相关两类。在判断缺失信息时,消费者也会推论其与已有信息呈现正相关或者负相关关系(Broniarczyk and Alba 1994a;Ford and Smith 1987;Huber and McCann 1982)。其中,前者被称为同化推论(Assimilative inference),后者被称为补偿推论(Compensatory inference)。这两种经典的消费者推论类型也是本节要讨论的重点。

同化推论也被称为评价一致性推论(Evaluative consistency inferences),与社会心理学中的同化效应(Assimilation effect)有着千丝万缕的联系(Ajzen 1977;Cooper 1981;Kelly 1955)。其中最经典的例子当属晕轮效应(Halo effect)。经典的社会心理学研究指出,当观察者在判断他人时,他们很少采用混合和复杂的模式进行判断。相反,他们会倾向于认为被判断对象在其自身的各个属性上具有一致性。因此,观察者更愿意采用先入为主的思维模式,即通过对被观察者的第一印象(例如最先接触和了解到的某一方面的行为特征)来解释和预测被观察者在其他方面的表现(Nisbett and Wilson 1977; Schneider 1973)。一个经典的例子就是外貌出色的个体会比外貌一般的个体更容易被认为拥有积极的人格特征和更高的技能水平(Asch 1946)。个体在判断产品属性时,也会采用类似的策略(Beckwith and Lehmann 1975; Bettman, John, and Scott 1986)。具体而言,根据这种同化推论原则,当 A 产品在可观察属性上的表现优于 B 产品时,那么消费者也更倾向于推断 A 产品在其他无法被直接观察到的属性上的表现也胜过 B 产品(Dick, Chakravarti, and Biehal 1990; Janiszewski and Van Osselaer 2000)。就这个角度而言,从价格、品牌、保险这三条线索信息去推断产品和服务的质量都更加类似于同化推论(Huber and McCann 1982; Lalwani and Shavitt 2013; Lichtenstein and Burton 1989)。

同化推论是建立在消费者认为两个属性之间存在正相关关系(或者存在评价一致性)的基础上。与同化推论相对,一些研究指出,消费者也会采用补偿推论的办法来推断不能被观察到的属性和信息。简单地说,消费者更倾向于认为已经观察到的属性和未被观察到的属性呈现负相关关系。补偿推论更接近于社会心理学中的对比效应(Contrast effect)。这种情况的发生主要是由于消费者预期在一个选择集中的选项应该呈现一种平衡态。例如选项 A 如果在 X 属性上好于选项 B,那么其在 Y 属性上的表现应该低于选项 B,只有这种情况才能使得选项 A 和 B 在总体上形成相似的吸引力。因此,当消费者在只知道两个选项在 X 属性上的相对表现的情况下,会试图在 Y 属性上做出相反的判断以平衡两者的总体效用。例如,试想消费者考虑选择同一个商家推荐的两款电视屏幕时,如果一款屏幕在可观察属性(例如面积和价位)上优于另一款,那么消费者会推论该屏幕在其他无法观察的属性上也许存在劣势(例如分辨率、耐用度、防水性)。这种补偿推论既可以是正面补偿(Positive compensation),即消费者在做推断时提高对处于比较劣势选项的评价,也可以是负面补偿(Negative compensation),即降低对处于比较优势选项的评价。

过往研究指出,补偿推论常见于社会知觉(Social perception)、概率判断(Probability judgment)、产品信息推断(Inference of missing attributes)中(Fiske, Xu, Cuddy, and Glick 1999; Kay and Jost 2003; Lerner 1980)。例如,研究者发现,社会知觉中的补偿推论取决于个体在多大程度上认可世界是公平的(Just world belief)。为了达到这一平衡态,那些在某一方面处于领先地位的群体,会被消费者认为在另一方面更差。基于这一信念,穷困群体会更容易被知觉为快乐和善良的,富裕群体更容易被知觉为不快乐和虚伪的(Kay and Jost 2003; Lerner 1980)。相似效应也出现在对人格和能力的判断上。那些微笑程度高的个体被认为为人温和但是能力欠佳(Wang, Mao, Li, and Liu 2017),外貌美丽的个体则被认为善于社交却缺乏思维能力(Peng, Cui, Chung, and Zheng 2020)。在概率判断上,经典的赌徒谬误(Gambler's fallacy)和随机感知偏差(Biased perception of randomness)都是补偿推论的绝佳案例。赌徒谬误理论认为,在彼此独立的多次赌博中,赌徒会更倾向于认为之前一直没有出现的结果相较于已经出现的更容易发生,哪怕其实这一结果出现的概率依然是随机的(Tversky and Kahneman 1974)。同样,随机感知偏差则指出,当两个事件(事件 A 为投币正面朝上,事件 B 为投币背面朝上)出现概率事实上都是 50%时,让这两个事件出现的序列看上去符合某种规律会减少消费者对这个事件随机程度的感知,这是因为消费者会认为随机应该建立在两个事件发生互相补偿的基础上。在产品的缺失属性推断上,我们也时常能观察到类似的效应。例如,Maimaran 和 Fishbach

(2014)发现,当告知学龄前儿童某种食物(例如胡萝卜)具有功能性的益处时(例如可以提高儿童智力表现),这些儿童会更倾向于推断该食物的味道较差。由此可见补偿推论在个体年幼的时候就已经形成。Kim等人(2016)发现,当游戏提供拟人化游戏助手时,个体会觉得游戏的乐趣下降,因为他们倾向于认为游戏助手承担了赢得游戏的主要功劳,会损害玩家的自主性。Newman等人(2014)则发现一家刻意强调自己进行环保和绿色事业的企业会被认为旗下产品质量堪忧,这是因为消费者认为绿色和环保上的投入会导致产品在技术投入上的牺牲。总的来说,补偿推论建立在人们寻求平衡的动机上。这种动机可能来自对市场本身的判断(选择集中的选项应该各有利弊),也有可能来自认为世界公平公正的信念(失去的应该会弥补,得到的也有可能失去),还有可能来自资源有限的假设(在总体资源有限且固定的情况下,分配资源到其中一个方面必然会导致另一个方面得到的资源减少)。

第二节 对于感官信息的推论

上文介绍的消费者推论研究主要集中在语义信息上,这些信息包含价格判断、质量判断等。然而在现实生活中,作为消费者的我们还经常需要对产品的感官信息(Sensory information),例如味道和重量,进行相应评价。与语义信息不同的是,感官信息更加具体,也更需要调动个体的机体(例如触觉和味觉相应的神经系统)参与到判断过程中。这也使得感官信息的推论过程更加复杂,不同于语义信息可以基于已知属性和内隐理论进行简单和快速推断。下面将结合神经科学、心理学与营销学中相关研究,讨论个体推断缺失的感官信息时所采用的信息加工模式。

Krishna(2012)指出,一个人对感官信息的判断是由感觉(Sensation)和知觉(Perception)共同构成的。感觉是指外来刺激作用在感觉器官的受体细胞上的生理学过程。知觉则是对这种感觉的觉知(Awareness)和解读(Interpretation)。例如,当向观察者呈现一些经典的视角错觉现象(例如艾宾浩斯错觉)时,视觉图像的光影与线条(两个一样大小的圆形分别被不同规格的圆形环绕)作用于观察者视觉器官的过程是感觉,然而最终观察者的知觉却会扭曲感觉信息,从而产生有偏差的判断(认为艾宾浩斯错觉中的两个被围绕的圆形大小不一)。

感觉主要分为几个大类:视觉(Vision)、听觉(Audition)、触觉(Haptics)、嗅觉(Olfaction)、味觉(Taste)。从感觉产生到知觉形成的过程中,这些感官信息的输入大多会受到环境因素(例如零售环境)和个人因素(例如动机和需求)的扭曲,从而最终影响到消费者对感官信息的判断。而这些感官信息的判断往往又会激发相应的情感和认知因素,从而决定消费者之后的购买和消费行为。例如,在营销学领域的部分学者关注消费者在对产品信息进行加工时产生的视觉偏差(Visual perception bias)(Raghubir and Krishna 1996, 1999; Wansink and Van Ittersum 2003)。这些偏差往往会体现在消费者对产品容量和规格的判断上,而这些判断又会反过来影响他们的购买意愿和购买数量(Chandon and Wansink 2007; Chandon and Ordabayeva 2009; Krider, Raghubir, and Krishna 2001)。

现有的感官营销(Sensory marketing)研究探讨的大多是感官信息的判断在形成后如何影响消费者后续的购买过程。例如,

Peck 和 Childers(2003a,2003b)的研究发现,对于那些具有更高的触觉需求(Need for touch)的消费者,触摸产品可以增强他们对产品评价的信心。在 Peck 和 Wiggins(2006)的后续研究中,他们发现在捐赠广告中设计可触碰的元素可以增强那些高触摸需求个体的捐款意愿。在嗅觉研究领域,Morrin 和 Ratneshwar(2003)发现环境中的香气可以促进消费者对观察到的品牌的回忆和再认。在听觉领域,Shen 和 Sengupta(2014)则发现看似无关的声音提示也会引导消费者对产品的选择。而味觉上的苦涩感,也被发现会改变消费者付出金钱的意愿(Cai,Yang,Wyer,and Xu 2017)

在感官信息判断的形成上,目前的研究主要探讨了产品呈现形式(Product display)、消费场景(Consumption context)、个体自身期望(Expectation)、知识背景(Knowledge background)、动机水平(Motivation)对消费者推断感官信息的影响。其中研究最为深入的是消费者对视觉、触觉、味觉的相关信息的推断过程。

推断视觉信息。已往研究主要基于认知心理学中的视觉偏差(Leong,Hughes,Wang,and Zaki 2019)。Dunning 和 Balcetis(2013)指出,人们对事物的视知觉会受到其动机和渴望的影响(Wishful seeing)。例如,关于"两可刺激"(Ambiguous stimuli)的研究(Balcetis and Dunning 2006)发现,针对模棱两可的图案(例如经典心理学教科书中都会出现的"花瓶—人脸"两可图案),观察者自身不同的动机和背景知识会左右他们对图形的判断与识别(更快看到花瓶 vs.更快看到人脸)。除开这种对于视觉图案的识别,另一些研究者着重考察了其他线索和因素如何影响消费者对产品大小(Size)、容量(Volume)乃至色彩光泽(Color and light)的判断。例如研究者发现,容器摆放的方式(长边朝上 vs.长边朝下)会导致消费者对同样的容器产生不同的容量估计(Perfecto,

Donnelly, and Critcher 2019）。广告中产品移动的速度越快,越容易让消费者认为该产品体积较小（Jia, Kim, and Ge 2020）。与此同时,一系列关于亮度错觉（Brightness illusion）的研究也发现个体对物体光亮的判断取决于周边场景的对比作用（Roe, Lu, and Hung 2005）。

推断触觉信息。已往研究探讨了视觉信息如何影响消费者对触觉和味觉信息的推断。例如,Deng 和 Kahn（2009）发现,针对同样产品进行不同的包装布局（包装上的图案出现在下方 vs.上方位置）会导致人们形成不同的关于产品重量的推断。Hagtvedt 和 Brasel（2017）则发现产品色彩的饱和度越高,越容易让消费者推断产品具有更重的重量。Dai 和 Hsee（2013）则发现,个体的生理状态（例如饥饿程度）和对食物的拥有状态（拥有 vs.不拥有）会共同影响他们对食物重量的判断。

推断味觉信息。一系列研究发现,视觉信息（例如颜色）会影响消费者对产品口味的判断（Hoegg and Alba 2007; Zhang, Wadhwa, and Chattopadhyay 2016）。例如 Zhang 等人（2016）发现消费者容易将较深的颜色和美味联系在一起。Si 和 Jiang（2017）则发现当消费者需要依次判断产品 A 和 B 的味道时,他们对产品 A 的味觉体验（即便是想象出的体验）会对之后产品 B 的味觉体验产生影响。Machiels 和 Karnal（2016）则发现产品加工程度的信息也会影响消费者对其口味的期望和判断。

与对抽象概念（Abstract concept）的推断不同,对具体的感官体验（Sensory experience）的推断往往涉及机体反应（Bodily responses）的加入（Barsalou 2010; Gallese and Sinigaglia 2011）。换句话说,机体状态本身会成为消费者用于推断感官体验的线索式信息。扎根认知（Grounded cognition）理论认为:在成长的过程中,个体的知觉和判断会与特定的机体反应结合起来（Barsalou 1999，2008；Gallese 2005；Gallese and Lakoff 2005；Wells and Petty 1980）。基于这一逻辑，一旦在评价某种产品的过程中这些机体反应被重新激活，那么个体也会做出相应的知觉和判断。例如，当个体面部和微笑相关的肌肉活动被增强，那么个体也将在情绪判断上更倾向于认为自己是快乐的（Strack，Martin，and Stepper 1988）。而当个体背着沉重的背包时，这种肌肉上的沉重感和劳累感会让其感到面前的山峰更加高耸陡峭（Proffitt，Stefanucci，Banton，and Epstein 2003）。

研究者进一步发现，这种机体状态上的改变既可以是物理干预的结果，也可以通过个体的想象来达成（Krishna 2012；Krishna and Schwarz 2014）。心理学和神经科学的研究发现，个体可以在思维中生成类似于图片或者真实场景的信息（心理表象）来帮助他们进行理解、想象和回忆（Kosslyn，Ganis，and Thompson 2001），这一过程研究者称之为心理模拟（Mental simulation）（Escalas 2004a，2004b）。心理模拟意味着个体在知觉上对事物的发生场景进行构建（Barsalou 2008；Escalas 2004；Taylor，Pham，Rivkin，and Armor 1998），这包括对未来事件的想象，对过去事件的重温，以及对过往经历其他可能性的假设。

当心理模拟发生的时候，与该事物相关的体验和感受也会被激活。例如，当消费者吃一块巧克力时，大脑会将所有和这段经历相关的感官信息进行编码与整合（例如巧克力的视觉形态，吃巧克力时的味觉感受）。而之后再看到巧克力广告或者回想起吃巧克力的场景时，消费者会在心理上模拟之前关于巧克力的这些感官信息，从而激活与真实品尝巧克力时相同的神经反应（Barsalou 2008）。除味觉之外，神经科学研究者发现其他的身体系统也会参与到心理模拟过程中。例如,当想象贝多芬的乐章时,人们的听觉神经活动会增强(Zatorre and Halpern 2005)。思考类似于肉桂和大蒜这些词语的时候,人们的嗅觉神经系统会被激活(González et al. 2006)。而阅读关于踢腿的动作描述也会激发读者的腿部肌肉活动,如同读者真的在执行这一动作(Pulvermüller, Shtyrov, and Ilmoniemi 2005)。

来自营销学的研究证据指出,呈现形式生动的或者类似故事叙述的产品描述信息更容易激发个体的心理模拟过程(Petrova and Cialdini 2005;Wyer, Adaval, and Colcombe 2002)。此外,通过改变广告和产品本身的视觉设计也可以达到类似效果。例如有学者发现,如果调整产品在广告中的摆放角度,使其朝向消费者的惯用手,消费者会更容易对使用该产品的过程进行心理模拟,从而增进自身购买意愿(Elder and Krishna 2012)。有的学者(Cian, Longoni, and Krishna 2020)的研究则显示,在减肥广告中呈现产品用户身材的渐变过程,比只呈现用户减肥开始和结束时的状态,更容易引发消费者对产品使用过程的模拟,从而增加广告的可信度。

在很多情况下,通过外在物理刺激或者内部心理模拟形成的机体反应,都可以对消费者其后的推断和决策产生影响(Herbert and Pollatos 2012;Schwarz and Clore 2003)。值得注意的是,这种影响的程度取决于消费者心目中该机体反应和判断目标之间的关联性。Schwarz(2011)的"感觉作为信息理论"(Feeling-as-information theory)指出,个体在做出最后的判断时,往往会先衡量体验到的感觉信息的重要性。一旦个体认为这种感觉信息与最终的判断目标之间并不存在关联(甚至干扰到了他们的最终判断),他们就会尽可能修正这种感觉信息对他们判断形成的影响。例如,来自营销学的研究发现,当个体体验到加工信息的困难时,他们更容易将这种困难感归结为信息本身质量的低下（Schwarz and Clore 1983；Shen，Jiang，and Adaval 2010），然而一旦他们被告知这种加工上的困难感是由外界环境因素（例如房间灯光灰暗）造成的,那么他们就不再使用这种感知的加工困难作为评判广告质量的信息线索。

综上所述,本节回顾了消费者进行感官推断的机制和相关发现。值得注意的是,尽管这些研究从多个层面探寻了个体、环境、设计等因素如何影响消费者对产品感官信息的推断,但是它们却很少探讨品牌相关信息在其中产生的影响和作用。品牌的信息既包括品牌知识（Brand knowledge），也包含品牌的战略行动（Branding strategy）。研究这个领域也有助于我们在品牌营销和消费者判断这两个领域之间搭建桥梁,从而发掘出全新的值得研究的问题。

第三章

品牌相关信息如何
影响消费者推论

已往关于品牌影响消费者推论的研究,大多集中于品牌自身特质(例如品牌形象、品牌觉知、品牌资产)如何影响消费者对品牌的评价以及对其旗下产品的偏好。然而有趣的是,现有的研究却少有探讨品牌的战略选择(例如品牌延伸、品牌代言)如何影响消费者对品牌/产品某些具体属性(例如品牌人格、产品感官体验)的推断。这意味着,过去的研究在自变量选择上没有考虑到品牌战略这一元素,并且在因变量选择上也更多局限在考察消费者的总体态度和反应,没有细化到考虑消费者对品牌/产品更细分的属性的推断。而在本书中,笔者试图对这一问题进行深入探讨。本章首先回顾已往研究中品牌信息影响消费者推论的相关研究,然后在此基础上引入本书的研究焦点:品牌联名战略如何影响消费者对品牌人格与产品感官体验的推断。

第一节 品牌相关信息如何影响消费者对品牌的推断

关于消费者对品牌的推断的早期研究,主要集中在消费者对品牌质量(Brand quality)的推断上。例如,研究者发现,品牌的价格、名称、产品属性可以共同影响消费者对品牌质量的推断(Jacoby, Olson, and Haddock 1971)。研究者也发现,品牌旗下产品的多元化程度(Compatible variety)越高,消费者越倾向于认为品牌的质量高(Berger, Draganska, and Simonson 2007)。

随着品牌人格理论的发展,研究者开始探讨不同的品牌信息如何影响消费者对品牌人格的推断。这一理论缘起于学者对消费者—品牌关系(Consumer-brand relationship)的探索(Fournier 1998; Kervyn, Fiske, and Malone 2012; Shimp and Madden, 1988; Thomson, MacInnis, and Park 2005)。相关研究认为,消费者会将品牌进行人格化,会采用类似于与他人相处的模式来对待品牌(Aggarwal 2004; Aggaarwal and Law 2005; Albert, Merunka, and Valette-Florence 2008; Batra, Ahuvia, and Bagozzi 2012)。以此类推,消费者也会认为品牌具有自己的人格,并会采用类似于判断他人人格的思维模式来判断品牌的人格(Aaker, Vohs, and Mogilner 2010; Fournier and Alvarez 2012)。

社会心理学中的刻板印象内容模型(Stereotype content model)(Fiske, Cuddy, and Glick 2007)指出,对他人进行社会判断(尤其是人格判断)的两个主要维度是温暖(Warmth)和能力(Competence)。很多学者在自己的研究中也提出了其他的社会判断维度。例如,Asch(1946)用"冷"(Cold)和"暖"(Warm)来对个体对他人形成的印象进行分类。Rosenberg等人(1968)则指出对他人的社会判断可以分为社交性(Social)和智力性(Intellectual)两个维度。Wojciszke等人(2009)还提出了能动性(Agency)和社群性(Communion)的划分方式。来自文化心理学领域的研究者(Fiske, Kitayama, Markus, and Nisbett 1998; Hui 1988; Markus and Kitayama 1998; Schwartz 1990; Singelis 1994)则强调独立性(Independent)和互依性(Interdependent),抑或是个人主义(Individualism)和集体主义(Collectivism)。尽管这些双维度结构采用了不同的称谓,但是其核心概念依然具有相近之处(Abele and

Wojciszke 2007;Fiske,Cuddy,and Glick 2007;Fournier and Alvarez 2012)。具体来说,温暖维度和其他诸如集体主义、社交性等维度均反映了人与人之间的互动和社会资本,而能力维度和其他诸如智力、能动性等维度则更多反映了个体自身的技能因素。

个体会结合一系列线索来推断人和品牌的温暖性与能力性。例如,研究发现模特微笑程度越高,观察者对模特在温暖维度上的评分会越高,然而在能力维度上的评分却会下降(Wang, Mao, Li, and Liu 2017)。Durante等人(2017)的研究则发现穷困(vs.富裕)的个体会被认为更温暖(vs.更有能力)。甚至在职场中,相对于未生育的职业女性,已生育的职业女性会被其他观察者认为更温暖,但是也更欠缺能力(Cuddy, Fiske, and Glick 2004)。除开对他人的判断,学者也探讨了公司的类型对于消费者品牌推断的影响(Aaker, Vohs, and Mogilner 2010),研究显示非营利性(vs.营利性)的公司会更容易被认为是温暖的(vs.有能力的)。

综上所述,尽管研究者已经指出对于品牌的人格推断近似于对他人的人格推断,这一推断的前因变量和后续结果研究还处于起步阶段。而探讨品牌战略(例如品牌联名)对于品牌人格推断的影响则可以同时对品牌营销理论和实践提供有益的补充。

第二节 品牌相关信息如何影响消费者对产品属性的推断

品牌自身的关联属性往往可以直接迁移到消费者对产品的属性判断上。例如品牌自身的定位(例如强调奢侈)和价格也会影响消费者对其产品属性(例如设计、材质、健康程度)的推断(Cornil, Chandon, and Krishna 2017; Gneezy, Gneezy, and Lauga 2014; Salerno and Sevilla 2019)。近年来,有不少研究者更进一步,开始探讨品牌相关信息对于产品感官体验的影响。这其中的主要研究集中在品牌信息对于消费者味觉体验的影响。

例如,关于饮料口感的研究发现,个体对产品(例如可乐)的感官体验会受到产品品牌的影响(Allison and Uhl 1964; Makens 1965; McClure, Li, Tomlin, Cypert, Montague, and Montague 2004)。具体而言,当消费者品尝贴有熟悉品牌标识(例如可口可乐)的食物或饮料时,他们的味觉体验会显著优于品尝没有品牌标识的或者品牌不出名的食物或饮料(哪怕事实上这两份餐饮一模一样)。而品牌中价格和营养信息的呈现形式,也会影响消费者对食物或饮料的感受。例如,Almenberg 和 Dreber(2011)发现红酒的价格可以影响消费者饮用该红酒的感受。而 Levin 和 Gaeth(1988)发现在品牌宣传中标榜自己"免去 75% 脂肪"的肉制品会让消费者觉得口感更胜那些标榜自己"仅含 25% 脂肪"的肉制品。这些研究发现的作用机制均离不开一个经典的理论——"安慰剂效应"(Placebo effect)(Price, Finniss, and Benedetti 2008)

安慰剂效应最早起源于医学研究领域(Bienenfeld, Frishman, and Glasser 1996; Stewart-Williams and Podd 2004)。相关研究发现,当向病人传递他们已经接受了治疗的信息时(例如给予一个没有对症效果的糖丸),病人会容易感觉自己在某些症状上出现了好转。可靠的"安慰剂"在医学上可以帮助患者缓解心理或者生理上的病痛,甚至起到治愈部分轻症的作用(Montgomery and Kirsch 1996; Price, Milling, Kirsch, Duff, Montgomery, and Nicholls 1999)。来自神经科学(例如功能性核磁共振 FMRI)的研究证明,这种安慰剂效应并非只是病患一厢情愿的口头报告,事实上,病患的相应生理指标的确出现了改变(Colagiuri, Schenk, Kessler, Dorsey, and Colloca 2015; Benedetti, Mayberg, Wager, Stohler, and Zubieta 2005)。

已往研究中安慰剂效应主要由两种理论进行解释(Kirsch 2018; Montgomery and Kirsch 1997; Stewart-Williams and Podd 2004):一种是期望理论(Expectancy theory),另一种则是经典条件反射理论(Theory of classical conditioning)。期望理论指出,安慰剂效应的产生是基于人们所抱有的信念:他们接受的治疗会带来一定的治疗效果。这种信念使得他们在主观感受上和身体具体反应上都出现相应的变化。经典条件反射理论则认为,真正产生疗效的药物成分是非条件反射刺激(例如药物中的化学成分),而承载该成分的载体(例如药片、胶囊、糖浆)则是条件反射刺激。当这两种刺激长期匹配时,即便只呈现条件反射刺激(例如没有对症化学成分的药片),患者也会产生相应的治疗效果反应。越来越多的实证研究指出,这两种机制本质上有共通之处(Kirsch 2004; Rescorla 1988)。回顾推论形成的相关研究,读者也不难发现这两种解释安慰剂效应的理论本质上都是个体建立和应用"出现 A 条件,则出现 B 结果"的逻辑链接的过程(Berns 2005; Deval, Mantel, Kardes, and Posavac 2013; Irmak, Block, and Fitzsimons 2005; Shiv, Carmon, and Ariely 2005a, 2005b)。因此安慰剂效应的形成本质上也是一种推论过程。

安慰剂效应及其背后的推论机制,同样可以用于解释熟悉或者流行品牌如何影响消费者对产品的感官推断。在 McClure 等人(2004)的经典研究中,他们发现消费者的偏好形成与大脑中的两套独立系统有关。而这两套系统均位于大脑的前额叶皮层内。其中,腹内侧前额叶皮层(Ventromedial prefrontal cortex)的活动和基于感官信息(例如可乐口感)做出偏好判断有关,背外侧前额叶皮层(Dorsolateral prefrontal cortex)、海马(Hippocampi)、中脑(Midbrain)的活动则和依靠品牌信息的决策有关。因此,在知晓品牌信息的情况下,品牌熟悉度自身造成的期望会扭曲纯粹依靠味觉进行的判断。而这样的效应甚至可以出现在孩提时期。例如,Robinson 等人(2007)以儿童作为实验被试,发现相比于被标榜为来自不知名品牌的餐饮,那些被标榜为来自麦当劳的餐饮,其口感更易使儿童感到满意。

随后的营销研究者进一步发现,不只是品牌的知名度或者熟悉性,品牌自身所含有的品牌人格、文化属性和价值观也会影响消费者的产品体验(Paasovaara, Luomala, Pohjanheimo, and Sandell 2012)。例如,当品牌强调道德上的价值观(Ethical claim)时,消费者对产品的体验和口感也会发生变化。除此之外,消费者会更倾向于认为贴有有机品牌标签的食物具有更低的卡路里含量(Besson, Lalot, Bochard, Flaudias, and Zerhouni 2019),而拥有公平贸易(Fair trade)这种社会公益性或者伦理性品牌标签的食物被认为口感更好(Lee, Shimizu, Kniffin, and Wansink 2013; Lotz, Christandl, and Fetchenhauer 2013; Poleman, Mojet, Lyon, and Sefa-Dedeh 2008; Schuldt, Muller, and Schwarz 2012)。研究者进一步指出,消费者对产品的味觉与嗅觉体验取决于产品/品牌的象征意义和消费者自身的价值观的匹配程度(Allen, Gupta, and Monnier 2008; Paasovaara, Luomala, Pohjanheimo, and Sandell 2012)。具体而言,如果该产品/品牌传达的象征意义和消费者自身的价值观具有一致性(Value-symbol congruency),消费者会感受到更好的味觉和嗅觉体验,从而提高对产品的喜爱程度。而在产品的触觉、听觉等相关领域,品牌的影响作用则有待于进一步的挖掘。

在本书的第四章和第五章,笔者将通过基于行为实验法的实证研究来探讨品牌联名如何对消费者的产品感官体验以及消费者对品牌人格的推断产生影响。其中,第四章的实证研究通过具身模拟理论(Barsalou 2008;Elder and Krishna 2012)探索联名品牌强调的品牌价值观(例如怀旧)如何改变消费者对联名产品的触觉体验。具体来说,笔者研究探讨了品牌价值观与消费者个体对该价值观的感知重要性如何共同对消费者产品重量感知造成影响。该研究不但丰富了品牌信息影响产品推断的领域(例如自变量从品牌要素延伸到品牌联名战略,因变量则首次考察了消费者对产品重量的体验),也解决了具身认知领域一个重要的理论问题。根据具身认知理论,心理上感知的"重要性"和生理上感知的"重量"具有紧密的关系。因此激活"重要"这一抽象概念也会导致个体高估"重量"。然而过去的相关研究却发现了矛盾的结果(Schneider, Parzuchowski, Wojciszke, Schwarz, and Koole 2015;Zhang and Li 2012)。笔者的研究结果表明,当与目标产品联名的品牌传达价值观 A(例如社会公平)时,激活该价值观的感知重要性会让消费者高估联名产品的物理重量。但是当联名品牌传达无关甚至相矛盾的价值观 B(例如效率至上)时,激活价值观 A(社会公平)的重要性不会影响人们对联名产品重量的判断。通过调节作用,笔者的研究表明这种价值观的感知重要性对于联名产品重量判断的影响是通过具身模拟(Embodied simulation)过程实现的。换言之,这意味着激活一个特定价值观的感知重要性可能会触发消费者的机体反应(Barsalou 1999,2008),而该机体反应成为消费者用于推断产品重量的线索。这些发现共同表明,消费者的推论过程不仅可以依赖于内隐理论、语义关联或者启发式,还可以通过由具身模拟过程激发的机体反应。

第五章的实证研究则以已往关于社会判断和品牌人格的研究(Abele and Wojciszke 2007; Kervyn, Fiske, and Malone 2012)为基础展开。在该研究中,笔者检验了初创品牌与知名品牌联名(vs.不联名)开发新产品时,消费者对该初创品牌的品牌人格推断将如何被影响。通过多个行为实验,笔者研究发现,与知名品牌进行联名会增加消费者在初创品牌"温暖"属性上的评分,但会降低其在初创品牌"能力"属性上的评分;当消费者相对更多关注初创品牌的温暖(vs.能力)维度时,与知名品牌的品牌联名可以增强(vs.降低)消费者对初创品牌的好感。该研究结果也整合了过去相关研究中不一致的发现(与知名品牌合作在何种情况下会对初创品牌有益 vs.有害),这对初创公司执行品牌联名战略,也具有管理学上的借鉴意义。

第四章

从感知重要性到物理重量判断：品牌联名如何改变消费者对产品的重量感知

本章探索在品牌联名的情况下,合作品牌传递的价值观如何影响消费者对联名产品物理重量的判断。通过五个行为实验,本章研究结果表明,当消费者认为价值观 A(例如社会公平)非常重要时,会高估与传递该价值观的品牌联名的产品的物理重量。而当目标产品不进行联名,或者与传递无关价值观 B(例如效率至上)的品牌进行联名时,消费者对价值观 A 的感知重要性不会影响到他们对产品物理重量的判断。结合具身模拟理论和信息可用性理论,本章研究认为当目标产品与传递价值观 A 的品牌进行联名时,激发消费者对价值观 A 的感知重要性会引发消费者的具身模拟过程,从而触发与承受重物相应的机体反应(例如更大的肌肉张力)。而该机体反应也会被消费者作为判断产品重量的信息线索,从而导致他们高估联名产品的物理重量。相反,当目标产品不进行品牌联名或者与传递无关价值观 B 的品牌进行联名时,激活价值观 A 的感知重要性无法引发消费者的具身模拟过程,从而不会影响他们对目标产品重量的判断。为了支持这种具身模拟机制,本章研究通过进一步实验发现上述"感知重要性—物理重量判断"效应会在消费者不持有产品就进行重量判断,以及消费者将具身模拟引发的机体反应进行错误归因时被削弱。本章还讨论了"感知重要性—物理重量判断"效应在营销学领域的下游变量。具体而言,本章研究指出该效应会进一步扩展到影响消费者对产品容量的判断和对产品卡路里含量的判断。在本章的最后,笔者讨论了本章研究的理论和实践意义。

第一节 研究背景

请大家想象以下的消费场景：张志和陈明正在考虑在同一家咖啡店购买一袋咖啡豆。在某品牌前驻足时，他们发现该品牌咖啡豆和一个关注社会公平的慈善机构（旨在增进发展中国家和边缘化地区生产者的生活水平）进行了品牌联名。张志认为社会公平这种价值观非常重要，而陈明对此则是觉得无所谓。那么这两位消费者对社会公平这一价值观的感知重要性是否会影响他们对同一袋咖啡豆的感官体验呢？类似于这种情况，很多商家会通过品牌联名或是其他营销渠道（广告代言、品牌社区、公益活动）宣扬自身品牌的价值观来吸引消费者。而消费者往往持有自己的价值观（追求不同的生活方式，认为生命具有不同的意义，采纳特定的文化价值与态度），或是会被外界信息（例如和朋友的交谈、观看到当天的新闻、当日生活遭遇）临时激发对某些价值观重要性的感知。那么，消费者感知到的某种价值观的重要性是否会影响到他们对传递相关或者无关价值观的产品物理性质（例如重量）的判断呢？

在消费者购物过程中，产品的重量体验是消费者的感官体验的重要组成部分（Deng and Kahn 2009; Krishna, Cian, and Aydınoğlu 2017）。根据自然科学或者工程类科学中对于重量的定义，个人对一个特定物体的重量判断应该仅仅取决于该物体的物理性质（例如质量，Bar, Brosh, and Sneider 2016）。然而，越来越多的营销学研究发现，消费者对产品重量的判断更多是一种主观

第四章 从感知重要性到物理重量判断：品牌联名如何改变消费者对产品的重量感知

的感官体验。这种主观的感官体验可能会受到各种因素的影响。例如，产品的包装设计(Deng and Kahn 2009; Van Rompay, Fransen, and Borgelink 2014)被发现对于产品重量感知有极大的影响。Deng 和 Kahn(2009)在研究中发现，当产品的图片被打印在外包装的右下角而不是其他位置时，消费者会更容易高估这一袋产品的重量。除开产品的设计因素，研究者还指出个体的生理和心理状态也会影响其对产品重量的判断。例如 Dai 和 Hsee (2013)发现，处于饥饿状态的消费者更倾向于高估同一块还未得到的蛋糕的重量。

具身认知(Embodied cognition)相关的理论表明，"重要性"这一抽象的语义概念和"重量"这一具体的感官概念在人类的知识和记忆系统中紧密相关(Jostmann, Lakens, and Schubert 2009; Schneider, Parzuchowski, Wojciszke, Schwarz, and Koole 2015)。因此，激活消费者的感知重要性可能会影响他们对物理重量的感觉和估计。然而，关于这一问题，已往研究却出现了不一致的结果(Schneider, Parzuchowski, Wojciszke, Schwarz, and Koole 2015; Zhang and Li 2012)。因此，现有的研究尚不能解释激活感知重要性是否以及如何影响消费者对产品重量的判断(Schneider, Rutjens, Jostmann, and Lakens 2011; Zhang and Li 2012)。而本章研究则基于营销场景，探讨了消费者感知到的特定价值观的重要性如何以及何时影响他们对和相应价值观品牌联名的产品重量的判断。这一研究可以整合已往研究中看似矛盾的结果，从而填补相关领域的研究空白。

已往关于感知重要性与物理重量关系的研究，主要集中在后者对前者的影响和作用上。具体而言，感受到较重的物理重量会影响个体对感知重要性的判断("物理重量—感知重要性判断"效应)。例如,Zhang和Li(2012)在实验中让被试提着装有瓶装水的购物袋(vs.不提重物),然后回答和消费者福利相关的议题是否重要。研究结果发现,当携带重物时,消费者会倾向于高估该议题的重要性。他们进一步发现,出现该效应的原因是携带重物的感官体验激发了语义上的"重量"概念。而由于语义上的"重量"和"重要"这两个概念是直接相关联的,因此也会导致被试认为判断目标更为"重要"。这一研究也证实了Jostmann等人(2009)的观点。

由于在语义上"重量"和"重要"这两个概念高度相关,研究者也开始关注是否先激活心理上的"重要"这一概念也会影响人们对物体重量的判断。然而有趣的是,已往研究却出现了不一致的结果。一些研究表明,激活感知重要性会使消费者高估他们持有的产品的物理重量(Schneider, Rutjens, Jostmann, and Lakens 2011)。而另一些研究却发现,感知重要性的激活并不会影响消费者对产品重量的判断(Zhang and Li 2012)。因此,如果能够找到研究框架以整合这些不一致的发现,将为这一研究领域提供充分的理论贡献。

此外,已往研究指出,抽象的概念(例如"重要")和具体的感官体验(例如感知的物理重量)之间的具身联系主要通过语义链接(Semantic association)来实现。语义链接是一种更加自动化(Automatic)的概念组织形式(Zhang and Li 2012)。一旦激活概念A,那么与该概念在语义上相关联的概念B应该会自动被激活。然而这一理论无法解释已往研究中关于"感知重要性—物理重量判断"效应的不一致发现。鉴于此,感知重要性对物理重量判断的潜在作用机制有待进一步研究。

具体来说,关于"物理重量—感知重要性判断"效应的研究(Jostmann, Lakens, and Schubert 2009; Zhang and Li 2012)支持前

者对后者的主效应。然而,通过分析已往关于"感知重要性—物理重量判断"效应的研究结果,笔者却发现前者对后者的影响受到某些因素的调节作用。Zhang和Li(2012)认为,物理重量的体验无论何时均可激活与感知重要性相关的语义概念。他们的研究进一步指出,哪怕并没有直接体验物理重量,而仅仅是通过语义上激活"重量"相关的抽象概念,也足以达到类似的效果。例如,通过社会认知研究中常用的启动范式(Priming paradigm)激活与重量相关的抽象概念(例如吨、秤),便足够让被试在下一个任务中高估消费者相关议题的重要性。然而他们的实验却发现语义上激活感知重要性并不能改变个体对物理重量的判断。因此,语义关联这一理论无法解释已往研究发现的"感知重要性—物理重量判断"效应。

近年来心理学和神经科学相关研究陆续指出,个体对具体感官体验(例如触觉、视觉、味觉)的判断会受到自身所处机体状态的影响(Si and Jiang 2017)。具体来说,个体会将自身的机体状态作为一种线索式信息(Cues),用以推断相关的感官信息。更有趣的是,这种机体状态的改变可以通过心理模拟来实现(Si and Jiang 2017)。而本章研究认为,激活感知重要性也将通过影响和重量感知相关的机体反应,来影响个体对物理重量的判断。由于从抽象概念到身体的具体感官反应是自上而下的认知过程(Top-down process)(Demanet, Verbruggen, Liefooghe and Vandierendonck 2010; Sarter, Givens, and Bruno 2001),会受到个体的目标、需求以及其他信息框架等因素的影响,因此从感知重要性到物理重量判断的影响路径也会受到其他因素的制约和调节。本章研究希望通过营销学情景中的实验解决两个问题:一是确认感知重要性到物理重量判断的影响机制;二是检验这一机制中潜在的边界条件或者调节作用。

在本章研究中,笔者采用了具身模拟机制来解释"感知重要性—物理重量判断"效应。根据这一机制,消费者对物理重量的感知会被他们当时机体所处的状态(例如持有重物时体会到的手臂肌肉紧张度)影响(Gallese and Caruana 2016)。而这种机体状态的改变则可能发生在消费者对一些与该状态相关的抽象概念(例如心理上或者概念上的"重要性")进行信息加工(例如进行心理上的模拟和想象)的时候(Kappes and Morewedge 2016)。值得注意的是,具身模拟机制(用于解释本章的"感知重要性—物理重量判断"效应)和语义关联理论(用于解释本章的"物理重量—感知重要性判断"效应)存在三个重要差别:其一,结合之前的讨论,笔者认为"物理重量—感知重要性判断"和"感知重要性—物理重量判断"分属自下而上加工和自上而下加工两个过程。其二,"感知重要性—物理重量判断"效应的出现,取决于感知重要性是否能引发和重量感知相关的机体反应,也就是说是否能成功激发心理模拟过程。其三,在"物理重量—感知重要性判断"效应中,物理重量的感知可以自动在语义网络中激活心理上或者概念上的"重要性"(Zhang and Li 2012)。这种效应不需要经过具身模拟过程(也就是说即便没有个体的机体反应参与,这一效应依然会出现)。然而,对于具身模拟过程来说,因为个体是将机体反应作为概念判断的线索,因此机体反应是必需的(Xi, Gong, and Wang 2019)。基于此,即便感知重要性激活了和重量感知相关的机体反应,如果该机体反应不能作为最终判断的线索,那么"感知重要性—物理重量判断"效应依然不会出现。

为了论证以上问题,笔者选择了品牌联名和价值观营销这样的研究情景。如前文所述,商家会选择和一些传递特定价值观的

第四章 从感知重要性到物理重量判断：品牌联名如何改变消费者对产品的重量感知

机构或者品牌进行合作,以帮助自己进行相关的价值观宣传(Srivoravilai, Melewar, Liu, and Yannopoulou 2011)。而过去的价值观营销研究主要是考察消费者对该类营销的态度和偏好,很少关注价值观营销如何影响消费者对产品的感官体验(Lotz, Christandl, and Fetchenhauer 2013; Poelman, Mojet, Lyon, and Sefa-Dedeh 2008)。基于该情景,本章研究指出,如果某产品选择和传递某种价值观(例如价值观A)的品牌联名,那么个体感知到的该价值观重要性会影响其对该产品重量的判断。相反,如果该产品没有选择和传递该价值观的品牌联名,或者联名品牌传递的价值观与价值观A无关甚至相矛盾,那么个体感知到的价值观A的重要性则不会对产品重量判断产生影响。例如,当我们增加消费者对"社会公平"这一价值观重要性的感知时,消费者会更容易高估与强调"促进社会公平"的公益机构进行品牌联名的产品的重量。我们将这种联名品牌强调价值观和消费者被激活的价值观彼此相关的情形称为"价值匹配情形"。相反,如果该产品是与强调"奢侈"或"优惠"的品牌进行联名,那么增加"社会公平"的感知重要性不会增加消费者对产品重量的判断。因为"社会公平"这一价值观和"奢侈"或是"优惠"存在价值不匹配的情况。简而言之,在我们的研究情景中,"感知重要性—物理重量判断"效应只出现在价值匹配的情况下,而不会出现在价值不匹配的情况中。

基于具身模拟理论,笔者解释了为什么上述的价值匹配对于"感知重要性—物理重量判断"至关重要。首先,笔者假设"感知重要性—物理重量判断"效应的发生不是由于两者之间单纯的语义联系,而是由于激活感知重要性(例如某价值观的感知重要性)成功导致了消费者对重量感知的机体反应(让消费者感觉自己像是在持有重物),也就是具身模拟过程。回到上述例子,当增强消费者对"社会公平"重要性的感知时,如果接下来消费者手持一个和强调公平的公益组织联名的产品,他们更容易在机体上模拟持有重物的体验(例如感受到更多的机体紧张和努力)。而这种机体上的体验便成为消费者用于判断产品重量的最直接依据。然而,一旦产品联名品牌传递的价值观(价值观 B)和消费者自身被激活感知重要性的价值观(价值观 A)之间不存在匹配性,那么消费者对价值观 A 重要性的感知将不适用于对目标产品的判断。也就是说,消费者不会将感知到的重要性用于对产品的判断。在这样的情况下,也就无从观察到"感知重要性—物理重量判断"效应。因此,价值匹配是该效应成立的一个决定性条件。

而另一个决定性条件,则是消费者与持有重物相关的机体反应(具身模拟过程的产物)是否能够被消费者作为判断产品重量的线索。一方面,尽管具身模拟过程为消费者的感官判断提供了充足的信息依据,但是这种效应也只有在消费者与产品存在感官接触时才能发生(例如品尝食物、持有物品)。另一方面,即便消费者与产品产生感官接触且具身模拟过程切实发生,消费者也必须要将该机体反应作为一种信息用于判断目标产品,否则具身模拟过程也无法影响最终的重量判断。

基于以上讨论,本章研究检验了两个调节变量来揭示"感知重要性—物理重量判断"效应背后的具身模拟机制。第一,笔者预测当消费者在没有实际与产品产生接触(即手持产品)的情况下估算产品重量时,即便在价值匹配的情况下,操纵价值观的感知重要性也不会显著改变消费者对产品物理重量的判断。这是因为当个体不与产品产生接触时,他们的机体反应(具身模拟过程)会被抑制,而且他们也无法直接将机体反应作为一种线索信息运用在对产品物理重量的判断上(Niedenthal 2007; Schneider, Rutjens,

Jostmann, and Lakens 2011)。因此,第一个调节变量是消费者是否持有产品。第二,笔者预测,在价值匹配的情况下,即便消费者手持产品,"感知重要性—物理重量判断"效应的发生还取决于消费者是否能够将自己在具身模拟中产生的机体反应运用到对物理重量的判断上。基于此,笔者预测,即便满足价值匹配和消费者手持产品两个条件,如果消费者将自己的机体反应归因于与重量判断的目标产品无关(不是由持有产品造成的),那么增加消费者的感知重要性也不会增加他们对产品物理重量的判断。具体而言,根据 Schwarz 和 Clore(1983)的研究,如果消费者将自己感受到的肌肉紧张归结为产品之外的情景因素(例如房间环境和设置),那么"感知重要性—物理重量判断"效应将消失。因此,第二个调节变量是消费者对机体反应的归因(归因于持有的产品 vs. 归因于与产品无关的因素)。

本章研究的理论贡献:第一,本章研究的假设提供了价值匹配这一研究框架,从而可以解释为什么已往关于"感知重要性—物理重量判断"效应的研究存在不一致的结果。第二,本章研究进一步指出在价值匹配的情况下,激活感知重要性是通过引发消费者的具身模拟过程来影响他们对产品物理重量的判断,从而提供了一种有别于已往研究的新机制来解读"感知重要性"和"物理重量"的关系。第三,为了证明这一机制,本章研究采用了调节检验的方法,通过对两个调节变量的探索来检验具身模拟的作用,丰富了过去具身认知研究中机制检验的方法论。第四,本章研究的理论框架也可以用于解读具身认知中的一个经典理论问题,即抽象概念和感官体验的联系究竟是双向的还是单向的。本章研究指出,从抽象概念到感官体验的联系相对来说会受到更多因素的制约,这也解释了为什么在具身认知研究中更多是发现感官体验对抽象概念判断的影响和作用。第五，本章研究在营销场景(价值观营销、品牌联名)中检验感知重要性和物理重量判断的关系，并探讨了这一效应的延伸作用(例如对产品卡路里含量的判断)，从而将价值观营销、品牌联名、感官营销(具身认知)和健康消费连接起来，这也可为产品设计师和品牌经理提供参考和借鉴。

第二节 文献综述

一、感知重要性和物理重量体验的关系

关于具身认知和语言学的实验研究为感知重要性与物理重量体验之间的关联提供了证据(Ackerman, Nocera, and Bargh 2010; Jostmann, Lakens, and Schubert 2009; Schneider, Parzuchowski, Wojciszke, Schwarz, and Koole 2015)。而这种关联也在个人的日常交流语言中得到了充分的支持(Jostmann, Lakens, and Schubert 2009)。例如，词语"重量级"既可以用来指代高于平均水平的物理重量，又可以在日常交流中用于描述一个人在能力、影响力、地位、资源上的重要性。在英文中也可以发现类似现象，短语"Add weight to"通常等同于日常交流中的"Attach importance to"。可见，感知重要性和物理重量之间的语义联系，在东方和西方文化中都可以得到佐证。

研究者试图探讨感知重要性和物理重量之间的因果关系，即激活感知重要性是否会影响物理重量判断，若反过来效应是否也会成立。目前大多数实证研究证明了激活物理重量体验会对消费

第四章　从感知重要性到物理重量判断：品牌联名如何改变消费者对产品的重量感知

者的感知重要性判断产生影响。也就是说，当个体在感知到更重的物理重量的状态下对某些事物的重要性进行判断时，其对该事物重要性的感知也会增加（Ackerman，Nocera，and Bargh 2010；Chandler，Reinhard，and Schwarz 2012；Maglio and Trope 2012；Zhang and Li 2012）。例如，Jostmann 等人（2009）在实验中发现，当实验被试在较为沉重（vs.较为轻便）的写字板上完成调查时，他们会认为调查中被问及的社会议题（例如"大学委员会是否听取学生的意见"）更为重要。与此相关的是，Zhang 和 Li（2012）则采用双任务范式（Two-task paradigm）重复了这一效应。具体来说，他们让实验的参与者连续完成两个任务。在第一个任务中，一半被试携带（vs.不携带）沉重的购物袋，这也是操纵感知的物理重量的方法。而在第二个任务中，他们需要完成一个调查。这个调查的一个核心问题是，他们在多大程度上觉得选择包装食品时阅读营养信息是重要的。结果显示，相对于在第一个任务中不携带重物的实验被试，那些在第一个任务中携带了重物的实验被试更加容易认为阅读营养信息是重要的。

尽管已往研究在"物理重量—感知重要性判断"效应上得到了一致的结果，但是在"感知重要性—物理重量判断"效应上却到了不一致的结论。一部分研究发现了支持该效应的证据。例如，Schneider 等人（2011）在研究中要求实验被试手持一本书并估算其重量。对于一半的实验参与者，他们通过实验操纵增强了被试对这本书重要性的感知。而在另一组中，这种重要性感知没有被操纵。结果表明，当书的重要性被强化时，实验被试会认为这本书的物理重量也更重。在 2015 年的一项研究中，研究者用 U 盘为实验材料，重复了这一发现（Schneider，Parzuchowski，Wojciszke，Schwarz，and Koole 2015）。在他们的研究中，一半的被试被告知手持的U盘存储有重要的数据,而另一半的被试则被告知这些数据已经过期。结果显示,当人们认为U盘存储有重要的数据时,他们会更倾向于高估U盘的重量。虽然以上两个研究提供了对于"感知重要性—物理重量判断"效应的支持,但其他的研究者却未能得到支持的结论。例如,在Zhang和Li(2012)的一项研究中,实验参与者首先被要求回忆自己做出的重要决定(vs.控制信息)以操纵感知重要性。接下来,在随后的任务中,他们被要求拿着产品并判断其重量。他们的研究结果表明,在实验中激活感知重要性不会影响消费者对手持产品物理重量的判断。

为了整合以上研究中关于"感知重要性—物理重量判断"效应不一致的发现,笔者指出这一效应与"物理重量—感知重要性判断"效应涉及不同的机制。具体而言,笔者提出了基于具身模拟理论的解释,并指出了具身模拟机制引发"感知重要性—物理重量判断"效应的几个先决条件。在以下的部分,笔者将首先就具身模拟机制进行阐述,并结合具体的营销情景,讨论"感知重要性—物理重量判断"效应成立的条件。

二、影响物理重量的机体反应

来自生理学和心理学的研究表明,个体对物体的重量感知会受到人们手持物体时自身机体运动系统相应活动的影响(Aniss, Gandevia, and Milne 1988; Gandevia and McCloskey 1977; Jones 1986)。这些机体运动系统的活动主要受到大脑中与自主肌肉收缩有关的神经系统的影响(Marcora 2009; Morree, Klein, and Marcora 2012)。当个人携带或者持有物体时,大脑中的相应区域会发出信号,通知自己的身体接下来将要进行大量的体力劳动。接下来大脑中相应区域会与相关的运动神经元进行通信,使身体的肌肉进行自主的收缩并产生肌肉张力,帮助个体施加力量(Aniss, Gandevia, and Milne 1988; Gandevia 1987; Gandevia and McCloskey 1977; Widmaier, Raff, and Strang 2004)。根据这些研究,个体对物理重量的感知取决于个体在承载物体重量时所处的身体状态(例如神经和肌肉系统中的活动)。因此,个体对物理重量的感知,一部分来源于该物体的实际重量,而另一部分则来源于个体的主观感受(受到其机体状态的影响)。来自认知科学的研究为该观点提供了实证支持。例如,研究者发现,如果他们改变实验参与者同负重有关的身体状态(例如抑制运动神经元、增加运动神经元兴奋度,抑或是使肌肉麻痹),那么这些实验参与者对物体的重量估计会产生偏差(Aniss, Gandevia, and Milne 1988; Gandevia and McCloskey 1977; Jones 1986)。

改变个体在持有重物时的机体状态并不仅限于通过生理和神经上的干预。具身模拟理论(Barsalou 1999, 2008; Gallese and Lakoff 2005; Gibbs 2006)指出,个体可以在心理上模拟自己在某特定状态下的机体反应,并促使相应机体部分产生"身临其境"的反应。而这种心理模拟过程,可以来自个体对抽象概念进行加工的过程,也可以来自个体的想象和回忆。具身模拟理论的大量研究文献表明,激活抽象概念会触发相关的身体状态并影响人们对机体感觉和体验的判断(Barsalou 1999, 2008; Decety and Grèzes 2006; Niedenthal, Winkielman, Mondillon, and Vermeulen 2009; Pecher, Zeelenberg, and Barsalou 2003)。来自神经科学的研究发现,当被试思考关于不道德行为这一抽象概念时,他们会更多感觉到自身的肮脏感。这种肮脏感会体现在个体相应的神经皮层活动上,并进而影响他们对清洁产品的评估与判断(Denke, Rotte, Heinze, and Schaefer 2016)。此外,Pulvermüller(2005)的研究显示,阅读有关特定动作(例如踢脚)的单词会触发被试相应运动系统中的机体活动(例如腿部肌肉活动和运动神经元的兴奋),就好像读者真的正在执行该动作一样。

在重量感知领域,具身模拟理论也提供了对于"感知重要性—物理重量判断"效应的一种可能解释。加工"感知重要性"可能会通过具身模拟导致和持有重物相关的机体反应。已往研究表明,处理重要问题需要个体投入更多的认知上和体力上的努力(Chaiken and Maheswaran 1994;Duffy 1951)。而投注努力(无论是认知上还是体力上)通常会激发身体的紧张反应。例如个体会在神经系统上体会到紧张感,并在肌肉系统中感受到更多的张力(Cacioppo, Petty, and Morris 1985;Duffy 1951;Gandevia and McCloskey 1977)。如前文所述,这些机体反应已被证明与个体对物理重量的感知有关(Gandevia and McCloskey 1977)。综上所述,笔者假设激活感知重要性可以通过具身模拟过程使持有物体的人产生类似于负重的机体状态。而这种机体状态也被人们当作判断物体重量的线索,导致他们高估所持物体的物理重量。

值得注意的是,如果"感知重要性—物理重量判断"效应是由具身模拟过程驱动,那么已往研究没有观察到该效应的一个可能原因是该具身模拟过程的运作受到了抑制或干扰。在本章研究中,笔者指出,要想观察到"感知重要性—物理质量判断"效应,整个实验需满足三个条件:价值匹配的作用和具身模拟机制的两个调节变量。笔者假设感知重要性的来源(可以感知到重要性的事物)和物理重量判断涉及的目标(需要被判断物理重量的事物)之间应该存在直接的关系。这一点在成功发现"感知重要性—物理重量判断"效应的研究中得到了佐证。例如操纵消费者对一本书重要性的感知,可以影响他们对同一本书的重量的判断

(Schneider, Rutjens, Jostmann, and Lakens 2011)。再或者是感知到 U 盘中存储数据的重要性会影响到被试对该 U 盘重量的判断(Schneider, Parzuchowski, Wojciszke, Schwarz, and Koole 2015)。这一研究中感知重要性的来源是存储在 U 盘中的数据,而重量判断涉及的目标则为承载数据的载体,即 U 盘。因此这两者之间也是密切相关的。相比之下,在 Zhang 和 Li(2012)的研究中,"感知重要性—物理重量判断"效应未能被发现,一定程度上可能是因为其感知重要性的来源(例如生活中的重要决定)和物理重量判断的目标(一个消费产品)之间并不存在必然的联系。基于这一观察,笔者在品牌联名和价值观营销的场景中试图检验以上的猜想。具体而言,当消费者的某种价值观(例如价值观 A)的感知重要性被激活时,他们对和传递同样价值观的品牌进行联名的产品重量的判断也会增加。然而如果目标产品选择与传递无关价值观(例如价值观 B)的品牌联名,那么感知重要性不会影响消费者对目标产品重量的判断。我们把前者的情形称为价值匹配(即感知重要性对应的价值观和联名品牌涉及的价值观相同),而将后者的情形称为价值不匹配(即感知重要性对应的价值观和联名品牌涉及的价值观不相关)。本章研究假设价值匹配是"感知重要性—物理重量判断"效应成立的前提之一。

三、"感知重要性—物理重量判断"效应成立的条件一:价值匹配的作用

如本章研究开篇的示例所言,在生活中消费者对某些价值观重要性的感知会在很多场景中被激活(例如短视频、公众号文章、被推送的公益广告)。在现实的商业世界中,很多营销者都试图在品牌中传递一些价值观或者象征意义,例如"扶贫""怀旧""本土

精神""绿色消费"(Barham 2002; Onozaka and McFadden 2011; Schuldt, Muller, and Schwarz 2012; Schuldt and Schwarz 2010)。在品牌联名的场景中,很多初创品牌为了增强品牌觉知和树立品牌形象,也会选择和这些传递特定价值观的品牌进行联名。而根据前文讨论,笔者预测,只有在价值匹配的情况下,我们才能观察到"感知重要性—物理重量判断"效应。例如,激活消费者对"怀旧"重要性的感知,会使得消费者高估和怀旧品牌进行联名的产品的重量。然而消费者对"怀旧"重要性的感知却不会影响他们对和传递"奢侈""现代感"等价值观(和怀旧无关甚至相矛盾)的品牌进行联名的产品的物理重量。换言之,本章研究认为,价值匹配是决定"感知重要性—物理重量判断"效应的一个先决条件。

值得注意的是,尽管同为对"感知重要性—物理重量判断"效应的研究,本章的研究思路与已往相关研究不同(Schneider, Parzuchowski, Wojciszke, Schwarz, and Koole 2015; Schneider, Rutjens, Jostmann, and Lakens 2011)。首先,本章研究致力于在营销情景中对该效应进行检验。例如,笔者考察了价值观营销和品牌联名的研究场景。其次,本章研究操纵感知重要性的方式与已往研究不同。具体来说,已往研究操纵产品自身的成分或者内容,例如书的内容或U盘中存储的内容,而本章研究操纵消费者在日常生活或是消费场景中会遇到的价值观的重要性。最后,由于笔者的目标是考察价值匹配在激发"感知重要性—物理重量判断"效应中的必要性,故本章研究通过品牌联名的场景来操纵目标产品所展示的价值观,而并没有改变目标产品本身的属性(例如不涉及基本内容或者制造工艺等属性上的变动)。值得注意的是,为了能够增加研究的说服力,笔者专门选择了双任务范式。这是因为Zhang和Li(2012)采用这种方式未能观察到显著的"感知重要性—物理重量判断"效应。因此,如果笔者采用这种范式成功观察到该效应,那么更能证明笔者提出理论的准确性。

本章研究假设,只有当感知重要性涉及的价值观与目标产品联名品牌的价值观相匹配时,才能观察到"感知重要性—物理重量判断"效应。笔者认为这出于两个原因:第一,基于前文关于具身模拟理论的讨论,笔者认为从抽象概念激活到引发感官体验的机制与反向作用(从感官体验到抽象概念判断)涉及的机制不同。第二,感知重要性本身是一个比较特殊的概念。与涉及个体情绪和感受的抽象概念(例如压力、快乐)不同,研究者指出感知重要性并非自动地对应基于重量感知的机体反应(Zhang and Li 2012)。也就是说,激活感知重要性可能不会自动触发与负重经历相关的机体状态和机体反应。当感知重要性无法自动指向与负重相关的机体体验时,就需要一些线索因素将两者联系起来。笔者在本章研究中假设激活特定价值观的感知重要性仅在价值匹配的状态下才会显著影响消费者对产品物理重量的判断。这是因为,当产品与具有相关价值观的品牌联名时,关于该价值观的重要性才能直接被链接到对目标产品的判断上。也就是说,当个体认为价值观 A 很重要,而产品又和具有价值观 A 的品牌进行联名时,消费者对价值观 A 重要性的感知才可能被纳入对产品的判断中。在这种情况下,激活价值观 A 的感知重要性才会引发消费者的具身模拟过程,进而导致消费者高估手持产品的物理重量。相反,当产品与具有无关价值观的品牌进行联名时,消费者对价值观 A 重要性的感知并不能作为一种适用于判断目标产品的信息。关于价值匹配的这一讨论,事实上基于自上而下加工中的目标导向加工(Goal-directed processing)和信息加工理论中的信息适用性原则(Applicability of information)。这些原则也在另外的具身认知的研究中得到了证实。例如 Lee 和 Schwarz(2012)探索了抽象概念"社会怀疑"和具体感官体验"鱼腥味"在西方文化中的联系。他们研究发现,只有当实验参与者认为社会怀疑这一抽象信息可以用于判断产品的感官体验时,激活这一抽象信息才可能会扭曲人们对产品气味的判断。基于以上讨论,笔者提出本章研究的第一个假设:

假设 1:增加消费者对某特定价值观(例如价值观 A)的感知重要性会导致其高估与相关价值观品牌联名的产品的物理重量。而当该产品与传递无关价值观(例如价值观 B)或者不传递任何价值观的品牌联名时,激活价值观 A 的感知重要性不会显著影响消费者对产品物理重量的判断。

四、"感知重要性—物理重量判断"效应成立的条件二和条件三:具身模拟机制的两个调节变量

本章研究认为"感知重要性—物理重量判断"效应是由具身模拟机制所引起的。如果这一解释成立,那么用于抑制和干扰该机制的调节变量便会削弱或者消除"感知重要性—物理重量判断"效应。在本章研究中,笔者主要探究了两个重要的调节因素:其一,用于抑制感知重要性对于具身模拟过程影响的调节变量;其二,当具身模拟过程发生之后,可以干扰该过程对最终物理重量判断产生直接影响的调节变量。而对这些调节变量的检验,既可以探查"感知重要性—物理重量判断"效应成立的条件,又可以为具身模拟机制提供必要的实证支持,同时还可以排除其他备选解释。

针对第一个问题,笔者认为消费者在判断产品重量的过程中是否持有该产品是一个重要的调节变量。对于这一调节变量的检验基于以下的推理过程。如前文所述,笔者认为"感知重要性—物理重量判断"效应是由具身模拟过程而不是语义链接过程(Zhang

第四章　从感知重要性到物理重量判断：品牌联名如何改变消费者对产品的重量感知

and Li 2012)来实现。具身模拟过程意味着个体机体反应和机体状态参与到了判断形成的过程中。而语义链接过程仅仅通过语义和概念在人脑中的知识网络链接就可以实现。例如，如果从语义链接过程解释"感知重要性—物理重量判断"效应，那么激活"感知重要性"可以导致在知识网络中和"重量"相关的抽象概念的激活。但是，这一过程不必通过机体的反应。为了支持具身模拟理论并排除掉这个替代性解释，笔者认为有必要检验个体在不持有产品的状态下对产品进行重量判断时，"感知重要性—物理重量判断"效应是否会消失。这是因为如果具身模拟是核心机制，那么当消费者在不实际持有产品的情况下进行重量判断时，他们的机体参与将会被抑制。换言之，具身模拟的过程将会被抑制，从而直接削弱感知重要性对于物理重量判断的影响。但是，如果"感知重要性—物理重量判断"效应是通过语义链接完成的，那么无论消费者是否在持有产品的情况下做重量判断，应该都能观察到激活感知重要性对于产品物理重量判断的影响。基于以上讨论，笔者提出本章研究的第二个假设：

假设2：在价值匹配的情景下，"感知重要性—物理重量判断"效应的产生取决于消费者在判断产品物理重量时是否持有该产品。当消费者持有该产品时，激活感知重要性会显著影响他们对产品物理重量的判断。而当消费者不持有该产品时，激活感知重要性不会显著影响他们对产品物理重量的判断。

针对第二个问题，笔者基于前文中提到的"感觉作为信息理论"(Schwarz 2011；Schwarz and Clore 1983)提出了另一个调节变量。基于这一理论，个体会将因为偶然因素（或者和目标无关的因素）引发的感受作为信息线索，导致其对目标事物的判断受到影响。例如，当个体处在良好的天气条件中，他们会将这种好天气带来的积极情绪引入对他人或者产品的判断中。反过来,如果个体将和目标判断相关的感受信息归结为来自目标以外的无关因素(例如外来的环境因素),那么他们将通过减少对该感受信息的依赖来修正自己对目标的判断(Schwarz 2004; Shen, Jiang, and Adaval 2010)。例如,研究发现如果个体将判断服务商时悲观的感受归结为来自空气污染,那么他们会避免使用这种感受作为判断依据(Zhang, Hou, Li, and Huang 2020)。根据以上讨论,本章研究假设消费者对自身机体反应的归因是具身模拟机制的另一个调节变量,也是决定"感知重要性—物理重量判断"效应是否发生的第三个因素。具体来说,笔者假设,如果消费者将自身的机体反应(即具身模拟的产物)归因于和目标产品无关的情景因素(例如房间设置、灯光等环境因素),那么即便在价值匹配的情况下,"感知重要性—物理重量判断"效应也不会发生。对这一调节变量的检验不但可以为具身模拟过程提供另一种实证支持,也从另一个方面排除了语义关联假设。如果"感知重要性—物理重量判断"效应是由语义关联驱动,那么无论个体是否将机体反应归因于场景因素,激活感知重要性都能影响物理重量判断。反之,则说明激活感知重要性对于物理重量判断的影响依然取决于个体的机体反应和机体状态。基于以上讨论,笔者提出本章研究的第三个假设:

假设3:在价值匹配的情况下,"感知重要性—物理重量判断"效应的产生也取决于消费者对自身机体反应的归因。即便在价值匹配的情况下,如果个体将自己的机体反应(即具身模拟产物)归因于和产品无关的外来因素(例如房间设置),那么激活感知重要性不会显著影响消费者对产品物理重量的判断。反之,则依然可以观察到感知重要性对于物理重量判断的影响。

第三节 实证研究部分

一、本章研究的实验架构

为了检验本章研究提出的三个假设,笔者采用了行为实验的方法。每一个实验均采用了类似于 Zhang 和 Li(2012)研究中的双任务范式。在第一个任务中,笔者将操纵某种特定价值观的感知重要性。在第二个任务中,笔者则将让被试判断目标产品的物理重量。值得注意的是,在第二个任务中,本章研究将同时操纵与目标产品联名的品牌的价值观,使得该价值观和第一个任务中涉及的价值观相关(价值匹配)或是无关(价值不匹配)。为了增加本章研究的可推广性,笔者在实验中操纵和测量了不同价值观的感知重要性,涵盖社会公平、怀旧、所属学校的精神。笔者之所以选择这几种价值观,主要是因为这些价值观被广泛运用于当前的营销情景中(Barham 2002)。例如,怀旧营销是很多经典食品品牌常用的营销手段,旨在通过对产品的怀旧化包装或是宣传使消费者回想起"过往的美好时光"(Roberts 2016)。强调增加社会公平、关爱弱势群体的价值观宣传也常见于各种社会公益广告和产品善因营销中(Cheng 2015)。因此,对这些价值观的感知重要性进行操纵或者测量也有助于增强研究的管理实践意义。笔者在双任务范式中选择操纵和目标产品联名的品牌传递的价值观,这样可以避免直接对目标产品的相应属性进行改变。具体来说,由于人们可能认为具有不同价值观的同类产品也可能存在其他方面属性的差异(例如制作工艺、制作材料),因此本章研究特地采用品牌联名的研究情景,排除由产品品类带来的混淆因素,更干净清晰地检验"感知重要性—物理重量判断"效应。

  本章研究的行为实验采用如下逻辑框架进行组织。首先,在研究的方法论上,本章研究的实验1和实验3测量了消费者对特定价值观重要性的感知,实验2、实验4、实验5则采用了社会心理学中的启动范式(Priming paradigm)来操纵消费者感知到的特定价值观的重要性。其次,实验1和实验2的目标是检验价值匹配对于"感知重要性—物理重量判断"效应的必要性(假设1)。实验3和实验4则通过检验两个调节变量(是否持有物品,是否对机体反应做出其他归因)的方法为具身模拟机制提供了实证支持(假设2和假设3)。而实验5则试图检验"感知重要性—物理重量判断"效应是否能扩展影响消费者对产品其他属性的判断。本章研究特别探讨了感知重要性对于物理重量判断的影响是否会延伸影响人们对产品卡路里含量的判断,从而增强了研究的实践意义。值得注意的是,这些实验不仅用于检验本章研究的三个假设,也试图排除掉一些潜在的备选解释。例如,实验4既可以排除语义关联对于"感知重要性—物理重量判断"效应的解释,也可以排除本效应是由消费者对产品态度的变化所引起的。此外,笔者在实验2和实验3中记录了实验被试花费在目标产品物理重量判断上的时间,也在实验5中要求被试报告他们对花费在重量判断任务上的时间的主观感受。通过这两项指标,我们可以排查"感知重要性—物理重量判断"效应是否源自消费者在物理重量判断任务中投入了不同的精力和注意力。排除这些解释,有助于我们进一步巩固具身模拟理论的解释。

二、实验1

实验1的研究目标主要是检验第一个假设。根据身份认同营销(Identity marketing)的相关研究(Bhattacharjee, Berger, and Menon 2014;Dalton and Huang 2014),笔者选择了消费者所属机构的相应价值观(例如所在学校的学校精神)作为研究对象。根据群体心理学的相关研究,个体从属的群体往往存在一个被群体内成员所共同支持的价值观。个体对其所属群体的认同强度也揭示了该共同价值观在他们心中的重要程度(Dalton and Huang 2014;Hitlin 2003;White, Argo, and Sengupta 2012)。基于这一前提,实验1选择了学生被试参与研究,并首先在第一个任务中测量学生被试对自己所属学校的认同感,来作为学校价值在他们心目中感知重要性的相关指标。然后,在第二个任务中,参与实验的被试被要求手持目标产品(例如运动水壶)并判断其物理重量。价值匹配则通过操纵该目标产品联名品牌所宣传的价值观来实现。实验1假设,当联名品牌宣传和被试所在学校相近的价值观时(强调该联名生产的运动水壶是为被试所在学校的周年庆专门设计),被试对自己所处学校的认同感越强,他们越倾向于认为该水壶具有较重的物理重量。相反,当联名品牌宣传的价值观和被试所在学校无关时(强调该联名生产的运动水壶是为其他学校设计),被试对母校的认同感不会影响他们对目标水壶物理重量的判断。

(一)实验方法

被试与实验设计:来自中国香港某高校的125名大学本科生(女性占比为73%,平均年龄为20.39岁)参加了该有偿行为实验。实验1采用2(所在学校价值观的感知重要性:高重要性 vs.低重要性)×2(联名品牌的价值观:价值匹配 vs.价值不匹配)的被试间设计。其中,所处学校价值观的感知重要性采用测量的方式,而品牌联名类型则进行实验操纵。根据我们在前文的讨论,联名品牌为被试所处高校周年庆设计运动水壶即是一种价值匹配情形,而联名品牌为其他高校周年庆设计运动水壶即为一种价值不匹配情形。

实验步骤与测量:实验1采用双任务的实验范式,也意味着被试将连续完成两个任务。在第一个任务中,被试被要求完成一个关于校园生活的调查。而这个调查的核心问题是测量被试感知的学校价值观的重要性。在第二个任务中,被试将手持一个运动水壶并判断其物理重量。具体内容如下:

任务1:测量被试对所处学校价值观重要性的感知。在这个所谓的校园生活调查中,被试需要先回答人口学相关问题(例如性别、年龄、母语、专业、年级、学历类型),然后填写关于学校价值观感知重要性的量表。该量表为9点量表,含有4个题目,改编自前人的相关研究(Cameron 2004; Dalton and Huang 2014)。具体来说,被试将阅读每个题目中的陈述,然后回答在多大程度上他们同意或者不同意该陈述。例如,"我的性格和[所在学校的名称]的特征之间有很多相同之处",1=完全不同意,9=完全同意。总分越高则代表在被试心目中自己所处学校的价值观越重要。

任务2:判断产品的物理重量。被试被告知需要手持一个运动水壶并判断其物理重量。被试会被随机分成两组(价值匹配组 vs.价值不匹配组)以接受不同的关于该运动水壶的信息。所有的被试均会被告知该运动水壶是由一家运动产品制造商设计,而这家制造商正在与当地大学进行品牌联名来为当地大学设计运动水壶。在价值匹配情形下,被试被告知该运动产品制造商与被试所在的大学进行联名,专门为该校校庆设计了这款运动水壶。而在价值不匹配情形下,被试被告知该运动产品制造商与当地另一所大学(不是被试所在的大学)进行联名,专门为该校校庆设计了运动水壶。事实上,所有被试持有的水壶均是相同水壶,实际重量约为368克。为了增加研究操纵的效果,笔者在电脑屏幕上向被试呈现关于这款水壶的相关介绍,并在该水壶上粘贴相应的品牌标签。例如,在价值匹配组中,水壶上粘贴有被试所在大学的校徽,而在价值不匹配组中,水壶上则会被贴上本地其他大学的校徽。通过这样的手段,可以让被试清晰了解该水壶生产商是与哪一所大学联名。接下来,所有被试被要求用自己的惯用手去持有该运动水壶,然后在电脑屏幕上拖动滑块(在100克至800克的范围之间)来标明他们估计的该运动水壶的物理重量(以克为单位)。最后,被试提交问卷,获得参与实验的报酬。

(二)实验结果

首先,笔者将被试在测量学校价值观重要性的四个题目上的得分进行平均值计算($\alpha=0.82$,说明信度良好)。较高的平均分代表被试认为所在学校价值观更重要。与此同时,笔者将价值匹配组进行相应编码(1=价值匹配,-1=价值不匹配)。随后,笔者首先将感知学校价值观重要性和价值匹配组分别进行标准化,并基于这两个变量标准化的结果生成交互项。接着,笔者以产品物理重量判断(以克为单位)为因变量,以感知学校价值观重要性(标准化)、价值匹配(标准化)、交互项为预测变量进行回归分析。回归分析的结果显示,学校价值观的感知重要性($p>0.30$)和价值匹配($p>0.50$)的主效应均不显著。更重要的是,这两者之间的交互作用在统计学上显著($\beta=0.18$, $t(121)=2.01$, $p=0.047$,使用非标准化数据绘制的交互作用请见图4-1）。Simple Slope Test结果显示，在价值匹配的情况下，学校价值观的感知重要性与运动水壶的物理重量判断之间存在正向的相关关系（$\beta=0.27$，$t(121)=2.34$，$p=0.021$）。也就是说，当被试认为他们所在学校的价值观越重要，他们就越容易高估和自己学校联名的运动水壶的物理重量。相比之下，在价值不匹配情景中，所处学校价值观的感知重要性与运动水壶物理重量判断之间不存在显著相关关系（$\beta=-0.09$，$t(121)=-0.65$，$p>0.50$）。换言之，当运动水壶没有和被试所在学校进行品牌联名时，那么被试感知到的自己母校价值观重要性不会影响他们对运动水壶物理重量的判断。

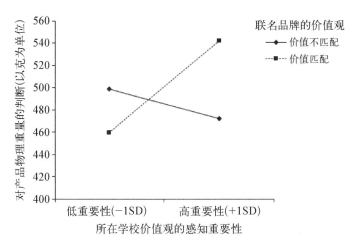

图4-1 感知重要性与联名品牌的价值观对于产品物理重量判断的影响（实验1）

（三）结果讨论

实验1的研究结果为假设1提供了实证支持。具体来说，实验1发现，即便在双任务范式中也能重现"感知重要性—物理重量判断"效应。而这一效应出现的关键在于价值匹配,因为其提供了人们将感知重要性信息运用到产品重量判断上的路径。实验1的研究结果和前人研究结果相似(Zhang and Li 2012),这也再次证明了感知重要性对物理重量判断的影响并非是单纯的语义关联作用。值得注意的是,实验1采用品牌联名和价值观营销的研究场景,对产品设计师和营销者具有一定的借鉴意义。由于实验1选择了功能型的产品(Utilitarian products),因此有必要检验"感知重要性—物理重量判断"效应是否也可以在享乐型产品上(Hedonic products)得到重现。所以在实验2中,笔者选择了咖啡这一享乐型产品。实验1采用测量的方法测量了某种价值观的感知重要性,实验2则直接操纵消费者对某种价值观重要性的感知,从而更好地提供因果关系(而不是相关关系)的检验。实验1采用学生对学校价值观重要性的感知进行研究,实验2则采用市场中的其他价值观进行研究,从而扩大了研究的外部效度。

三、实验2

实验2旨在通过不同实验情景、不同实验范式和不同产品品类来为假设1提供额外的实证支持。笔者选择"社会公平"这一价值观作为研究对象,并操纵其在被试心中的感知重要性。同时,选择盒装咖啡粉这一享乐产品来让被试估计其物理重量。实验2不仅希望通过操纵价值观感知重要性来检验其与产品物理重量判断的因果关系,还希望通过这一实验排除一些备选解释。具体来说,与实验1相同,实验2会排除语义关联解释。除此之外,实验2还将检验是否感知重要性激活和价值匹配一起影响到了被试在物理重量判断任务上的投入度与注意力。基于这种观点的假设是:当认为某种价值观很重要的消费者在估计目标产品重量时,如果发现该产品与传递相同价值观的品牌联名,那么这些消费者会认为该重量评估任务更加重要。于是他们会倾向于投入更多时间和精力参与到该任务中,以便更精确地做出评估。而这种在任务中时间和精力的投入差异(以及追求精确估计的动机),也许造成了对物理重量估计的影响。值得注意的是,这种解释的核心驱动因素是被试对任务的动机和投入(例如更多时间付出在重量估计上)。然而与之不同的是,笔者认为只要处于价值匹配的情况下,操纵感知重要性就足以快速激活个体的机体反应,这并不需要通过改变对任务的投入度来实现。因此,为了排除关于任务投入度的解释,为之后实验的具身模拟机制检验奠定基础,笔者测量了实验被试在重量估计任务中手持产品的时间作为控制变量。

(一)实验方法

被试与实验设计:来自中国香港某高校的 125 名本科生参加了该有偿行为实验。在实验过程中,有 2 名被试未遵循研究者的指示,因此被排除在最终的数据分析之外。剩余的 123 名被试(女性占比为 75%,平均年龄为 20.07 岁)最终被纳入数据分析。实验 2 采用了 2(社会公平的感知重要性:高重要性 vs.控制组)×2(联名品牌的价值观:价值匹配 vs.价值不匹配)的被试间设计。笔者选择以盒装咖啡粉作为目标消费产品,并预测激活社会公平的感知重要性将使被试高估与代表公平价值观的公益机构联名的盒装咖啡粉的物理重量。然而如果该咖啡粉没有与代表公平价值观的公益机构进行联名,则激活社会公平的感知重要性不会显著影响被试对盒装咖啡粉物理重量的判断。

实验步骤与测量:与实验 1 相同,实验 2 依然采用双任务范式,但是在此基础上做出了一些调整。为了避免被试猜出实验的

第四章 从感知重要性到物理重量判断：品牌联名如何改变消费者对产品的重量感知

真实目的,同时也为了增强无意识启动的效果,实验2在感知重要性激活任务(任务1)和产品物理重量判断任务(任务2)之间加入了一些无关题目(Filler questions)。具体内容如下：

任务1：操纵社会公平这一价值观的感知重要性。为了隐藏这一任务的真实目的,所有被试都会被告知他们将参与一个阅读理解任务。在这个任务中,被试关于社会公平的感知重要性将被操纵。被试首先被随机分成两组(高重要性 vs.控制组)。处于高重要性组的被试被告知需要阅读一篇解释如何促进落后地区的生产者的公平待遇的文章。这篇文章也强调了为什么保持社会公平对人类社会是极其重要的。处于控制组的被试则被要求阅读一篇和社会公平完全无关的文章。这篇文章主要是介绍一种新型的太空船的相关属性和性能。为了增强实验操纵的效果,这两个组的被试均被要求使用自己的语言文字总结所读文章的要点。为了检验和控制被试在该阅读理解任务中参与度差异和文章难度差异潜在的影响,笔者首先记录了被试在阅读理解任务上花费的时间(以"秒"为单位)。同时,笔者还通过一个9点量表测量了被试感知到的理解文章的难度("理解本文的内容有多难?"1=非常容易,9=非常困难)。

在完成第一个阅读理解任务之后,被试接下来完成了一些无关题目的问答。这些问题主要是测量消费者在日常生活中的偏好,例如对电影类型的喜爱或者对音乐风格的选择。完成这些无关题目之后,所有被试进入下一个任务。

任务2：判断产品的物理重量。在该任务中,被试需要手持一盒研磨咖啡粉并判断其物理重量。该盒咖啡粉的实际重量为520克。为了尽可能减少产品品牌和营养成分等信息对实验结果可能的影响,笔者统一告诉被试这是来自某品牌(虚构的)的盒装咖啡粉。此外,笔者事先对该盒咖啡粉进行了包装,遮盖了相关的营养信息,并且全程不允许实验被试拆开包装盒。所以被试对该款盒装咖啡粉产品信息的了解,都是来源于笔者在计算机屏幕上呈现的产品描述信息,以及笔者在咖啡粉包装盒上粘贴的标签。产品描述信息和标签主要是用于操纵品牌联名的类型。被试被随机分为两组(价值匹配 vs.价值不匹配)。价值匹配组的被试被告知,该款咖啡产品与某公益组织进行联名。该组织旨在扶助发展中国家和边远地区的生产者,从而促进社会公平(见本章附录4-1)。在价值不匹配组,被试被告知该款咖啡产品与当地一家零售商联名。该联名信息并不包含促进社会公平的价值观诉求。然后,所有的被试被要求用自己的惯用手去持有该盒咖啡粉并估计其重量。他们需要拖动滑块,在0克到800克的范围中做出选择。如前文所述,笔者也专门记录了被试在该重量估计任务中手持咖啡粉并做重量判断的时间。

(二)实验结果

在开始检验主要的研究假设之前,笔者先分析了一系列混淆因素的潜在作用。独立样本 t 检验的结果表明,高重要性组被试($M=371.66$ 秒,$SD=177.30$)和控制组被试($M=357.99$ 秒,$SD=195.29$)在阅读理解任务中的时间花费没有显著差异,$t(121)=0.41$,$p>0.60$。因此,实验2对于社会公平价值观的感知重要性的操纵方式并没有改变实验被试在该操纵中的任务参与度。但是需要引起注意的是,另一项独立样本 t 检验结果表明,那些在控制组中的被试($M=4.68$,$SD=2.00$)感觉自己所阅读文章的理解难度显著高于那些在高重要性组的被试($M=2.87$,$SD=1.48$,$t(121)=5.71$,$p<0.001$,$d=1.03$)。之所以出现这种差异,一个可能的原因

是在控制组中的被试阅读的是高技术相关文章(宇宙飞船),而在高重要性组中的被试阅读的内容则更少涉及专业的技术信息(社会公平)。因此,有必要将被试感知的阅读理解难度作为控制变量来分析实验 2 中的"感知重要性—物理重量判断"效应。

首先,将感知阅读理解难度作为协变量,然后执行 2(社会公平的感知重要性:高重要性 vs.控制组)×2(联名品牌的价值观:价值匹配 vs.价值不匹配)ANCOVA。结果表明,社会公平价值观的感知重要性与价值匹配程度呈现显著的交互作用($F(1,118)=4.96$,$p=0.028$,$\eta_p^2=0.04$,如图 4-2)。与此同时,社会公平价值观和价值匹配程度均未出现显著的主效应(对应的 p 值均大于 0.10)。此外,笔者也检验了不含协变量时的统计结果。2(社会公平的感知重要性:高重要性 vs.控制组)×2(联名品牌的价值观:价值匹配 vs.价值不匹配)ANOVA 结果显示,当不包括协变量时,社会公平价值观的感知重要性与价值匹配程度依然呈现显著的交

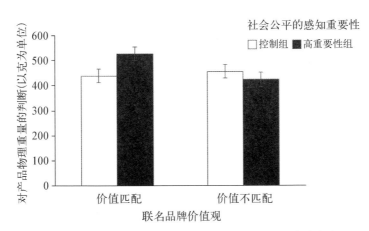

图 4-2　价值观(社会公平)的感知重要性与联名品牌的价值观
如何共同影响消费者对产品物理重量的判断(实验 2)

互作用($F(1,119) = 4.67$, $p = 0.033$, $\eta_p^2 = 0.04$)。也就是说,两种分析下感知重要性和价值匹配的交互作用的趋势与显著性相对一致,从而证明了结果的稳健性。

然后,笔者对显著的交互作用进行简单主效应分析。Planned Contrast 分析的结果显示,当咖啡产品选择与强调社会公平价值观的机构联名时,在高重要性组中的被试对手持的咖啡物理重量的估计($M = 519.00$ 克,$SD = 150.75$)要显著高于在控制组中被试的估计($M = 447.88$ 克,$SD = 146.49$,$F(1,118) = 4.69$,$p = 0.032$)。相反,当咖啡产品没有与强调社会公平价值观的机构联名时,在高重要性组中的被试对咖啡物理重量的估计($M = 417.52$ 克,$SD = 142.22$)并没有显著不同于控制组中被试的估计($M = 462.65$ 克,$SD = 156.36$,$F(1,118) = 0.63$,$p > 0.40$)。这些结果证明,在价值匹配的情况下,通过实验操纵提高消费者关于社会公平的感知重要性,会导致他们显著高估和传递该价值观的机构联名的咖啡产品的物理重量。但是在价值不匹配的情况下,这种"感知重要性—物理重量判断"效应会消失。

为了检验是否消费者在不同情形下在物理重量判断任务中投入的时间存在差别,笔者还进行了类似的2(社会公平的感知重要性:高重要性 vs.控制组)×2(联名品牌的价值观:价值匹配 vs.价值不匹配)的 ANCOVA 分析,只是这次以被试在手持和判断咖啡重量上花费的时间作为因变量。分析结果表明,无论是社会公平的感知重要性还是价值匹配的主效应,均不显著。更重要的是,这两者的交互作用也不显著(所有 p 值均大于 0.30)。这一结果表明,实验2中发现的"感知重要性—物理重量判断"效应并不能用消费者在感知重要性操纵任务和物理重量判断任务中的投入度与参与度差异来解释。

（三）结果讨论

实验 2 的结果通过操纵而不是测量某种特定价值观的感知重要性来进一步为假设 1 提供了实证支持。同样，实验 2 的研究结果不但为"感知重要性—物理重量判断"效应排除了语义关联这一种解释，还排除了另一种看似与具身模拟机制相似，实则类型不同的解释（即被试在不同任务中的投入度存在差异）。从实验 3 开始，笔者将直接对具身模拟机制进行检验。根据具身模拟理论的相关研究（Barsalou 1999,2008），笔者假设在价值匹配的情形下，激活某种价值观的感知重要性会触发与手持重物相关的机体状态（例如在肌肉上体会到更多的紧张感和疲劳感）。这种机体的状态被消费者归结为来自手持的产品自身，因此导致消费者判断他们所持有的产品更加沉重。如果具身模拟机制真的可以有力解释"感知重要性—物理重量判断"效应，那么阻碍具身模拟的发生，就能从一定程度上削弱感知重要性对物理重量判断的影响。基于这一假设，笔者推断如果被试在不实际持有产品的情况下对产品的物理重量进行判断，那么由于被试的机体活动被抑制，具身模拟也无法发生（假设 2）。同时，实验 2 的结果也可以从另一个方面排除语义关联解释。具体而言，如果感知重要性对物理重量判断的影响真的是因为"重要"（抽象概念）与"沉重"（物理体验）在语义上的联系，那么无论被试是否手持产品，我们都应该能观察到前者激活后对后者的显著影响。但是如果该效应在被试不手持产品的情况下消失，那么就说明被试的机体反应和状态依然是该效应成立的必要条件，如此便可再次排除语义关联假设。

四、实验 3

如上文所讨论的，实验 3 集中关注价值匹配的情形（即消费者被激活感知重要性的价值观与联名品牌传递的价值观相一致),并检验被试在不手持(vs.手持)产品的情况下,激活感知重要性对于物理重量判断的影响是否具有显著差别。由于具身模拟理论将个体的机体反应作为"感知重要性—物理重量判断"效应成立的必要条件,因此检测这一调节变量可以为具身模拟理论提供最直接的证明(假设2)。与实验2不同,实验3再次采用测量的方法量化被试感知的社会公平的重要性,这也有助于以一种不同的形式检验实验2结果的稳健性。该研究结果也可以为进一步排除语义关联假设提供实证支持。

(一)实验方法

被试与实验设计:来自中国香港某高校的156名本科生参加了该有偿行为实验。1名在实验过程中不遵循实验说明的被试被排除在最终数据分析之外。剩下的155名参与者(女性占比为68%,平均年龄为20.25岁)被纳入了最终的数据分析。与实验1、实验2不同,在实验3中笔者只关注价值匹配的条件。具体来说,笔者依然选择社会公平这一价值观,但是在实验设计时只保留目标产品与强调公平价值观的公益机构联名的情形。换言之,所有被试都对联名信息完全相同的产品进行物理重量判断,只是判断的方式被操纵成不同模式。笔者在实验3中采用了2(社会公平的感知重要性:高重要性vs.低重要性)×2(判断模式:持有产品vs.不持有产品)的被试间设计。其中,社会公平为被测量因素,而判断模式为被操纵因素。

实验步骤与测量:所有被试均参与了两项任务。首先,实验被试会完成一个问卷调查,该问卷中包含了测量"社会公平"这一价值观的感知重要性的题目。然后,在接下来的第二个任务中,被

第四章 从感知重要性到物理重量判断：品牌联名如何改变消费者对产品的重量感知

试将完成一项消费品调查。与实验2相同，实验3中的被试将对同样的咖啡产品的物理重量进行判断。具体内容如下：

任务1：测量社会公平的感知重要性。所有实验被试首先被告知填写一份关于他们日常生活中信念与偏好的调查问卷。在一系列的无关问题中，被试需要完成关于社会公平的感知重要性的核心测量。所有被试会阅读有关分配公平（社会公平的一个重要方面）与生产效率（即在资源固定的情况下使收益最大化）的简短介绍。同时，他们也被告知，在现实世界中人们往往需要在这两者之间做出权衡取舍。这是因为在很多时候，专注于生产效率的提高可能伴随着分配公平性的下降，反之亦然。然后，所有被试完成一个9点量表来回答社会公平这一价值观的感知重要性（"分配公平对您有多重要？"1=完全不重要，9=非常重要）。选择分配公平作为社会公平的一个指标，是因为增加财富的分配公平被认为是实现社会整体公平的最重要途径。接下来，所有被试回答一些无关问题，例如他们在电影和音乐等方面的兴趣和偏好。

任务2：判断产品的物理重量。所有实验被试都被要求参与一个关于咖啡产品（盒装现磨咖啡粉）的调查。由于实验3集中在价值匹配的情景，所有被试均被告知该咖啡产品和一个致力于推动社会公平的公益组织进行品牌联名。接下来，所有被试均见到该盒装现磨咖啡粉。每盒咖啡粉的实际重量为523克。被试将被随机分成两组。在持有产品组，被试被要求用自己的惯用手去持有该盒装咖啡粉，并判断其重量。在不持有产品组，被试则被告知不要手持产品，而仅仅是通过观察来判断该盒装咖啡粉的重量。此外，两个组的被试均被告知不能打开包装盒。但是为了强化品牌联名的操纵，笔者在外包装上贴上了联名公益组织的相关徽标和号召社会公平的宣传语。被试需要在电脑上拖动滑块，在0克到 800 克之间选择他们估计的该盒装咖啡粉的物理重量。与实验 2 相同,笔者在实验 3 中也记录了被试在手持盒装咖啡粉并估算其重量的过程中所花费的时长。测量该指标一方面是为了如实验 2 一样检验是否感知重要性的操纵改变了被试在物理重量估计任务中的参与度和投入度,另一方面则是由于手持产品做判断和不手持产品做判断本身存在较大差异,从而使得测量和控制任务时间花费显得更加有必要。

(二) 实验结果

笔者分析了社会公平的感知重要性和产品判断模式对于消费者对产品物理重量的判断的影响。首先,笔者对产品判断模式进行了编码(1=持有产品,-1=不持有产品)。接着,笔者将社会公平的感知重要性和产品判断模式这两个变量进行标准化(转化为 z 分数),并在此基础上创建两者的交互项。随后,笔者通过回归模型进行分析,以被试对产品的物理重量判断为因变量,以社会公平的感知重要性、产品判断模式、两者标准化之后生成的交互项为预测变量。回归模型分析结果显示,社会公平这一价值观的感知重要性($p>0.60$)和产品判断模式($p>0.80$)的主效应在统计学上不显著。实验 3 最关注的是感知重要性和产品判断模式的交互作用,而该交互作用在统计学上呈现显著($\beta=0.16$,$t(151)=2.00$,$p=0.048$,图 4-3 为使用未标准化的原始分数所描绘的交互作用趋势)。

随后,笔者进一步分析了在持有产品和不持有产品这两种不同情况下,社会公平的感知重要性对于产品物理重量判断的不同影响。通过简单斜率测试(Simple Slope Test),笔者发现,当被试在持有产品的情况下判断该产品的物理重量时,社会公平价值观

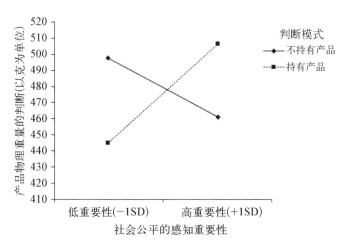

图4-3 价值观(社会公平)的感知重要性与
产品判断模式的交互作用(实验3)

的感知重要性与该产品物理重量判断之间呈现正相关趋势,尽管这种正相关在统计学上是边缘显著的($\beta = 0.20$,$t(151) = 1.78$,$p = 0.078$)。也就是说,当被试持有与宣传公平价值观品牌联名的盒装咖啡产品时,他们越是认为社会公平重要,就越倾向于高估所持产品的物理重量。相较之下,在不持有该产品的情况下,社会公平这一价值观的感知重要性则与该产品物理重量判断呈现负相关趋势($\beta = -0.12$,$t(151) = -1.05$,$p > 0.20$)。这一结果支持了假设3。

除此之外,笔者还检验了被试花费在产品物理重量判断任务上的时间对于结果的潜在影响。首先,检验了是否产品判断模式会影响被试在重量估计中的参与度。独立样本 t 检验的结果显示,被试在持有产品并做物理重量判断时所花费的时间($M = 27.51$ 秒,$SD = 15.86$)和不持有产品并做物理重量判断时所花费的时间($M = 26.35$ 秒,$SD = 16.40$)没有显著差异,$t(153) = 0.45$,$p > 0.60$。

随后,以被试在物理重量估计任务中的时间花费为因变量,以社会公平的感知重要性、产品判断模式、两者标准化后生成的交互项为预测变量进行回归分析。回归分析结果显示,无论是感知重要性和产品判断模式的主效应,还是两者的交互效应,在统计学上都不显著(所有 p 值均大于 0.70)。因此被试在任务中花费的时间不受到实验操纵或者测量的影响。

(三)结果讨论

实验 3 的发现为假设 2 提供了实证支持。具体来说,实验 3 的结果证明了对于"感知重要性—物理重量判断"效应而言,被试的机体参与(例如手持产品)是驱动该效应发生的必要条件。而这一结果也从另一方面排除了语义关联假设。如果激活感知重要性对物理重量判断的影响仅仅是通过语义关联就可以实现,那么即便在被试机体不参与的情况下(不手持产品),也应该能观察到感知重要性对物理重量判断的影响和作用。然而实验 3 的结果却发现,一旦被试不手持产品,则"感知重要性—物理重量判断"效应随即消失。此外,由于实验 3 涉及不同的产品判断模式,一种潜在的混淆影响是不同判断模式下被试在产品物理重量判断上花费的时间应该不同。笔者通过考察感知重要性、判断模式及其交互项对于被试时间花费的影响,排除了这一混淆解释。总而言之,实验 3 的发现为"感知重要性—物理重量判断"效应背后的具身模拟机制提供了实证支持。

具身模拟机制建立在两个先决条件上:第一,关于感官体验的机体模拟需要被激活;第二,个体需要将自己因具身模拟产生的机体反应归结到目标产品上。实验 3 的发现其实是在探索第一个先决条件,即如果被试的具身模拟过程被抑制,是否还能观察到感知重要性对于物理重量判断的影响。而接下来的实验4则是检验第二个先决条件。具体来说,如果被试不能成功将自己因具身模拟产生的机体反应(例如感受到的肌肉紧张)归因到目标产品上,抑或是被试将自己的机体反应归因到与目标产品无关的环境因素(例如所在房间的环境和设置)上,那么依照具身模拟机制,"感知重要性—物理重量判断"效应应该会被削弱甚至消失,这也为该机制提供了另一种实证支持。实验4还对实验3的潜在缺陷进行了修正。实验3虽然发现在个体不持有产品的情况下,感知重要性对于物理重量判断的影响消失,但是一种可能的解释是个体在不持有产品时做出的重量判断准确性较低(重量判断呈现更多的随机特征)。因此,实验4直接让所有被试都在持有产品的情况下做出判断,只是改变他们对机体反应的归因。如此一来,重量估计的准确性这种混淆解释就可以得到排除。此外,这种实验范式依然可以排除"感知重要性"和"物理重量"之间的语义关联解释。

五、实验4

在实验4中,笔者希望进一步为具身模拟机制提供实证支持。实验4和实验1、实验2、实验3在实验范式等方面存在一系列差异。第一,实验4选择了"怀旧"这一价值观。选择该价值观既可以提升研究的普适性,也更具有营销实践意义。因为怀旧营销目前是价值观营销中最常见的形式之一(Roberts 2016)。第二,与之前实验选择水壶和咖啡不同,实验4选择了饼干来作为实验材料,增加了研究结果的可推广性。第三,之前三个实验均用产品重量的估计数字作为因变量,实验4则直接采用9点量表测量了被试对产品主观沉重程度的感受,使因变量测量更加多元化。第四,实验4采用了不同的方式来操纵特定价值观（怀旧）的感知重要性。尤其是，笔者根据社会心理学中的语义启动技术（Semantic priming）来改变被试对怀旧这一价值观重要性的感知。第五，实验4采用了社会心理学中的错误归因范式（Misattribution paradigm）来检验具身模拟机制。具体而言，已往研究表明，如果个体将自身在当下的感受归因于其他外部环境因素（而不是归因于其判断的目标），他们将较少依赖这种感受来对目标做出判断（Schwarz 2004；Shen，Jiang，and Adaval 2010）。基于这一逻辑，笔者预测在价值匹配的情况下（即产品与代表怀旧价值观的品牌进行联名），激活怀旧这一价值观的感知重要性将导致消费者高估手持产品的物理重量。而在价值不匹配的情况下（即产品未与传递怀旧价值观的品牌进行联名），激活怀旧这一价值观的心理重要性并不会显著影响被试对产品重量的判断。这样，也重复了前三个实验中的核心发现。更重要的是，即便在价值匹配的情况下，如果实验被试将他们的机体反应归因于所处房间的环境与设置，那么怀旧的感知重要性不会显著影响被试对目标产品物理重量的判断（假设3）。通过这一系列设计，实验4可以为具身模拟机制提供不同角度的实证检验。值得注意的是，有人可能认为"感知重要性—物理重量判断"效应是由于被试对产品的态度发生了改变。例如，在价值匹配的情况下，被激活某种价值的感知重要性会让被试对目标产品产生更为积极的态度，而这种积极的态度最终影响到他们对产品物理重量的判断。尽管目前并不清楚个体对产品的态度会如何影响他们对产品物理重量的判断，但笔者仍然探讨了这种可能性。为了检验这一潜在解释，实验4直接测量了实验被试对产品的态度（积极或是消极）并分析了其可能的作用。

(一) 实验方法

被试与实验设计：来自中国香港某高校的 340 名本科生参加了该有偿行为实验。其中有 22 名实验被试表达了对实验步骤的不理解和怀疑（例如对研究目的、感知重要性启动任务、最终向他们呈现的饼干产品抱有怀疑），因此被排除在最终的数据分析之外。剩余的 318 名被试（女性占比为 68%，平均年龄为 20.08 岁）被纳入了最终的数据分析。实验 4 采用了 3（怀旧的感知重要性：控制组 vs.高重要性 vs.归因）×2（联名品牌的价值观：价值匹配 vs.价值不匹配）的被试间设计。其中，归因组意味着该组被试既要被激活怀旧的感知重要性，又要对自身机体反应进行归因。

实验步骤与测量：实验 4 在双任务范式的基础上做了一些调整。在第一个任务中，所有被试都将参加一个重组句子的任务（Scrambled sentence task）。通过这一任务，可以操纵怀旧这一价值观的感知重要性。接下来，高重要性组被试和控制组被试直接进入第二个任务，即产品物理重量判断的任务。归因组被试则在被激活怀旧的感知重要性之后继续完成一个关于所处房间环境设置的调查。笔者通过该调查来引导归因组被试对自身的机体反应进行归因。完成这一调查之后，归因组被试才能进入第二个任务，即产品物理重量判断的任务。具体内容如下：

任务 1：操纵怀旧价值观的感知重要性。所有被试均被要求参加一个重组句子的任务，这也是社会心理学中操纵心理状态的经典范式。在这个任务中，被试需要完成 10 轮句子重组。在每一轮，被试都会获得几个被打乱的单词，被试需要将重组好的完整句子填写在电脑屏幕上呈现的空格中。值得注意的是，由于笔者想通过这个句子操纵怀旧价值观的感知重要性，因此被试将被随机分为三组，所面对的需要重组的句子也有所差别。具体而言，在高重要性组和归因组中,被试要面对的 10 个句子均表达怀旧这一价值观的重要性。例如,被试需要重组完成"The old days are crucial to me."(过去对我来说至关重要)以及"It is important for me to recall past events."(对我来说,回顾过去的事件很重要)这样的句子。控制组中的被试则将重组 10 个与怀旧无关的句子,例如"I love painting on the weekends."(我喜欢在周末画画)以及 "I enjoy watching TV dramas."(我喜欢看电视剧)。

对机体反应归因的操纵。在完成句子重组任务之后,归因组的被试还需要额外完成一个关于所处房间环境和设置的简短调查。这个调查的目标是引导被试对自己的机体反应做出归因(Shen, Jiang, and Adaval 2010)。具体而言,归因组的被试被告知大学设施管理办公室会定期评估行为实验室的环境与设置以撰写报告。而最新的报告称,当前的房间环境设置(例如笔记本电脑、座椅和书桌的布置)可能会使人们感到压力与肌肉紧张。然后,归因组的被试被要求完成一项简短的调查,以表明他们对房间设置的意见。被试需要完成 9 点量表(例如,"您在多大程度上认为房间的照明应该被改善?"1 = 完全无必要,9 = 非常有必要)。另外两个组(高重要性组和控制组)的被试则直接跳过该项房间环境调查。

任务 2:判断产品的物理重量。在此项任务中,所有被试均需要手持一盒饼干并判断其物理重量。一盒饼干的实际重量为 490克。为了尽可能减少无关信息对于实验的干扰,笔者依然采用类似于实验 2 和实验 3 的方法,只给予被试限定的信息。这其中包括在计算机屏幕上呈现的关于该款饼干产品信息的描述,以及粘贴在饼干盒上的联名品牌徽标和价值观口号。与之前三个实验类似,被试也被随机分为价值匹配组和价值不匹配组。在价值匹配组中,屏幕上的产品说明指出该款饼干由商学院研究组与一个怀旧的食品品牌联名推出。该品牌的目标是用这种怀旧的饼干让消费者重新回味过往的美好时光。在价值不匹配组中,屏幕上的产品说明仅显示该款饼干由商学院研究组与一个强调美味体验的食品品牌联名推出(详见本章附录4-2)。为了强调品牌联名的操纵效果,笔者分别在两组的饼干包装盒上粘贴了相应的联名品牌的徽标和价值观口号。紧接着,实验被试用自己的惯用手去持有一盒饼干,并通过一个9点量表报告其对该产品重量的感知("您认为这盒饼干有多重?"1=完全不重,9=非常重)。同时,如前文所述,实验4也计划检验"感知重要性—物理重量判断"效应是否随消费者对目标产品的态度而在不同组中发生改变。因此,被试被要求完成一个包含五道题目的9点量表(例如,"您对这盒饼干有何看法?"1=不好,9=很好)。

(二)实验结果

笔者首先检验了"感知重要性—物理重量判断"效应。具体而言,笔者使用消费者关于饼干产品的感知沉重性作为因变量,进行了3(怀旧的感知重要性:控制组 vs.高重要性 vs.归因)×2(联名品牌的价值观:价值匹配 vs.价值不匹配)的 ANOVA 分析。分析结果表明,怀旧的感知重要性和联名品牌的价值观的主效应均不显著(所有 p 值均大于0.20)。更重要的是,这两个变量的交互作用在统计学上呈现边缘显著($F(2,312)=2.98$, $p=0.053$, $\eta_p^2=0.02$;如图4-4)。接着,笔者进行了简单主效应分析。Planned Contrast 分析结果显示,在价值匹配的情况下(与强调怀旧价值观的品牌联名),高感知重要性组的被试($M=6.20$, $SD=1.90$)会比控制组被试($M=5.46$, $SD=1.78$, $F(1,312)=4.54$, $p=0.034$)和归因组被试($M=5.41$,$SD=1.90$,$F(1,312)=5.46$,$p=0.020$)更易高估饼干产品的物理重量。控制组被试和归因组被试之间则在产品物理重量判断上没有呈现显著差异($F(1,312)=0.02$,$p>0.80$)。相比之下,在价值不匹配时(即联名品牌未强调怀旧价值观),三个组(高重要性组、控制组、归因组)被试对饼干产品物理重量的判断没有显著差异($M_{高重要性组}=5.77$,$SD=1.66$ vs. $M_{控制组}=6.07$,$SD=1.71$ vs. $M_{归因组}=5.98$,$SD=1.41$,所有两两比较的p值均大于0.30)。综合这些结果可以发现,当不存在对机体反应的归因操纵时,实验4的结果重复了前三个实验的发现(支持了假设1)。而一旦被试将自身的机体反应归因于和目标产品(饼干产品)无关的因素(房间的环境设置),即便处于价值匹配情况下,激活价值观的感知重要性也不会显著增加被试对目标产品物理重量的估计,因此支持了假设3。

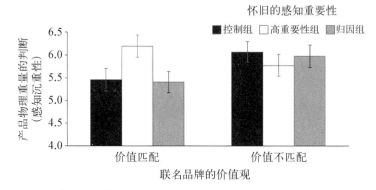

图4-4 检验具身模拟过程在"感知重要性—物理重量判断"效应背后的作用机制:基于错误归因范式的结果(实验4)

为了检验"感知重要性—物理重量判断"效应是否由消费者对目标产品态度的改变所驱动,笔者检验了这一变量的潜在影响。具体来说,笔者首先对衡量实验被试对产品态度的五个题目计算了平均得分($\alpha=0.91$,代表信度良好),并以该平均评分作为因变量,进行了3(怀旧的感知重要性:控制组 vs.高重要性 vs.归因)×2(联名品牌的价值观:价值匹配 vs.价值不匹配)的 ANOVA 分析。分析结果表明,怀旧的感知重要性和联名品牌价值观的主效应不显著,同时这两者之间的交互作用也不显著(所有 p 值大于 0.20)。因此,在不同组别下,被试对目标产品的态度不存在显著差异。然后,笔者将被试对产品的态度作为控制变量,以感知的饼干产品的重量作为因变量,进行了3(怀旧的感知重要性:控制组 vs.高重要性 vs.归因)×2(联名品牌的价值观:价值匹配 vs.价值不匹配)的 ANCOVA 分析。结果显示,即便在控制了被试对目标产品态度的情况下,怀旧的感知重要性和联名品牌价值观的交互作用依然呈现类似的趋势($F(2,311)=2.96$,$p=0.053$,$\eta_p^2=0.02$)。因此,"感知重要性—物理重量判断"效应的发生不是由于被试对产品的态度发生了变化。

(三)结果讨论

实验 4 的发现具有重要意义。首先,采用不同的目标产品、不同的价值观、不同的感知重要性操纵、不同的因变量测量方式,实验 4 重复了前三个实验的研究结果,也证明了"感知重要性—物理重量判断"效应的稳健性和可推广性。更重要的是,通过错误归因范式(Misattribtion paradigm),实验 4 发现即便在价值匹配的情况下,如果被试将自己的机体反应(例如肌肉紧张感)归因于目标产品之外的因素(例如房间环境和设置),那么即便激活价值观的感知重要性也不会显著改变被试对目标产品物理重量的判断。这一实验结果支持了假设 3,也从另一个角度证实了具身模拟机制在解释"感知重要性—物理重量判断"效应中的作用。这一实验结果也有助于排除实验 3 中因为任务类型不同（持有产品做判断 vs. 不持有产品做判断）带来的混淆影响，并进一步排除了语义关联这一解释。此外，实验 4 通过直接测量和分析不同组被试对目标产品的态度，排除了态度变化对于"感知重要性—物理重量判断"效应的解释作用。

在实验 5 中，笔者致力于采用不同的方式激活价值观的感知重要性。与此同时，笔者也计划检验"感知重要性—物理重量判断"效应是否可以扩散到其他与重量相关的下游变量上，例如产品的卡路里含量。检验这些问题不但可以扩大本章研究的可推广性，也使本章研究结果具有更强的管理实践意义。

六、实验 5

实验 5 具有四个目标。第一，笔者采用了不同于前面四个实验的方法来操纵价值观的感知重要性。笔者采用了社会心理学中常用的反馈操纵范式（Bogus feedback paradigm），通过给予被试人格测验的反馈结果来操纵社会公平这一价值观的感知重要性。值得注意的是，在实验 5 中，笔者对控制组（与高重要性组对照）做出了调整。在实验 2 和实验 4 中，没有向与高重要性组做对照的控制组被试呈现在高重要性组中被提及的价值观。例如在实验 2 中笔者操纵社会公平的感知重要性，采用的方式是在实验组中向被试展现社会公平的重要性。对于控制组的被试，则不呈现和社会公平相关的信息，只是呈现无关的中立信息（太空飞船）。这种设计带来的一个潜在混淆解释是，在控制组中的被试根本没有接收到与"社会公平"相关的信息。也许是这种信息上的不对称，而不是个体感受到的价值观的感知重要性差异造成了前四个实验的结果。尽管为了避免这一问题，实验 1 和实验 3 都采用了直接对价

第四章　从感知重要性到物理重量判断：品牌联名如何改变消费者对产品的重量感知

值观的感知重要性进行测量的结果（在这种情况下不存在价值观未被提及的问题）作为自变量，但是为了研究的严谨性，依然有必要再设计一个实验来解决这种价值观重要性操纵的缺陷。因此，在实验 5 中，向控制组的被试呈现一个和社会公平相对冲突的概念——社会自由。由于公平和自由在一定程度上存在一些权衡取舍，因此当个体感觉社会公平相对重要时，就不得不降低对社会自由重要性的评价，反之亦然。因此，通过在高重要性组和控制组中分别呈现这两个概念，可以更干净地操纵社会公平的感知重要性。同时，这一实验范式也可以证明价值匹配在"感知重要性—物理重量判断"效应中的关键作用。具体来说，由于笔者在高重要性组中激活了社会公平的感知重要性，在控制组中激活了社会自由的感知重要性，因此在两组中其实"重要性"这个语义上的抽象概念都会被激活。如果实验结果与价值匹配无关，仅和语义关联有关（换句话说，仅和"重要"这个词相关，而和"什么是重要的"无关），那么在两组中被试对产品物理重量的判断应该不存在显著差异（毕竟两组中都出现了"重要"这个词）。基于这一讨论，如果采用这一设计依然能重复"感知重要性—物理重量判断"效应，则可以从另一个方面排除语义关联假设，并证明价值匹配这一先决条件的必要性。

第二，实验 5 只关心价值匹配场景，将实验 4 的饼干产品和实验 2 的社会公平价值观结合起来，从而进一步增加了研究结论的可推广性。

第三，实验 5 不仅希望重复价值匹配情况下的"感知重要性—物理重量判断"效应，还希望能检验该效应是否会延伸去影响到其他和产品重量相关的下游变量（Downstream variable）。尤其是，已往研究（Deng and Kahn 2009）指出在高卡路里产品类别（例如巧克力棒、牛油曲奇等零食）中，消费者感知到的产品重量和感知到的产品卡路里含量呈现显著的正相关关系。基于这一发现，实验5选择了曲奇饼干作为实验材料，并检验"感知重要性—物理重量判断"效应是否也会延伸去影响消费者对产品卡路里含量的判断。这一基于消费者营养信息判断的探索，也可以使"感知重要性—物理重量判断"效应彰显更强的市场管理实践意义。

第四，实验5也希望排除被试主观感受的任务参与度对"感知重要性—物理重量判断"效应的影响。在实验2和实验3中，笔者测量了实验被试在重量判断任务中投入的客观时间，并排除了其对实验结果可能的影响和作用。这种任务参与度的度量是客观指标，和被试的主观感知的参与度不同。例如，尽管事实上花费了同样的时间，但是被试对同一段时间间隔却会有不同的感知（对自己时间投入的感知：高估 vs. 准确估计 vs. 低估）。这种被试感知的时间投入也许影响个人在疲劳程度以及持有物品困难程度上的感知，并进而影响他们对目标产品物理重量的判断。例如，那些认为自己花了更多时间手持并判断产品物理重量的实验被试，可能会更倾向于觉得握住产品更加耗费气力，从而导致他们对产品物理重量的高估。为了排除这种潜在的解释，在实验5中，笔者直接测量了实验被试在持有和判断产品物理重量上花费时间的主观感知，并检验了其对核心结果的可能影响。

（一）实验方法

被试与实验设计：来自中国香港某高校的107名本科生参加了该有偿行为实验。其中有5名被试对研究目的和过程产生怀疑，另有4名被试告知研究人员不记得自己看到的实验操纵信息，因此均被排除在最终的数据分析之外。剩下98名实验被试（女性

第四章　从感知重要性到物理重量判断：品牌联名如何改变消费者对产品的重量感知

占比为72%,平均年龄为20.19岁)则被纳入最终的数据分析。实验5采用单因素(社会公平重要性:高重要性 vs.控制组)的被试间设计。

实验步骤与测量：与实验2类似,实验5也在双任务范式的基础上加入了无关题目。第一个任务是一个性格测试。被试需要完成该测试以获得关于自身性格的反馈。通过这个测试,笔者旨在操纵社会公平这一价值观的感知重要性。在这个任务完成之后,被试需要完成一些无关题目。插入这些无关题目的目的是让被试无法知晓实验的真实目的。其后,所有被试均进入第二个任务。在这个任务中他们将手持一盒巧克力饼干并判断其物理重量。具体内容如下:

任务1:操纵社会公平的感知重要性。所有被试均被要求完成一项性格测试。这个性格测试由五道选择题组成。在每个问题中,被试均被要求根据自己的直觉选择五张塔罗牌中的一张。例如在其中一道问题中,被试被告知"请选择引起您注意的第一张塔罗牌"。而这五张塔罗牌分别呈现关于太阳、地球、魔术师、月亮、人类的图像。所有的被试都完成了相同的性格测试题目,但是他们得到的反馈却是被操纵的结果。具体而言,当被试完成这五道题目后,系统会呈现类似于读取进度的标识,并告知被试该测试系统正在分析他们的性格得分。被试会被随机分至(社会公平)高重要性组和控制组,并接收到相应的关于他们性格特点的反馈信息。其中,处于高重要性组的被试会被告知他们的性格特点是更重视社会公平,处于控制组的被试则被告知他们的性格特点是更重视社会自由(参见本章附录4-3)。为了检验关于社会公平感知重要性的操纵是否成功,被试被要求就该测试结果提供评论和反馈。笔者也可以从中分析被试是否对实验流程和目的产生了怀疑。

任务2：判断产品的物理重量。在完成任务1之后，被试首先要完成一系列无关题目以尽可能减少他们对实验目的的怀疑。其中，被试回答的问题包括其获取新闻信息的方式（例如，"您使用手机观看新闻有多频繁？"1=从不，9=非常频繁）。随后，所有被试参与了任务2。他们被要求用自己的惯用手去持有一盒巧克力饼干，并判断它的物理重量。这盒巧克力饼干的实际重量为478克。由于实验5只关注价值匹配的场景，因此所有实验被试都会被告知该款巧克力饼干是商学院与一个旨在促进社会公平的公益组织进行品牌联名推广的。如之前的四个实验，为了尽可能控制无关信息对实验结果的干扰，笔者对巧克力饼干的包装盒进行了修饰，遮挡其本身的品牌信息和营养成分，并且不允许被试将包装盒拆开。被试只能通过限定的信息了解该款巧克力饼干产品，包括电脑屏幕上呈现的指导语，饼干包装盒表面粘贴的联名品牌（公益组织）徽标，以及该公益组织促进社会公平的价值观口号。所有被试都被要求用自己的惯用手去持有一盒巧克力饼干，然后拖动电脑屏幕上的滑块，在0克到1200克的范围内选择他们所估计的该款巧克力饼干的物理重量。接下来，被试将通过一个9点量表估计他们对该款巧克力饼干卡路里含量的看法（"该盒饼干在多大程度上让您感觉含有高脂肪？"1=完全不含高脂肪，9=含有非常高的脂肪量）。紧接着，实验被试报告他们在持有该产品并判断其重量的过程中自我感知的时间花费（"我花了很多时间拿着该盒饼干并判断其重量"，1=非常不同意，9=非常同意）。最后，实验被试被要求回忆其在调研一开始的性格测验的结果。通过这一方式，笔者可以确认并排除那些感知重要性操纵失败的个案。

（二）实验结果

首先,笔者检验了"感知重要性—物理重量判断"效应是否可以被重复。独立样本 t 检验的结果显示,处于(社会公平)高重要性组中的实验被试($M=643.28$ 克,$SD=246.49$)比处在控制组中的实验被试($M=545.65$ 克,$SD=198.68$)更倾向于高估该款巧克力产品的物理重量,$t(96)=2.17$,$p=0.033$,$d=0.44$。这一结果重复了前面四个实验的发现,即在价值匹配的情况下,激活价值观的感知重要性会造成被试高估目标产品的物理重量,从而支持了假设1。

接下来,笔者探究了该"感知重要性—物理重量判断"效应是否可以延伸去影响关于产品卡路里含量的判断。独立样本 t 检验的结果显示,处在高重要性组中的被试($M=7.11$,$SD=1.26$)会比控制组中的被试($M=6.45$,$SD=1.60$)更倾向于高估产品的卡路里含量,$t(96)=2.24$,$p=0.027$,$d=0.45$。因此在价值匹配的情况下,激活价值观的高感知重要性也会影响被试对享乐型或者是高脂类型产品的卡路里含量的判断。

随后,笔者检验了"感知重要性—物理重量判断—产品卡路里估计"这一完整的中介模型。笔者使用了学者开发的 INDIRECT SPSS Macro(Preacher and Hayes 2008;Sokolova and Krishna 2016),然后通过路径分析和 Bootstrap 分析检验了物理重量判断作为中介变量的作用。具体而言,笔者将社会公平这一价值观的感知重要性进行了编码(1=高重要性,-1=控制组)。随后路径分析结果显示,社会公平的感知重要性与产品物理重量判断呈现显著的正相关关系($\beta=0.22$,$t(96)=2.17$,$p=0.033$)。同时,社会公平的感知重要性也和产品的卡路里含量判断呈现显著的正相关关系($\beta=0.22$,$t(96)=2.24$,$p=0.027$)。而当笔者将社会公平的感知重要性(自变量)和产品物理重量判断(中介变量)均作为预测变量放入回归模型(以产品卡路里估计为因变量)后,产品物理重量判断对于产品卡路里估计的回归作用依然显著($\beta = 0.26$, $t(95) = 2.61$, $p = 0.010$),然而社会公平的感知重要性对于产品卡路里估计的影响作用则不再显著($\beta = 0.17$, $t(95) = 1.69$, $p = 0.095$,如图4-5)。因此路径分析证明了产品物理重量判断在"感知重要性"到"产品卡路里含量估计"效应中的中介作用。为了进一步检验该中介模型的稳健性,Bootstrap检验显示间接效应的95%置信区间(95% Confidence interval,简称95% CI)均大于0,间接效应 = 0.08,SE = 0.05,95% CI = [0.01 to 0.24]。由此可见,Bootstrap分析证明了"感知重要性—物理重量判断—产品卡路里估计"这一中介模型的稳健性。综上所述,在价值匹配的条件下,激活价值观的感知重要性可以通过影响被试对产品物理重量的判断来影响他们对产品卡路里含量的估计。

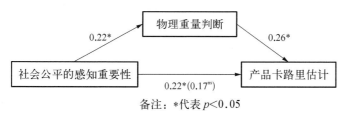

备注:*代表 $p<0.05$

图4-5 "感知重要性—物理重量判断—产品卡路里估计"中介模型(实验5)

此外,如前文所述,实验5也希望检验"感知重要性—物理重量判断"效应是否取决于被试主观感知的任务时间投入。独立样本 t 检验发现,在高重要性组和控制组中,被试感知的任务时间投入没有显著差异($M_{高重要性组} = 5.66$, $SD = 2.17$ vs. $M_{控制组} = 5.43$, $SD = 1.63$, $t(96) = 0.59$, $p > 0.50$)。因此,被试在重量估计任务中感知到的时间投入差异并不能解释核心的发现。

(三) 结果讨论

实验 5 的发现具有几个重要意义。首先,通过不同的自变量操纵模式,实验重复了价值匹配条件下的"感知重要性—物理价值判断"效应。与此同时,实验采用的自变量操纵方法也可以弥补前几个实验的缺憾,如排除了不同组之间信息量存在差异的解释,以及证明了只是激活语义概念中的"重要性"不足以影响产品的重量判断,必须在此基础上考虑到价值匹配的必要作用。其次,实验的结果通过测量被试主观感知的任务时间投入,排除了该混淆变量对于"感知重要性—物理重量判断"效应的影响。最后,实验通过检验在价值匹配情况下的"感知重要性—产品物理重量判断—产品卡路里含量估计"中介模型,发现价值观的感知重要性对于物理重量判断的影响可以延伸到影响消费者对产品健康营养因素的判断。当然,值得注意的是,由于已往研究主要是发现享乐型/放纵型产品中产品重量感知和产品卡路里估计之间的正相关关系,笔者假设这一中介模型只在类似的产品类型(例如巧克力曲奇)中才会成立。而在相对健康和低热量的产品品类(例如蔬菜汁和水果)中,这样的效应不大可能出现(也就是说增加价值观的感知重要性不会导致消费者高估产品卡路里含量)。

第四节 关于本章实证研究的综合讨论

一、研究发现的总结

已往研究显示,关于感知重要性对物理重量判断的影响的研究存在不一致的结论（Schneider, Rutjens, Jostmann, and Lakens 2011; Zhang and Li 2012）。为了整合过去这些看似矛盾的研究结果，本章研究在市场营销的情景下探索了为什么，以及在何时，激发感知重要性会对物理重量判断产生影响。其中，笔者指出已往的部分研究（Zhang and Li 2012）之所以无法观察到显著的"感知重要性—物理重量判断"效应，是由于该效应涉及的机制与单纯的语义关联不同。与此同时，决定该效应的核心机制（具身模拟过程）需要感知重要性的来源和物理重量判断涉及的目标之间存在匹配关系。为了检验这种假设，笔者选择了价值观营销和品牌联名的场景，指出激活特定价值观（价值观 A）的感知重要性可以导致消费者高估目标产品的物理重量，但是这种效应只会出现在目标产品和传递相同价值观（价值观 A）的品牌进行联名的情景（价值匹配情形）中。而一旦与目标产品联名的品牌未能传递同样的价值观，或者传递相矛盾的价值观（价值观 B），那么激活价值观 A 的感知重要性不会改变消费者对目标产品物理重量的判断。更进一步，笔者指出，价值匹配之所以成为"感知重要性—物理重量判断"效应的先决条件，是因为该效应不是通过"重要"和"重量"这两个概念之间的语义链接完成，而是通过具身模拟机制完成。根据这一解释，只有在激活感知重要性并能激活个体与负重相关的机体状态（例如体会到更多的肌肉紧张感）时，个体才会更倾向于高估产品的物理重量（Barsalou 1999, 2008）。根据信息的可用性原理（Lee and Schwarz 2012），只有在价值匹配的情况下，价值观的感知重要性才能被个体认为是可以用来帮助判断目标产品的可用信息，才更容易激发具身模拟的过程。而在价值不匹配的情况下，个体也许把价值观的感知重要性当作一种和目标产品判断无关的信息，所以激活该价值观的感知重要性无法引发具身模拟过程，也无法改变个体对产品物理重量的判断。

基于以上推理,本章研究的五个实验均发现了价值匹配对于"感知重要性—物理重量判断"效应的必要作用。例如,实验 1 和实验 3 测量了被试对特定价值观重要性的感知,而实验 2、实验 4 和实验 5 则操纵了特定价值观的感知重要性。这些实验都提供了一致的结果,即"感知重要性—物理重量判断"效应只有在价值匹配的情形下才会出现。本章研究也检验了该效应背后的机制——具身模拟机制。具身模拟机制包含两个关键要素:个体的机体反应被激活,以及该机体反应被归因到目标产品(从而导致对目标产品判断出现偏差)。因此本章研究试图从这两点入手,通过检验"感知重要性—物理重量判断"效应的调节变量来为具身模拟机制提供实证支持。通过实验 3,笔者发现即便在价值匹配的条件下,如果被试在不持有产品的情况下对产品物理重量进行判断,那么"感知重要性—物理重量判断"效应依然不会出现。这是由于不持有产品也就意味着被试的机体反应被抑制,从而削弱了具身模拟过程。而在实验 4 中,笔者则发现即便在价值匹配的条件下,如果被试选择将机体反应归因于和目标产品无关的外界因素(例如房间的环境和设置),那么依然无法观察到"感知重要性—物理重量判断"效应。综上,这些实验发现都为具身模拟机制提供了充分的实证支持。

除开寻找对具身模拟机制的支持性证据,本章研究也试图排除其他可能解释的混淆作用。首先,实验 1 至实验 5 均发现"感知重要性"对"物理重量判断"的影响和作用并非源于"重要"与"重量"两个抽象概念之间的语义关联。同时,实验 4 排除了被试对产品态度转变的潜在影响和作用。而实验 2、实验 3、实验 5 则通过测量和检验被试主观感受到的及客观记录的任务参与感(用时间投入来指代),排除了参与感对于"感知重要性—物理重量判断"效应的混淆作用。这些排除备选解释的工作也为具身模拟机制的检验提供了重要的实证参考。最后,实验5显示,对于高热量产品的品类(例如巧克力饼干),"感知重要性—物理重量判断"效应会进一步延展到消费者对产品卡路里含量的判断上。通过对完整中介模型("感知重要性—产品物理重量判断—产品卡路里含量判断")的检验,本章研究也进一步挖掘了该效应的下游结果。

二、本章研究的理论贡献和实践意义

第一,本章研究整合了已往研究中关于"感知重要性"和"物理重量判断"之间关系的不一致发现(Schneider, Parzuchowski, Wojciszke, Schwarz, and Koole 2015;Zhang and Li 2012)。价值匹配观点的提出,不仅可以作为一种调节变量检验何时"感知重要性—物理重量判断"效应会发生或是消失,还拓展了我们对信息可用性理论(Applicability of information)的了解。由于"感知重要性—物理重量判断"效应可以被看作一种自上而下的信息加工模式(从抽象概念到具体体验),那么在这个过程中,效应发生与否往往取决于前者作为一种信息是否会被个体运用到后者的判断中。这个思路也为其他具身认知的相关理论研究提供可以参考的视角。例如,在具身认知中一个经典的理论问题是:抽象概念和具体感官体验之间的链接究竟是单向(Unidirectional)的还是双向(Bidirectional)的。换言之,是否激活这两者之中的其中一个就一定会激活另外一个?已往研究中,既有支持单向的,也有支持双向的。例如感官上的温暖和人与人之间的社会温暖被发现是双向链接的,而关于感知重要性和物理重量判断之间的链接则被发现时而呈现双向链接,时而又呈现单向链接(Aggarwal and Zhao

2015；Koo，Wong，and Shavitt 2011；Lakoff and Johnson 1980；Lee and Schwarz 2012；Zhong and Liljenquist 2006）。本章研究的价值匹配观点，为建立两者之间的双向链接提供了一个前提条件，也为进一步探索具身认知中其他抽象概念与具体体验的具身组合提供了重要的参考价值。

第二，本章研究通过论证具身模拟过程，为相关领域的理论研究也做出了贡献（Barsalou 1999，2008；Gibbs 2006；Lakoff and Johnson 1980；Zhang and Li 2012）。具身模拟理论（Barsalou 1999，2008）认为，当个体在对抽象概念（例如描述情绪的词语，包括愤怒、忧伤、喜悦等）进行加工时会激发与该概念相对应的身体状态。例如，加工"愤怒"这个词会让个体体会到血压上升和心跳加速，而思考"微笑"或"悲伤"等词语还会激活与该情绪词相对应的面部肌肉活动（Niedenthal 2007）。通过研究"感知重要性"这一抽象概念和"物理重量感知"这一感官体验之间的关系，本章研究不但找到了一种新的可以运用具身模拟理论的组合，也揭示了"感知重要性—物理重量判断"效应背后的机制。更重要的是，过去对这一机制的检验更多要依靠神经和生理学相关的设备去检验机体反应的中介作用，本章研究则找到了通过调节作用检验这一机制的手段（Barsalou 1999，2008；Gibbs 2006）。具体而言，为了支持具身模拟理论，本章研究从具身模拟机制发生的先决条件入手，通过两个调节变量分别抑制具身模拟过程，以及干扰被试对机体状态的归因过程，从而为具身模拟机制提供了实证支持。此外，由于过去的具身认知研究往往涉及多种混淆解释，为了进一步支持具身模拟过程，本章研究排除了包括语义关联、任务参与（主观感受的时间投入 vs.客观记录的时间投入）、被试对目标产品的态度、实验操纵涉及的信息量差异等在内的一系列解释。

第三,本章研究的发现也有助于将具身模拟理论和重量感知的相关理论结合起来,为各自领域做出相应的理论贡献。根据重量感知与判断的相关研究,人们在判断产品重量时往往会依赖于他们持有产品时的身体状态。例如持有产品这个动作往往会涉及神经系统和肌肉系统的活动(Aniss, Gandevia, and Milne 1988; Jones 1986),而干扰这种机体状态也会影响到被试对产品重量的判断。因此,结合具身模拟理论,笔者假设只有当激活感知重要性可以影响承载产品的机体状态时(例如触发与持有重物相似的机体状态和反应),"感知重要性—物理重量判断"效应才会发生。这个激活感知重要性之后个体产生类似持有重物机体状态的过程被称为具身模拟过程。根据前文的讨论,与情绪相关的词语不同,感知重要性可能对应更加复杂和多元化的机体反应。因此单纯激活感知重要性未必就能唯一指向重量感知的机体反应。这也解释了为什么部分研究(Zhang and Li 2012)在激活感知重要性的情况下未能发现被试物理重量判断的改变。通过与前文所述的信息可用性原则相结合(Higgins 1996; Lee and Schwarz 2012),本章也指出了当研究对象为"感知重要性"这一类概念时具身模拟过程发生的前提条件。总结起来,当抽象概念本身直接对应于具体的感官体验时(例如"微笑"与面部肌肉活动的关联、"踢腿"与腿部运动系统活跃度的关联),激活抽象概念会自动引发具身模拟过程,并影响个体在感官体验上的判断。相比之下,当抽象概念与感官体验之间的关联不够自动化时,只有当情景线索将该抽象概念直接链接到特定的机体反应时,具身模拟过程才会发生。本章研究的"感知重要性—物理重量判断"效应则是这一大框架下的一个具体实例。因此,本章研究对于具身模拟过程发生的边界条件也做出了理论上的补充。

第四章　从感知重要性到物理重量判断：品牌联名如何改变消费者对产品的重量感知

值得注意的是，已往研究指出的"物理重量—感知重要性判断"效应不需要笔者在本章研究中提出的价值匹配条件。例如已往研究发现，只要激发沉重的感官体验（例如完成附在沉重的剪贴板上的问卷），便会改变人们对问卷中议题重要性的感知，即便沉重感觉的来源和重要性判断的目标无关（Jostmann，Lakens，and Schubert 2009）。这也进一步说明了"物理重量—感知重要性判断"效应和"感知重要性—物理重量判断"效应涉及不同的潜在机制（Landau，Meier，and Keefer 2010；Zhang and Li 2012）。具体而言，"物理重量—感知重要性判断"效应的产生，更大可能是因为"重量"和"重要"这两个概念之间的语义关联（Zhang and Li 2012）。也就是说重量的具体感知仅仅是一种信息来源，它激活了"重量"这一语义概念，并进而激活了在语义网络中与"重量"相关联的"重要"这一概念。换言之，即便没有具体的感官上的重量体验，只要其他因素能够激活语义上的"重量"概念（例如通过语义启动的方法给被试呈现和"重量"相关的词语），那么就能对被试之后的重要性判断产生影响。正是因为这一机制强调"重量"和"重要"这两个抽象的语义概念之间的自动化链接，因此并不需要"重量"的来源与"重要"的目标建立对应关系。换言之，用于本章研究的实验场景即便存在价值不匹配，持有重量不同的产品也会影响到个体对价值观感知重要性的判断。然而，一旦研究的问题变成"感知重要性—物理重量判断"效应，就包含了两个不同的前提：一是从"感知重要性"到"物理重量感知"涉及从抽象概念激活到物理体验的路径，因此必须有机体活动和机体状态的参与，也就是具身模拟过程；二是"感知重要性"的激活并不能快速唯一地链接到"物理重量"上，因此更需要一些线索（Cue）将两者链接起来。这正是价值匹配条件的作用，将感知重要性的来源和物理重量判断的目标直接关联在一起。

第四,本章研究的发现对于价值观营销、品牌联名和感官营销都具有重要的营销实践意义。在价值观营销层面,如今的许多营销人员都喜欢在产品广告中宣传自己独有的品牌精神和某种品牌价值观。尤其是很多商家还将价值观营销和消费者的身份认同结合起来,建立了身份认同营销(Identity marketing)这一营销模式。尽管过去的很多研究都发现了将产品价值观与消费者的身份认同(以及其认可的价值观/信念)相链接会带来积极的促销结果,但是这些研究主要是基于消费者对产品态度的判断。而本章研究则发现,采用价值观营销的手段(例如与传递某特定价值观的品牌进行联名)也会影响消费者对产品感官体验甚至是其他产品属性(例如营养价值)的判断。因此,这些发现也为商家的管理实践提供了借鉴。因为在很多时候,消费者行为不仅涉及消费者在当时对产品的态度(购买前行为),还涉及事后具体的消费和使用体验(购买后行为)。尽管价值观营销可以影响消费者的态度,促进购买行为,然而在进入事后消费阶段,消费者对产品属性的具体判断则会影响到其使用体验和使用口碑。以本章研究中的物理重量为例,产品的物理重量是一种重要的产品属性,是某些工具类产品用户体验的重要相关因素。例如,对于可穿戴设备(例如健康检测仪)或者体育运动产品(例如球鞋),消费者更希望产品能够轻巧便携。与此同时,由于本章研究也再次证实了高热量产品中消费者感知的产品重量和感知的卡路里含量之间的关联(Deng and Kahn 2009),因此对于有较强自我控制动机(例如减肥动机)的消费者来说,重量较高(往往意味着分量更足)的该类产品并不是合适的选择。基于这些讨论,尽管挑选重要价值观进行营销会影响消费者在购买前对产品的态度,但是在事后消费时,他们可能会更容易不满于产品的沉重不便;而在考虑选择礼物推荐给有追求健康目标的朋友时,高卡路里又会让他们更容易放弃使用这种感知卡路里含量较高的产品。因此对于产品营销者而言,他们也需要考虑到这种重要价值观营销所带来的潜在双刃剑效应。

三、本章研究的不足之处和未来展望

第一,尽管本章研究力图在概念、理论和研究设计上保持严谨,但是依然存在一些不足之处,这也为相关领域的未来研究提供了改进的空间。本章研究测量或操纵了特定价值观的感知重要性,并检验了激活感知重要性如何影响消费者对产品物理重量的判断,但是并未直接检验激活价值观的感知重要性是否也会改变目标产品的感知重要性。尽管实验4的错误归因范式以及将消费者对产品的态度作为控制变量可以在一定程度上排除感知产品重要性对于"感知重要性—物理重量判断"效应的解释作用,但是未来的研究依然需要直接测量并控制这一变量的潜在影响。

第二,本章研究选择了"感知重要性"这一概念作为研究对象。如前文所述,"感知重要性"并不唯一地或者自动化地指向物理重量感知,因此才需要价值匹配作为先决条件。未来的研究可以探索哪些抽象概念和重量感知可以产生更自动化的链接。例如"轻松""速度""灵活"这类抽象概念与沉重感会形成鲜明的反差。那么激活这些抽象概念,是否即便在价值不匹配的情况下,也能影响个体对产品物理重量的判断?探索这一问题可以让我们更好地完善具身模拟理论,深化我们对抽象概念激活对具体感官体验的影响和作用的了解。

第三,尽管本章研究采用了成本相对较低的行为实验范式,为"感知重要性—物理重量判断"效应背后的具身模拟机制提供了

支持,但是本章研究缺少对于该机制的直接中介作用的分析。为了弥补这一不足,未来的研究可以直接通过神经科学和生理学相关设备来量化这一具身模拟过程。例如,基于生理学的研究设备(例如皮肤电)可以测量个体当时的机体紧张感,相应的神经科学测量设备(例如功能性核磁共振 Fmri)可以测量与运动相关的脑区的激活状态,而与运动科学相关的设备可以测量当时个体手部肌肉承受的张力。这些生理指标的测量有利于进一步分解和具体化具身模拟的过程,从而为未来具身模拟理论的研究提供更多的参考指标和理论指引。

第四,如前文所述,本章研究从一定程度上解答了抽象概念(例如感知重要性)和具体感官体验(例如重量感知)如何实现双向关联,从而为这一具身认知研究中的理论问题提供一种解决思路(Aggarwal and Zhao 2015;Koo,Wong,and Shavitt 2011;Lakoff and Johnson 1980;Lee and Schwarz 2012;Zhong and Liljenquist 2006)。具体而言,一部分研究认为抽象概念和具体感官体验的链接是由于这两者相对的概念之间存在语义联系(Landau,Meier,and Keefer 2010;Zhang and Li 2012),而另一种解释则认为这种联系是具身模拟过程所致(Barsalou 2008;Gibbs 2006)。在本章研究中,笔者认为从抽象概念激活到具体感官体验的影响和作用更多是依赖后者。未来的研究可以直接对这一假说进行检验。与此同时,针对同样的具身关系,未来的研究还可以探索是否存在调节变量,可以在不同情形下引发不同的背后过程(语义关联机制 vs.具身模拟机制)。在前文的讨论中,本章研究就指出了一种潜在的调节变量,即抽象概念本身是否唯一和自动化地指向具体感官体验。在未来,学者们还可以就这一问题做出更多深入的研究。

第五,本章研究采用"信息可用性"理论来检验激活感知重要

第四章 从感知重要性到物理重量判断:品牌联名如何改变消费者对产品的重量感知

性何时会影响个体对产品物理重量的判断。具体而言,在本章研究的情景中,信息可用性更多是产品联名的品牌是否传递了和被试相关的价值观。未来的研究可以探索通过其他方法来操纵感知重要性信息的可用性。例如,未来研究可以考虑任务本身的性质,使得被试将感知重要性激活和物理重量判断知觉为相关任务,或是独立不相关的任务。这种任务的框架效应(Task framing)也可以为该领域提供全新的研究视角。

第六,如已往研究(Zhang and Li 2012)所述,感知重要性也许对应多种复杂的机体反应(而不仅限于与重量感知相关)。本章研究重点探讨了感知重要性对于与重量相关的身体机制的影响,未来的研究则可以探讨感知重要性如何对应其他的机体状态。例如,"重要性"这一抽象概念可能指向相对更高的位置或者程度更强烈的感官刺激(Aggarwal and Zhao 2015;Koo,Wong,and Shavitt 2011;Zhang and Li 2012)。其中前者和物理运动相关,后者则和更敏锐的感官感受(例如更浓烈的口感、更大的音量)相关。基于此,学者们也可以进一步做相关探索。

附　录

附录4-1　实验2中对联名品牌价值观进行操纵的实验材料(中文翻译版)

"我们正在和一个公益组织进行合作来推广一款现磨咖啡粉。该公益组织的宗旨是帮助发展中国家的边缘生产者得到更好的贸易条件,并促进自身的可持续发展。"

附录4-2　实验4中对联名品牌价值观(价值匹配vs.价值不匹配)进行操纵的实验材料(中文翻译版)

价值匹配组:

我们正在与一个擅长制作怀旧零食的品牌进行合作来推广一种新的曲奇饼。请认真阅读以下的产品描述:

"Retro(旧时光)"曲奇饼:带您回到过去。

传统工艺制作的曲奇饼,让您回顾那些美好的旧时光。

经典的包装,传统的形态和纹理,古典的制作工艺——这款曲奇饼能为您带来美好的怀旧体验。

价值不匹配组:

我们正在与一个擅长制作美味零食的品牌进行合作来推广一种新的曲奇饼。请认真阅读以下的产品描述:

"FEUT"曲奇饼:您的美味之选。

尽情享受这些曲奇饼吧!

时尚的包装,精心组织的形态和纹理,优良的制作工艺——这款曲奇饼能为您带来美味的体验。

附录4-3 实验5中对"社会公平"价值观的感知重要性进行操纵的方法(中文翻译版)

高重要性组:

这是您的性格测试结果的报告。请仔细阅读以下信息:

性格测试结果显示您在现在的人生阶段更接近第二类人格。

"根据第二类人格的特征描述,您是一个真诚且努力体谅他人的人。您看重社会的公平程度,并且关心那些处在穷困中的人们的处境。您有一颗柔软的心,使得您愿意去帮助那些有需要的群体。"

控制组:

这是您的性格测试结果的报告。请仔细阅读以下信息:

性格测试结果显示您在现在的人生阶段更接近第二类人格。

"根据第二类人格的特征描述,您是一个真诚且努力希望变得独立的人。您看重社会的自由程度,相信每一个个体都应该为自己的生活和处境负责。您是一个果敢的人,愿意依靠自己的能力去实现自己的目标。"

第五章

与知名品牌联名会帮助还是损害初创品牌?

——基于品牌不同人格维度(温暖 vs. 能力)推论的探索

通过六个行为实验,本章研究考察了一个在品牌联名领域少有研究的问题,即与知名品牌进行联名是会帮助还是会损害初创品牌。本章研究提供了一种基于品牌人格推论的框架来解答这一问题。具体而言,本章研究基于补偿式推论和同化式推论的相关理论,指出与知名品牌进行联名将降低消费者对初创品牌在"能力"这一品牌人格维度上的评价,但会提升消费者对初创品牌在"温暖"这一品牌人格维度上的评价(实验1A、实验1B、实验2)。随后,实验3至实验5进一步探索了对品牌人格维度的不同推断如何塑造消费者对和知名品牌联名的初创品牌的评价。这几个实验的结果指出,如果消费者将关注点集中在初创品牌的能力(vs.温暖)维度上,与知名品牌联名将不利于(vs.有利于)初创品牌。同时,实验4和实验5进一步发现,这种品牌联名与消费者关注维度的交互效应不仅会影响消费者对初创品牌的态度,还会延伸去影响消费者对该初创品牌独立开发的其他产品的偏好。综上所述,这项研究不仅整合了已往研究关于品牌联名对初创品牌影响的不一致的发现,还为品牌方如何开展品牌联名,如何进行品牌定位,以及如何向潜在消费者描述品牌联名信息等具体的营销实践问题提供了参考和启示。

第一节 研究背景

品牌联名,是指两个或多个品牌之间的合作和联盟。在过去的几十年中,品牌联名已成为一种广泛流行和被认为行之有效的品牌战略(Ahn and Sung 2012;Monga and Lau-Gesk 2007)。当共同创建新产品或一起提供新服务时,品牌联名战略可以使合作品牌相互借用对方资源,并最终实现互惠互利(Motion,Leitch,and Brodie 2003;Seno and Lukas 2007;Swaminathan,Gürhan-Canli,Kubat,and Hayran 2015;Washburn,Till,and Priluck 2000)。一些成功的例子,例如食品品牌好时(Hershey)和通用磨坊(General Mills)联名推出的新品牌贝蒂妙厨(Betty crocker),以及苹果(Apple)公司和耐克(Nike)公司在运动产品领域的品牌合作,都证明了这种品牌战略的普适性和有效性。

除了两个知名品牌之间进行联名的案例外,我们也能观察到初创品牌和知名品牌之间进行品牌联名的新案例与新趋势。根据IBM公司2014年对1 447家公司的商业技术趋势研究,被调研的行业知名公司中有40%—45%选择与初创公司进行品牌联名或其他品牌战略合作(IBM 2014)。例如,饮料品类的巨头可口可乐(Coca-Cola)从2015年开始与当时处于初创阶段的有机果汁品牌Suja合作(Kell 2015)。而在如今大受欢迎的音乐服务品牌Spotify当初还处于萌芽阶段时,它就与阿迪达斯(Adidas)合作创建了一个运动与音乐结合的手机软件,根据跑步者的运动状态推荐音乐(Millington 2015)。与此同时,越来越多的知名品牌正在尝试建立合作平台或项目,以鼓励与各种初创公司的合作和联名。例如,奢侈品行业的LVMH于2016年开设了"奢侈品实验室"。该实验室的宗旨就是推动自身与奢侈品行业的初创公司开展更多的合作(LVMH 2016)。

从商家或是营销从业人员的角度来看,品牌联名应该能同时为初创品牌和知名品牌带来增益。对于初创公司或品牌而言,通过与知名品牌进行合作,可以更好地借用知名品牌的资源(Ilicic and Webster 2013;Keller 2003;Leuthesser, Kohli, and Suri 2003)。研究者(Rao, Qu, and Ruekert 1999)指出,与知名品牌进行品牌联名可以为初创品牌进入市场提供有效路径。这是由于知名品牌本身在品牌觉知、品牌地位和品牌信誉上具有现成优势。例如,学者(Yoon and Hughes 2016)指出,知名品牌的优势在于更擅长扩大市场规模,因此至少可以帮助初创品牌提升制造、采购和分销的能力与效率。同时,知名品牌所拥有的品牌资产(例如品牌知名度和品牌形象)也可以在建立品牌联名关系时传递给该初创品牌(Keller 2003;Levin and Levin 2000;Cunha, Forehand, and Angle 2015)。

初创品牌与知名品牌之间的品牌联名不仅可以帮助初创品牌,也可以使知名品牌从这种合作中获益。首先,与初创品牌的品牌联名可以帮助知名品牌以较低的成本进行创新与开发(Freeman and Engel 2007;Michel 2015)。例如,Freeman 和 Engel(2007)认为,与初创品牌或者公司进行合作时,知名品牌可以"购买"新领域的创新发现和知识,这远比自己开发新产品线要划算。毕竟,开发新产品线意味着公司资源、人力等因素的重大调整,而且创新往往具有更多的不确定性和风险。与初创品牌联名,意味着知名品牌可以将创新潜在的成本和风险外包给对方。其次,初创品牌或者公司由于其关注点的不同,往往能够发现并释放市场中新兴的和潜在的消费者需求,而这反过来又有助于知名品牌进入新的细分市场并吸引潜在的新客户(Yoon and Hughes 2016)。最后,来自组织战略与管理的研究表明,随着知名公司或者品牌在规模上的不断扩大,其创新过程受制于庞大的机构和转型成本,逐渐变慢(Freeman and Engel 2007)。相较之下,由于初创公司或品牌通常专注于创新速度和对消费者快速响应的能力,这会使其有别于知名品牌或公司的官僚化和迟缓反应(Fishbein 2013)。基于这些讨论,与初创品牌进行品牌联名有助于知名公司维持自身的发展和创新速度,避免其陷入"大公司病"之中。综合以上讨论,初创品牌与知名品牌的联名可以说是一种双赢的品牌战略。

尽管初创品牌与知名品牌之间的品牌联名正逐渐盛行,但意外的是目前却少有实证研究来系统地检验这种品牌联名战略的效果。目前大部分的关于这种战略成败得失的讨论依然是基于已往研究的理论的推导。而在本章研究中,笔者将从消费者行为的视角入手,通过行为实验的手段,探究与知名品牌进行品牌联名如何影响消费者对初创品牌的评价。这个研究题目之所以重要,主要基于三个原因:第一,根据全球多个国家(例如美国)的社会调查数据,每年发达经济体的主要国家有超过40万家新公司和新品牌诞生(Clifton 2015),但最终能生存下来的公司屈指可数(Pryor 2016)。第二,尽管从直觉上讲,与知名品牌进行联名是初创公司或者品牌的合适选择,但是很少有实证研究从数据上检验这一预测,更不用说检验这种效应成立的条件和可能的调节作用。第三,即使已往研究对相关问题进行了前期的研究,其发现也呈现不一致的趋势(Washburn, Till, and Priluck 2000, 2004; Cunha, Forehand, and Angle 2015)。例如,支持该类品牌联名对初创品牌产生积极影响的研究(Washburn, Till, and Priluck 2000)发现,当品牌资产较少的食品品牌(例如知名度较低的薯片)和品牌资产较多的品牌(例如知名度较高的烤肉酱)进行品牌联名(例如合作推出使用该烤肉酱的薯片),消费者对品牌资产较少的食品品牌的评价在使用联名产品后得到显著提升。但是,另一批学者却发现,与知名品牌进行联名并不一定总是会为初创品牌带来积极效应(Cunha, Forehand, and Angle 2015)。这些研究发现与知名品牌合作既有可能会提升,也有可能会损害消费者对一个知名度较低的品牌的评价,这也从一定程度上证明这种品牌战略也存在潜在的风险。因此,如果本章研究能够整合已往研究的这些不一致发现,会为品牌联名研究领域带来明显的理论贡献。同时,本章研究之所以专注于探索与知名品牌联名对于初创品牌的影响,还因为有学者分析指出,相对于那些已经在市场上站稳脚跟的知名品牌,初创品牌更容易受到品牌联名战略的过程与结果的影响(Simonin and Ruth 1998;Washburn, Till, and Priluck 2000, 2004)。例如,这些学者指出,当品牌联名失败时,知名品牌更容易从失败中全身而退,而初创品牌则要承担更多的后果。当品牌联名取得成效时,初创品牌往往也能比知名品牌获得更多在品牌形象上的改进(一个原因是知名品牌本身的品牌形象已经相对成型和稳定)。综合以上讨论,本章研究主要关注与知名品牌进行品牌联名如何影响消费者对初创品牌的评价与判断。

为了整合已往研究看似矛盾的发现,笔者提出了一个基于消费者对品牌人格推论的理论框架来探讨与知名品牌联名给初创品牌带来的双刃剑效应。具体来说,结合消费者推论、社会判断和品牌人格的相关理论,笔者指出与知名品牌进行品牌联名会影响消费者对初创品牌品牌人格维度的判断。例如,与知名品牌进行品牌联名将减少消费者对初创品牌能力(品牌人格中涉及成就和技能的维度)水平的感知。然而有趣的是,这种品牌联名方式却反过来可以增加消费者对初创品牌温暖(品牌人格中涉及社会关系管理和社会资本的维度)水平的感知。换言之,与知名品牌进行联名可以使消费者对初创品牌的不同维度产生截然不同的推断。那么基于这一结果,消费者对该初创品牌的整体评价,就取决于在形成评价过程中温暖和能力这两个维度哪一个维度获得了更高的权重,扮演了更重要的乃至于决定性的角色。基于这一逻辑,当消费者更加关注初创品牌的能力维度(vs.温暖维度)时,与知名品牌的联名将会显著减少(vs.增加)消费者对初创品牌的整体评价。在接下来的文献综述部分,笔者将介绍相关的概念、理论,并基于这些讨论提出研究的假设。

第二节 文献综述

一、与知名品牌进行联名对于初创品牌的影响——已往研究中不一致的发现

已往研究主要从记忆的关联网络理论(Associative network theory)出发,肯定了与知名品牌进行联名对于初创品牌的积极作用(Anderson and Bower 1973;Cunha, Forehand, and Angle 2015;McCracken 1989;Miller and Allen 2012)。根据这一理论,消费者会在记忆网络中建立联名品牌之间的关联(Anderson and Bower 1973;Cunha, Forehand, and Angle 2015;Levin and Levin 2000)。一旦这种关联被建立,那么关联的每个联名品牌自身的属性(例如品牌资产)也可以被联名品牌所共享(Cunha, Forehand, and Angle 2015;James 2005;Levin and Levin 2000)。例如,已往研究(Levin and Levin 2000)发现,当两个品牌进行联名时,消费者对一个品牌的评价与对另一个品牌的评价会趋于近似。而这种评价的同化趋势在初创品牌与知名品牌之间的品牌联名上可能会表现得更加明显。这是由于相对于已建立稳定品牌形象的知名品牌,消费者对

一个初创品牌的了解几乎为零。在这种情况下,消费者只能根据与其联名的知名品牌(消费者对其有更多的了解)来形成和调整他们对初创品牌的评价(Aaker and Keller 1990;Cunha, Forehand, and Angle 2015)。于是,一旦建立品牌联名关系,知名品牌的品牌资产等属性可以快速和自动化地被初创品牌所共享,从而影响消费者对初创品牌的评价(Levin, Davis, and Levin 1996)。

有趣的是,尽管现有研究中的大多数都肯定与知名品牌联名对于初创品牌的积极影响,但研究者还是发现该类型的品牌联名也可能对初创品牌造成负面影响。有研究(Cunha, Forehand, and Angle 2015)指出该类品牌联名的影响取决于品牌联名的相关信息如何呈现给消费者。例如,向消费者披露品牌联名的信息时一般会涉及两种类型的信息,包括品牌联名的方式(例如两个参与联名品牌各自的名称信息)以及品牌联名的成果(例如两个联名品牌共创的服务或者产品)。该研究发现,当品牌联名的方式信息和品牌联名的成果信息同时呈现给消费者时,消费者没有足够时间将两个联名品牌视为一个整体,他们更倾向于计算每个品牌各自对于品牌联名成果的贡献度。由于知名品牌具有更高的知名度、更多的品牌资产,因而更能吸引消费者的注意。在此情况下,消费者更倾向于将知名品牌视为合作成果的主要贡献者,对初创品牌在合作中的贡献度的感知则相对减弱。这也意味着,消费者更倾向于认为初创品牌与知名品牌的联名是前者在"搭便车"。基于这一逻辑,消费者也更容易对初创品牌独立开发的产品持不信任的态度,从而对初创品牌造成整体上的负面影响。相反,如果实验者让消费者先了解到品牌联名的方式,例如先让消费者知晓这两个品牌已经建立了联名关系,经过一段时间的延迟(例如五秒钟的延迟)之后,再向消费者呈现关于联名品牌合作开发的产品的相关信息。由于消费者已经有足够的时间在记忆网络中将两个品牌关联起来,他们更容易将这两个品牌视为一个整体(同时也感知到这两个品牌更多的相似性)。在此基础上,呈现品牌联名的成果更容易让消费者认为两个品牌都做出了显著的贡献。此时,如果他们再被要求评价初创品牌独立开发的产品,他们也会感觉到更多的信心(因为此时的初创品牌已经被认为和知名品牌类似)。在这种情况下,品牌联名会对初创品牌带来更积极的整体影响。

值得注意的是,尽管 Cunha 等人(2015)的研究探讨了品牌联名对于初创品牌的负面影响,但是他们的研究情景与真实的商业世界存在一定的差异。具体来说,无论是线下还是线上的品牌联名广告一般都是同时呈现联名方式(参加联名的品牌名字)和联名结果(合作生产和推广的产品或者服务)。两种信息之间加入时间间隔的情景,在真实世界中几乎不存在。更重要的是,如果只考虑 Cunha 等人(2015)研究中的"信息同时呈现"条件,那么不难发现他们的研究结果其实是,在此类条件下与知名品牌进行联名会为初创品牌带来负面效应。这一结论恰好与在类似条件下其他学者(Washburn, Till, and Priluck 2000, 2004)发现的品牌联名对初创品牌的正面效应相矛盾。因此,无论是从该领域研究的理论体系还是实证检验角度,都有必要去整合已往研究中不一致的发现。

根据社会判断、消费者推论和品牌人格的相关研究,笔者认为与知名品牌进行品牌联名会影响消费者对初创品牌人格维度的评价(Abele and Wojciszke 2014; Bakan 1966; Rucker, Galinsky, and Dubois 2012)。具体来说,当初创品牌与知名品牌进行联名时,消费者会对初创品牌的温暖维度和能力维度做出方向不同的判断。

消费者对这两个维度相对重视的程度则会作为调节变量,影响他们对和知名品牌进行联名的初创品牌的态度。因此,笔者从不同的视角寻找到了可能调节品牌联名影响的变量。在下一部分,笔者将对相应的概念和假设进行梳理。

二、品牌人格的两个主要维度——温暖维度与能力维度

来自社会心理学的研究表明,个体对他人的社会判断主要围绕两个基本维度,分别是能力维度和温暖维度(Abele and Wojciszke 2014; Bakan 1966; Dubois, Rucker, and Galinsky 2016; Wiggins 1991)。能力维度是指个人成就和技能(Abele and Wojciszke 2014; Bakan 1966; Rucker and Galinsky 2016; Ybarra, Chan, Park, Burnstein, Monin, and Stanik 2008)。具体来说,能力维度涵盖了个人的竞争力、信心、实力等特征(Abele and Wojciszke 2014; Gebauer, Wagner, Sedikides, and Neberich 2013; Kurt, Inman, and Argo 2011)。相比之下,温暖维度则指向人际关系管理和社交资源的维护(Abele and Wojciszke 2014; Bakan 1966; Dubois, Rucker, and Galinsky 2016; Rucker and Galinsky 2016)。温暖维度的关键内容包括社交性、合作性、慷慨性等特征(Abele and Wojciszke 2014; Diehl, Owen, and Youngblade 2004; Trupin 1976)。

随着品牌心理学研究的日益深入,部分学者指出,一个公司或者品牌可以被看作一个有生命的个体(Kervyn, Fiske, and Malone 2012)。基于这一理论,消费者对一个品牌或公司的判断也类似于他们对一个活生生的人的社会判断(Fournier 1998, 2009; Ahuvia 2005; Swaminathan, Stilley, and Ahluwalia 2009; Dunn and Hoegg 2014)。已往研究指出,消费者对品牌的判断也可以落入类似的双

维度框架中。研究人员采用了不同的名称来表示这种二维区分,包括能动性与社群性(Agency vs. communion)(Van Marrewijk, 2003),温暖与能力(Warmth vs. competence)(Alvarez and Fournier 2012),男性化与女性化(Masculinity vs. femininity)(Grohmann 2009),等等。例如,Van Marrewijk(2003)提出,企业社会责任(CSR)这一公司常见战略与公司的社群性维度相关,而公司的长远发展则与公司的能动性维度相关。来自消费者行为学的研究(Aaker, Vohs, and Mogilner 2010)则发现,相对于营利性品牌,非营利性品牌被认为在温暖维度上得分较高,而在能力维度上得分较低。尽管这些研究各自使用了不同的术语,但从概念的核心成分上讲,它们都和温暖维度与能力维度相似(Abele and Wojciszke 2014; Dubois, Rucker, and Galinsky 2016)。因此,笔者主要使用温暖和能力这两个专有名词来描述这两个维度(Abele and Wojciszke 2007; Abele, Uchronski, Suitner, and Wojciszke 2008; Bakan 1966)。

三、与知名品牌联名如何影响消费者对初创品牌的评价——品牌人格推论的作用

在本章研究中,笔者指出,相同的与知名品牌进行联名的战略,也可能导致消费者对初创品牌的温暖维度和能力维度产生方向完全相反的评价。具体来说,与知名品牌进行联名会让消费者认为初创品牌缺少能力。而这一推论来源于个体在推断目标的能力时采用的补偿式推论思路。按照已往研究的定义,能力维度关系到个体的权力、控制感和主导支配地位(Tiedens and Fragale 2003; Wiggins 1991)。团体和组织行为方向的学者指出,当团队成员的关系是建立在一起完成目标任务的基础上时,地位和主导

权更像是一种有限的资源,不能平均地被每个小组成员获得(Dufner, Leising, and Gebauer 2016)。因此,为了确保合作顺利进行以及任务的成功完成,团队中的每一个个体将自动界定和划分自己的权力和控制范围(Tiedens, Unzueta, and Young 2007)。基于这一理论,已往研究发现,如果被试与其他成员(姑且称之为合伙人)一起被要求组队完成任务,一旦合伙人被被试感知为具有较高的能力和权力地位,则该被试会认为自己处在能力和地位较低的状态。换句话说,在这种任务导向的团队关系中,个体将自动采用互补式推论来推断自己和合伙人的能力维度(Carson 1969; Kiesler 1983; Tiedens, Unzueta, and Young 2007)。笔者推断,这种在能力维度上的补偿式推论也会发生在初创品牌与知名品牌进行联名的场景中。这是基于两个重要的前提条件:其一,当一个初创品牌与一个知名品牌联名开发产品或提供服务时,他们会建立面向任务的团队关系,这与日常生活中的人际友谊大不相同(Swaminathan, Gürhan-Canli, Kubat, and Hayran 2015)。其二,由于消费者缺乏对初创品牌的了解,因此他们更倾向于根据对知名品牌的了解来对初创品牌进行推断(Simonin and Ruth 1998; Vaidyanathan and Aggarwal 2000)。相对于初创品牌,知名品牌往往意味着拥有更高的品牌知名度、更多资源和更高的市场地位。因此,知名品牌在能力维度上的表现远比初创品牌显眼(Cunha and Laran 2009; Cunha, Forehand, and Angle 2015; Kruschke 2001)。基于以上两个前提条件,笔者认为消费者对初创品牌的能力维度的推断容易被能力维度上的互补式推论所驱动。因此,当初创品牌与知名品牌进行联名时,消费者会认为知名品牌在能力维度上表现突出,进而推论初创品牌的能力维度得分较低。综上,笔者正式提出以下假设:

假设 1：当初创品牌与知名品牌联合开发新产品时（vs.初创品牌独立开发新产品时），消费者会感知初创品牌在能力维度上表现更差（vs.更好）。

与知名品牌进行联名也可以被消费者进行另一种解读。笔者假设，当观察到初创品牌与知名品牌进行联名时，消费者会更容易认为该初创品牌具有较高的温暖属性。笔者的这一推断建立在品牌联名这一行为的特性上。温暖属性最直接对应的特质就是社会关系的建立与维护（Helgeson 1994；Trucco，Wright，and Colder 2014）。与其他类型的战略联盟不同，品牌联名并不是两个品牌在金钱和其他资源上的短期交换（Motion，Leitch，and Brodie 2003；Seno and Lukas 2007）。相反，品牌联名中的所有合作伙伴都寻求互惠互利并希望彼此提供持续的长期的支持（Keller 1993；Motion，Leitch，and Brodie 2003；Seno and Lukas 2007）。已往研究表明，寻求或提供支持都是展现社交性和温暖性的信号，因为这两者都反映出了对他人的信任以及对他人需求的考量（Chiaburu，Marinova，and Lim 2007；Helgeson and Fritz 2000）。而即便从商业交易或者商业战略的角度出发，与知名品牌进行合作也可以清晰地向消费者传递一种信息，即该初创品牌拥有强大的社交网络，并擅长与资源更丰富的合作伙伴建立和维持关系（这正是社会资本的表现）。无论是彰显信任感、关怀感，还是传递自身关系网的信号，这些都和温暖维度存在直接的对应关系（Abele and Wojciszke 2014；Cislak and Wojciszke 2008；Koka and Prescott 2002；Wiggins 1991）。综上，笔者正式提出以下假设：

假设 2：当初创品牌与知名品牌联合开发新产品时（vs.初创品牌独立开发新产品时），消费者会感知初创品牌在温暖维度上表现更好（vs.更差）。

四、整合已往研究中不一致的发现——消费者关注维度的调节作用

基于上文的讨论,与知名品牌进行联名可能会让消费者感知初创品牌具有更低的能力,但是也同时拥有更多的温暖。由于消费者对品牌的整体评价取决于其对品牌各个维度或者属性评价的总和,因此与知名品牌联名对于初创品牌的影响主要取决于消费者在评价初创品牌时更侧重该品牌的哪一个维度(温暖维度 vs.能力维度)。具体来说,若消费者在评价品牌时更侧重其能力维度,此时由于与知名品牌的联名衬托出了初创品牌的能力缺陷,因此消费者更容易对初创品牌抱有负面态度("背靠大树好乘凉")。相反,若消费者在评价品牌时更侧重其温暖维度,那么与知名品牌的联名便会彰显初创品牌的社交性和社会资本,消费者对初创品牌的整体态度也将得到提升。值得注意的是,这种消费者信息加工过程中的关注点(抑或是注意和权重的分配)既可以是来自消费者自身的个体差异和偏好,也可以是来自广告信息的刻意引导(例如强调品牌的能力维度或是温暖维度)。而且,这种品牌联名与消费者关注点对于初创品牌评价的交互效应,也可以进一步扩散到消费者对待初创品牌独立生产产品的态度上。综上,笔者正式提出以下两个假设:

假设3:在初创品牌与知名品牌联名开发新产品(vs.初创品牌独立开发新产品)的情况下,当消费者更多地关注初创品牌的能力维度时,消费者对初创品牌及其独立推出产品的评价将降低(vs.升高)。

假设4:在初创品牌与知名品牌联名开发新产品(vs.初创品牌独立开发新产品)的情况下,当消费者更多地关注初创品牌的温

暖维度时,消费者对初创品牌及其独立推出产品的评价将升高(vs.降低)。

第三节　实证研究部分

一、本章研究的实验架构

通过六个行为实验,本章研究考察了与知名品牌进行联名如何影响消费者对初创品牌的评价。在实验1A、实验1B、实验2中,笔者检验了在初创品牌与知名品牌进行联名的情况下,消费者对初创品牌温暖和能力这两个维度的判断(假设1和假设2)。在得到相应的结果之后,在余下的实验中笔者检验了消费者关注维度如何与品牌联名情况一起影响消费者对初创品牌的评价与判断。具体来说,笔者测量(实验3)或者操纵(实验4和实验5)了消费者在评价品牌时对品牌能力维度或者温暖维度的侧重,并进一步探索了其是否能调节"品牌联名—消费者对初创品牌评价"效应。实验4和实验5发现,品牌联名与消费者关注维度对初创品牌的影响也会体现在消费者对该初创品牌独立开发的其他产品的评价上。

二、实验1A

实验1A和实验1B分别检验了假设1和假设2。其中,实验1A旨在研究与知名品牌进行联名如何影响消费者对初创品牌能力维度的推断。已往研究指出,品牌联名是一种任务导向的团队合作关系,会促使观察者(例如消费者)采用补偿式推断的思维模式来评价每个合作方的能力维度(Tiedens, Unzueta, and Young 2007)。同时,在品牌联名的合作关系中,知名品牌的能力维度要远比初创品牌更显眼和突出。基于以上两个前提,实验1A假设,当初创品牌选择与知名品牌联名(vs.初创品牌独立)开发产品时,消费者会推断初创品牌在能力维度上表现更差(vs.更好)。

(一)实验方法

被试与实验设计:笔者从美国亚马逊网站Amazon Mechanic Turk(以下用Mturk表示)平台招募研究被试。Mturk是一个全球知名的众包服务平台,超过十万名志愿者在该平台上完成各种发布任务并获取金钱酬劳。在过去的十年中,Mturk是很多社会科学研究人员(例如社会心理学、市场营销、组织行为学)依靠的重要数据收集平台。来自美国的151名成年Mturk用户(女性占比为56%,平均年龄为36.68岁)参加了这一有偿行为实验。实验1A采用单因素(与知名品牌联名:是vs.否)的被试间设计。被试被随机分配到品牌联名组或者无品牌联名组,并将对初创品牌进行相应评价。

实验步骤与测量:在实验1A中,被试将首先阅读关于初创品牌及其开发产品的相应信息,然后对初创品牌的能力维度进行评分。具体内容如下:

首先是品牌联名的操纵。所有被试首先被要求阅读一份商业报告。这份商业报告简单介绍了冰激凌市场上的知名品牌,例如哈根达斯(Haagen-Dazs)、蓝兔(Blue Bunny)、布利斯(Breyers)。之所以要给所有被试做介绍,是为了尽可能平衡被试在冰激凌品牌相关知识上的个体差异。同时,告知这些美国被试在美国市场上的知名冰激凌品牌,有助于笔者随后进行品牌联名的相关操纵

(让被试相信与初创品牌合作的品牌的确是知名品牌)。

接着,被试被告知在这些知名品牌之外,一些新的冰激凌也正在进入市场,而这些冰激凌是由一些初创品牌开发生产的。紧接着,被试会被随机分成两组(品牌联名组 vs. 无品牌联名组)并接受不同的信息。在品牌联名组,向被试呈现一个关于某款新型莓果口味冰激凌的广告。为了控制消费者的品牌知识,笔者给予了这款冰激凌一个虚构名字——"Summer Dream Ice Cream"(夏日梦幻冰激凌)。被试被告知这款冰激凌是由一个初创品牌"Leisure-Time Snacks"(休闲时光零食,这是虚构的)和知名品牌哈根达斯联名推出的。与之不同的是,在无品牌联名组,向被试呈现同样的冰激凌广告,但是仅告知该款冰激凌是由"休闲时光零食"这个初创品牌开发的。换言之,在无品牌联名组,没有出现知名品牌参与合作的信息(详见本章附录 5-1)。

随后是能力维度评分。在阅读了对应的冰激凌广告之后,所有被试均被要求就该初创品牌"休闲时光零食"的能力维度进行评分。具体而言,被试需要完成一个六道题目的量表。在这个 7 点量表中,向被试呈现六条关于该初创品牌能力的陈述,他们需要回答在多大程度上自己同意或者不同意每一条陈述(例如,"该品牌是有竞争力的/有能力的/具有自信的",1 = 完全不同意,7 = 完全同意)。这一量表改编自已往研究对品牌温暖或是能力维度的经典测量,具有较好的信度和效度(Aaker, Vohs, and Mogilner 2010; Fiske, Cuddy, Glick, and Xu 2002)。最后,所有被试回答人口统计学相关问题并领取酬劳。

(二)实验结果

信度分析显示对于初创品牌能力维度进行评分的这六道题目

具有良好的信度($\alpha=0.90$)。因此,笔者将被试在这六道题目上的得分计算平均值来作为因变量。随后,独立样本 t 检验结果显示,在品牌联名组中被试对初创品牌"休闲时光零食"能力维度的评价($M=5.02, SD=1.08$)显著低于无联名组中被试对该品牌能力维度的评价($M=5.39, SD=0.89$),$t(149)=2.34, p=0.021, d=0.38$。因此,实验 1A 的结果支持了假设 1,即相比于不联名的情况,与知名品牌进行联名反而会降低被试对初创品牌能力的评价。而在实验 1B 中,笔者将用相同的范式检验与知名品牌联名如何影响消费者对初创品牌温暖维度的评价。

三、实验 1B

实验 1B 旨在用和实验 1A 同样的设计来检验假设 2。具体而言,和知名品牌进行联名既能体现初创品牌的社交性(信任商业伙伴、寻求和提供支持),又能传递该初创品牌拥有充足社会资本和外来资源的信号(擅长建立和维护合作关系网)。由于这些属性恰好也是温暖维度对应的核心属性(Conway, Pizzamiglio, and Mount 1996),因此笔者假设,与知名品牌进行联名可以显著提升消费者对初创品牌温暖维度的评价。

(一)实验方法

被试与实验设计:笔者通过 Mturk 招募了来自美国的 144 名成年被试(女性占比为 43%,平均年龄为 36.12 岁)来参加该有偿行为实验。如前文所述,与实验 1A 相同,实验 1B 也基于单因素(与知名品牌联名:是 vs.否)的被试间设计,并采用了与实验 1A 相同的研究场景和刺激物。不同的是,在实验 1B 中,笔者主要考察与知名品牌联名如何影响被试感知的初创品牌的温暖程度。

实验步骤与测量：实验1B的步骤与实验1A相同，先告知被试冰激凌市场的知名品牌，随后将被试随机分成品牌联名组与无品牌联名组。与实验1A不同的是，在实验1B中，当被试接受与实验1A同样的品牌联名操纵后，他们将完成一个由六道题目构成的量表以测量他们对"休闲时光零食"这一初创品牌温暖的感知。该量表同样改编自已往研究并具有良好的信度和效度（Cuddy, Fiske, and Glick 2004；Wojciszke and Abele 2008）。向被试呈现六条关于该初创品牌温暖程度的陈述，他们需要回答在多大程度上自己同意或者不同意每一条陈述（例如，"该品牌是善于社交的/具有合作倾向的/值得信赖的"，1 = 完全不同意，7 = 完全同意）。最后，所有被试回答人口统计学相关问题并领取酬劳。

（二）实验结果

信度分析显示，对初创品牌温暖维度进行评分的这六道题目具有良好的信度（$\alpha = 0.91$）。因此，笔者将被试在这六道题目上的得分计算平均值来作为因变量。随后，独立样本t检验结果显示，在品牌联名组中被试对初创品牌"休闲时光零食"温暖维度的评价（$M = 5.36$, $SD = 0.82$）显著高于无品牌联名组中被试对该品牌能力维度的评价（$M = 5.05$, $SD = 0.99$），$t(142) = 2.00$, $p = 0.048$, $d = 0.33$。因此，实验1B的结果支持了假设2，即相比于不联名的情况，与知名品牌进行联名会提升被试对初创品牌温暖的评价。

（三）对实验1A和实验1B结果的讨论

实验1A和实验1B分别检验了与知名品牌进行品牌联名如何影响消费者对初创品牌能力维度和温暖维度的感知。实验结果表明，与知名品牌进行品牌联名会显著降低被试对初创品牌能力的评价(支持假设1),但可以提升被试对初创品牌温暖的评价(支持假设2)。值得注意的是,实验1A和实验1B各自独立检验了品牌联名对初创品牌的能力和温暖的感知,这是因为采用分开检验的方法可以避免消费者在两种维度上的评分互相污染。这两个实验均选择了食物作为研究对象,而在接下来的实验2中,笔者将尝试通过测量非食品类别的初创品牌的能力感知和温暖感知,来重复实验1A和实验1B的发现。

四、实验2

实验2的主要目的是通过不同的实验范式和实验场景来复制实验1A和实验1B的发现,从而为假设1和假设2提供更多的实证支持。具体来说,实验2专注于汽车领域的品牌联名现象,并改编真实案例作为实验材料。与实验1A和实验1B不同,实验2同时测量了消费者对初创品牌能力和温暖的感知。笔者预测,即便在新的场景和实验范式下,与知名品牌联名开发新产品依然会降低消费者对初创品牌能力的感知并提高他们对初创品牌温暖的感知。

(一)实验方法

被试与实验设计:笔者从Mturk招募了138名来自美国的成年被试(女性占比为47%,平均年龄为38.24岁)来参加该有偿实验。实验2在设计时改编了曾真实存在于商业世界中的品牌联名案例:知名品牌(即梅赛德斯-奔驰)和一家对美国消费者而言相对较新的初创品牌共同开发新型电动汽车。实验2采用2(与知名品牌联名:是vs.否)×2(对初创品牌的感知类型:能力维度vs.温暖维度)的混合设计。其中第一个因素(品牌联名情况)为被试间因素,第二个因素(对初创品牌的感知类型)则是被试内因素。笔者预测,得知初创品牌与知名品牌联名制造电动汽车会降低消费者对初创品牌能力的感知,却会提高他们对初创品牌温暖的感知。

实验步骤与测量：在实验 2 中,被试同样将首先阅读汽车市场知名品牌相关信息,以减少被试对汽车品牌了解度的个体差异。之后,他们将阅读有关新型电动汽车的产品介绍。该介绍内容会根据被试所处的组别(品牌联名组 vs.无品牌联名组)进行调整。然后被试将同时对初创品牌能力维度和温暖维度进行评价。具体内容如下：

首先是品牌联名的操纵。所有被试首先阅读了一份有关汽车行业的简短商业报告。在该报告中,实验向参与者统一呈现了汽车市场上的知名品牌,例如梅赛德斯-奔驰、福特、奥迪。同时,被试被告知也有一些初创的品牌加入了汽车市场。而在之后一页,实验向被试呈现了一款新型全电动汽车(Denza 电动汽车)的广告。尽管都是关于同一款汽车的介绍,但是被试被随机分配到品牌联名组和无品牌联名组,以接受不同的制造商品牌信息。具体来说,在品牌联名组的被试被告知该款电动汽车是由一个初创品牌与梅赛德斯-奔驰联名共同开发的产品。与此相对,在无品牌联名组中,被试被告知该初创品牌是这款新型电动汽车的唯一制造商。

随后是能力维度与温暖维度评分。在阅读了上述电动汽车广告之后,所有被试被要求将该初创品牌想象成一个真实存在的人,然后通过 7 点量表对该品牌的温暖维度和能力维度进行评价。其中,对初创品牌温暖维度的评价通过三个题目来测量(例如,"该品牌具有合作倾向",1 = 完全不同意,7 = 完全同意)。对初创品牌能力维度的评价也通过三个题目来测量(例如,"该品牌具有自信",1=完全不同意,7=完全同意)。为了避免出现顺序效应,笔者将温暖维度评价题目和能力维度评价题目的出现顺序进行了随机化。

被试在完成这些品牌感知的题目之后,他们还将完成控制变量的测量题目。由于在本章实验中出现的电动汽车和初创品牌名字都是真实的,因此笔者需要检验 Mturk 上的美国被试是否对该初创品牌有足够了解(换言之,是否该初创品牌真的被他们视为知名度较低的初创品牌)。具体而言,被试需要完成一个 7 点量表("总的来说,您有多了解这个初创品牌?"1=完全不了解,7=非常了解)。最后,所有被试回答人口统计学相关问题并领取酬劳。

(二)实验结果

信度分析结果显示,对初创品牌能力维度进行评分的三道题目($\alpha=0.77$),以及对该品牌温暖维度进行评分的三道题目($\alpha=0.83$)均具有良好的信度。因此,笔者对被试在这两个品牌维度上的评分分别计算平均值来作为研究的因变量。2(与知名品牌联名:是 vs.否)×2(对初创品牌的感知类型:能力维度 vs.温暖维度)的 Repeated ANOVA(重复测量方差分析)结果显示,品牌联名和初创品牌感知类型之间的交互作用在统计学上较为显著,$F(1,136)=22.07$,$p<0.001$,$\eta_p^2=0.14$,如图 5-1。接下来,笔者通过 Planned Contrast 分析简单主效应,结果显示在品牌联名组中的被试对初创品牌能力的评价($M=5.10$)在趋势上低于在无品牌联名组中的被试评价($M=5.44$),尽管这种差异在统计学上呈现边缘显著,$F(1,136)=3.80$,$p=0.053$。相比之下,在品牌联名组中的被试对初创品牌温暖维度的评分($M=5.36$)显著高于在非品牌联名

组中的被试评分($M = 5.00$),$F(1, 136) = 4.80$, $p = 0.030$。同时,笔者还检验了 Mturk 上的美国被试是否的确认同实验 2 对初创品牌的选择。单样本 t 检验结果表明,消费者对该初创品牌的了解($M = 1.86$)显著低于 7 点量表的中间值 4(也就是中立态度),$t(137) = 17.81$, $p < 0.001$, $d = 1.52$。因此,实验 2 中对初创品牌的选择和阐述被实验被试所接受,实验操纵有效。

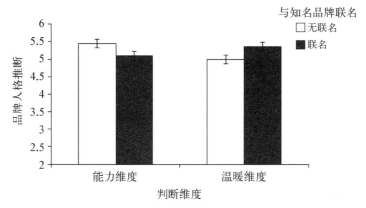

图 5-1　品牌联名如何影响消费者对初创品牌能力维度和温暖维度的评分(实验 2)

(三) 结果讨论

实验 2 改编自真实的商业案例,选择不同的产品品类(汽车而不是食物)并采用混合设计同时测量被试对初创品牌温暖和能力的感知。实验 2 的结果重复了实验 1A 和实验 1B 的结果,即与知名品牌进行联名会损害被试对初创品牌能力的感知,但是有益于他们对初创品牌温暖的感知。因此,实验 2 的结果同时为假设 1 和假设 2 提供了实证支持。由于消费者对品牌的整体态度取决于他们在品牌不同维度上评价的整合,并且同样的与知名品牌进行品牌联名的行为会让消费者在初创品牌的温暖维度和能力维度上产生截然相反的评价,因此消费者在评价品牌时对不同品牌维度的权重分配将成为决定品牌联名对初创品牌影响的调节变量。具体来说,如果消费者在评价品牌时相对更侧重品牌的能力维度(vs.温暖维度),那么与知名品牌联名造成的消费者对初创品牌的低能力感知(vs.高温暖感知)会更容易损害(vs.增加)他们对初创品牌的整体评价(假设3和假设4)。为了检验这两个假设,实验3将测量消费者在决策时关注维度的倾向(更侧重温暖维度 vs.更侧重能力维度),然后检验其是否影响了消费者在品牌联名和不联名情况下对初创品牌的态度。

五、实验3

实验3直接同时对假设3和假设4进行检验。与前面三个实验不同,实验3测量了消费者在评价品牌时侧重的维度(能力维度 vs.温暖维度),并检验其如何与品牌联名类型(与知名品牌联名 vs.不与知名品牌联名)共同影响消费者对初创品牌的整体态度。实验3以消费者对初创品牌的态度为因变量,既可以整合已往研究中不一致的发现,也可以为管理实践者提供直接的借鉴。笔者预测,消费者在评价品牌时若相对更关注品牌的能力维度(vs.温暖维度),与知名品牌进行联名会降低(vs.提升)消费者对该初创品牌的整体评价。

(一)实验方法

被试与实验设计:笔者从 Mturk 招募了293名来自美国的成年被试(女性占比为56%,平均年龄为36.51岁)来参加该有偿实验。实验3采用2(与知名品牌联名:是 vs.否)×2(消费者关注维度：能力维度 vs.温暖维度）的被试间设计，其中第一个因素需要进行实验操纵，第二个因素则通过量表测量连续得分。

实验步骤与测量： 在实验 3 中，首先让被试完成一个量表以测量他们在评价品牌时更侧重的维度。然后让被试完成一系列无关问题，以防止被试猜到实验目的。其后，他们阅读关于新款食品的广告信息，并对特定的初创品牌进行评价。具体内容如下：

首先是测量被试在评价品牌时的个人侧重（能力维度 vs.温暖维度）。为了测量消费者在评价品牌时的相对关注维度，笔者改编了已往研究对这两个维度进行测量的量表（Aaker, Vohs, and Mogilner 2010; Fiske, Cuddy, Glick, and Xu 2002; Fiske, Xu, Cuddy, and Glick 1999）。具体而言，被试需要完成一个五道题的 7 点量表。每道题目都在询问被试在评判一个品牌时更侧重哪一个维度（例如，"当您评价一个品牌时，以下两个品牌形象中的哪一个是您更看重的？"1＝合作的/7＝自立的，1＝友好的/7＝有效的，1＝慷慨的/7＝自信的）。

当被试完成上述量表的问题后，还需要让他们完成一系列无关题目以减少他们对实验设计的怀疑。例如，他们将回答一些关于他们睡眠质量和睡眠周期的问题。完成这些无关问题之后，所有被试进入下一个品牌评价任务。

接着是品牌联名操纵。所有被试首先阅读一份关于"高纤维膳食与早餐麦片"的科学报道。该科学报道改编自已往研究（Cunha, Forehand, and Angle 2015）。通过这一报告，笔者试图尽可能让被试了解在麦片市场上的知名品牌，以此控制被试个人对该产品和品牌知识度差异可能带来的混淆作用。在报告中，笔者既强调知名的麦片品牌，例如家乐氏（Kellogg's）、桂格（Quake）和亨氏（Heinz），也告知被试一些初创品牌开发的高纤维早餐麦片正在进入这一市场。接下来,向所有被试呈现一个新款高纤维早餐麦片"快乐日子早餐麦片"(Happy-Day Breakfast Cereal)的广告。被试会被随机分成品牌联名组和无品牌联名组,了解关于这款麦片的不同制造商的信息。具体来说,在品牌联名组中的被试被告知一个初创品牌"晨光食品"(For-Morning Foods,这是虚构的)和知名品牌家乐氏联名推出了这款高纤维早餐麦片。而在无品牌联名组中,被试被告知该初创品牌推出了这款高纤维早餐麦片(详见本章附录5-2)。

随后是关于消费者对品牌整体态度的测量。所有被试被要求用一个7点量表来评价初创品牌"晨光食品"。该量表包含两个测量问题(例如,"您对晨光食品这一品牌的看法是?"1=非常差/7=非常好,1=令人不喜欢的/7=令人喜欢的)。最后,所有被试完成人口统计学相关问题并领取报酬。

(二) 实验结果

由于因变量的测量(即消费者对初创品牌的整体态度)是由两道题目构成的,因此要通过相关分析来论证该因变量测量的信度。相关分析显示这两道题目呈现显著正相关($r=0.88$)。因此,笔者将被试在这两道题目上的得分计算平均值来作为因变量。

接着,由于信度分析显示测量调节变量(即消费者在评价品牌时的维度侧重)的量表具有良好的信度($\alpha=0.79$),因此,笔者计算了被试在该量表每个题目上的平均得分。平均分越高(vs. 越低),则说明被试在评判品牌时相对更看重品牌的能力维度(vs. 温暖维度)。

随后,笔者将自变量(即品牌联名情况)进行了分组编码(1=品牌联名,-1=无品牌联名)。接下来,笔者对上述的自变量和调节变量先各自进行标准化计算出 z 分数,再通过两个标准化分数的乘积(品牌联名 × 消费者关注维度)计算出交互项。

在此基础上,笔者以被试对初创品牌的态度为结果变量,以品牌联名、消费者关注维度以及两者的交互项为预测变量,进行了回归分析。回归分析结果显示,品牌联名($p>0.50$)和消费者关注维度($p>0.20$)的主效应均不显著。更重要的是,品牌联名和消费者关注维度之间的交互作用在统计学上显著($\beta = -0.13$,$t(289) = -2.25$,$p = 0.025$)。然后,笔者使用未标准化的原始数据进行 Floodlight 分析(Johnson and Neyman 1936;Spiller, Fitzsimons, Lynch, and McClelland 2013)。结果显示,如果消费者在调节变量的量表上的得分高于 5.42($B_{JN} = -0.17$,$SE = 0.09$),也就是说当他们在评价品牌时相对更侧重品牌的能力维度时,与知名品牌进行品牌联名会降低消费者对初创品牌的整体评价($p<0.05$)。相反,当消费者在调节变量的量表上的得分低于 1.30($B_{JN} = 0.26$,$SE = 0.14$)时,便意味着他们在评价品牌时相对更侧重品牌的温暖维度。此时与知名品牌进行联名会在趋势上提升消费者对初创品牌的整体评价,尽管该趋势呈现边缘显著($p = 0.077$)。因此,这些发现支持了假设 3 和假设 4,即与知名品牌进行联名对初创品牌的影响取决于消费者在评价品牌时究竟更关注品牌的能力维度还是温暖维度(见图 5-2)。

(三)结果讨论

实验 3 的结果同时为假设 3 和假设 4 提供了实证支持。本章研究通过测量被试在评判品牌时关注维度的个体差异,证明了这一变量可以调节品牌联名对初创品牌的影响。然而实验 3 依然具有改进的空间。首先,实验 3 先测量了被试的个体差异,然后操纵

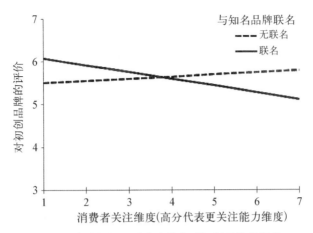

图 5-2 品牌联名如何影响消费者对初创品牌的评价——
消费者关注维度个体差异的调节作用(实验3)

品牌联名。尽管实验在两个阶段之间插入了无关任务以尽可能减少被试的怀疑,但是被试个体差异的测量可能会对被试造成某些提醒,并影响被试对自变量(品牌联名)操纵的反应。其次,实验3在理论和实证结果上支持了假设3和假设4,但是测量被试个体差异的方法较难为品牌管理者提供实践价值。毕竟在商业世界中,商家很难用量表去测量被试决策模式的个体差异(侧重品牌温暖维度还是侧重品牌能力维度)。因此,有必要寻找到干预被试的信息加工模式的手段,从而使得其在评判品牌时更侧重温暖维度或是能力维度。同样的关于管理实践的问题也出现在因变量的测量上。实验3以消费者对初创品牌的整体态度为因变量,但是在现实生活中更具有实践意义的测量应该来自消费者对该品牌的产品的态度和偏好。为了解决上述的问题和不足,接下来的实验4和实验5都将操纵被试在评判品牌时的关注维度,并测量他们对初创品牌旗下产品的态度。

六、实验 4

实验 4 有两个目的：首先，实验 4 并没有采用测量的方法来量化消费者关注维度的个体差异，而是直接操纵消费者在评价品牌时的注意分配（侧重温暖维度 vs.侧重能力维度）。其次，实验 4 探讨了实验 3 中发现的品牌联名和消费者关注维度的交互作用是否会进一步影响消费者对该初创品牌独立开发的其他产品的态度。具体而言，笔者预测，初创品牌与知名品牌共同开发产品 A 的行为会影响被试对初创品牌独立开发的产品 B 的态度，而这种影响取决于消费者在评价初创品牌时更关注品牌的温暖维度还是能力维度。当消费者关注初创品牌的能力维度（vs.温暖维度）时，与知名品牌联名开发产品 A 会降低（vs.提升）消费者对初创品牌产品 B 的评价。

（一）实验方法

被试和实验设计：笔者从 Mturk 招募了 128 名来自美国的成年被试（女性占比为 45%，平均年龄为 37.51 岁）来参加该有偿实验。实验 4 采用 2（与知名品牌联名：是 vs.否）×2（消费者关注维度：能力维度 vs.温暖维度）的被试间设计。两个因素都通过实验手段进行操纵。

实验步骤与测量：类似于实验 3，在实验 4 中所有被试会首先了解麦片市场的知名品牌，然后他们会阅读实验 3 中的麦片广告。但与实验 3 不同的是，笔者在麦片广告中将同时操纵品牌联名和消费者关注维度，并且在实验中将不再测量被试对初创品牌的整体态度。取而代之的是，被试将被要求完成一个额外的调研。在这个调研中，他们将就该初创品牌独立开发的另一款产品进行评

价。具体内容如下:

首先是品牌联名与消费者关注维度的操纵。与实验 3 相同,向所有被试呈现关于麦片市场知名品牌的报告,并告知被试一些初创品牌也在进入这一市场。品牌联名的操纵也和实验 3 相同,在品牌联名组的被试被告知初创品牌"晨光食品"(For-Morning Foods,这是虚构的)和知名品牌家乐氏(Kellogg's)联名推出了这款高纤维早餐麦片。而在无品牌联名组中,被试则被告知晨光食品是该新型早餐麦片唯一的制造商。

与实验 3 不同,被试在实验 4 中不需要直接填写对初创品牌的态度。将被试随机分成两组(关注能力维度 vs.关注温暖维度),并告知他们可以通过思考哪些方面来帮助他们形成对该初创品牌的态度。具体来说,在关注能力维度组,告知被试可以通过思考该初创品牌是否具有能力/是否有自信/是否具有竞争力来形成对该初创品牌的整体态度。相较之下,在关注温暖维度组,告知被试可以通过思考该初创品牌是否擅长社交/是否热情/是否值得信赖来形成对该初创品牌的整体态度。这一操纵的目的是在被试形成对初创品牌态度的过程中,人为干预他们评价品牌时更侧重的品牌维度。

接着是对初创品牌独立开发产品的评价。在完成上述任务之后,所有被试进入下一页。在这一页,他们会看到关于初创品牌的另一个广告。这个广告告诉被试晨光食品独立开发了新款的豆浆产品(详见本章附录 5-3)。所有被试阅读关于该产品的描述和介绍,并通过 7 点量表填写他们对这款豆浆产品的态度("您对这款豆浆的评价是?"1 = 非常差/ 7 = 非常好,1 = 令人不喜欢/ 7 = 令人喜欢)。最后,所有被试回答人口统计学相关问题并领取酬劳。

(二) 实验结果

由于因变量的测量(即消费者对初创品牌独立开发的豆浆产品的态度)是由两道题目构成的,因此要通过相关分析来论证该因变量测量的信度。相关分析显示这两道题目呈现显著正相关($r=0.91$),因此笔者将被试在这两道题目上的评分计算平均值作为实验的因变量。接着,2(与知名品牌联名:是 vs.否)×2(消费者关注维度:能力维度 vs.温暖维度)的 ANOVA 分析表明,品牌联名和消费者关注维度的主效应均不显著(所有 p 值均大于 0.30)。更重要的是,品牌联名和消费者关注维度之间的交互作用在统计学上显著,$F(1, 124) = 11.32$,$p = 0.001$,$\eta_p^2 = 0.08$(见图 5-3)。随后,笔者通过 Planned Contrasts 进行了简单主效应分析。分析结果显示,若被试在评价品牌时更关注品牌的能力维度,在品牌联名组中被试对初创品牌独立生产的豆浆产品的评价($M=4.61$)会显著低于无品牌联名组中被试对同样豆浆产品的评价($M=5.47$,$t(124)=-2.65$,$p=0.009$)。相比之下,若被试在评价品牌时更关注品牌的

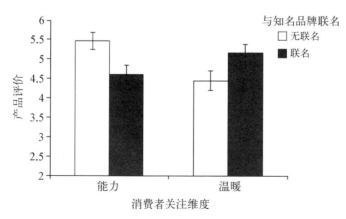

图 5-3 品牌联名如何影响消费者对初创品牌独立开发产品的评价——操纵消费者关注维度(实验 4)

温暖维度,在品牌联名组中被试对初创品牌独立生产的豆浆产品的评价($M=5.17$)会显著高于无品牌联名组中被试对同样豆浆产品的评价($M=4.45$,$t(124)=2.12$,$p=0.036$)。这些结果重复了实验3的发现,并进一步证明了与知名品牌联名和消费者关注维度的交互效应可以延伸去影响消费者对初创品牌独立开发的其他产品的评价,从而再次支持了假设3和假设4。

(三)结果讨论

实验4通过不同的研究设计(操纵消费者在评价品牌时关注的维度,并测量消费者对初创品牌独立开发的其他产品的态度)重复了实验3的发现,也为假设3和假设4提供了更多的实证支持。同时,实验4的发现也更具有管理学实践意义,因为在现实生活中消费者对品牌产品的态度和偏好是重要的营销效果指标。

尽管如此,实验4依然存在一些缺憾。例如,实验操纵消费者评价产品时的关注维度的方法相对比较学术化。因此在接下来的实验5中,笔者将用更自然、更贴合真实商业世界的方法(例如广告用语选择)来引导消费者更多关注品牌的能力维度或者温暖维度。之前的实验都是探讨处于相同行业中的两个品牌的联名,但是对于跨界联名(即参与联名的品牌来自两个较为不同的行业)的情形缺乏讨论。当联名品牌来自相同产业时,消费者可能会认为初创品牌比较多余,从而降低对该品牌能力的感知。选择不同产业品牌之间的跨界联名作为研究场景,可以帮助排除这种混淆解释,从而更加支持笔者的互补性推论机制。因此,在接下来的实验5中笔者将着力于解决这些问题。

七、实验 5

实验 5 包含五个目的：第一，希望通过操纵品牌联名类型和消费者关注维度来重复实验 4 的研究结果。第二，为了扩大研究的外部效度，选择了不同的产品品类（电子产品），并探讨了跨界联名的情形。具体来说，实验的知名品牌主营运动产品，初创品牌则主营电子产品，这样的品牌联名也能在真实商业世界中找到相关例证（例如苹果和耐克的合作）。第三，通过操纵品牌的品牌形象（能力型 vs.温暖型）来引导消费者在评价品牌时侧重的维度。这种操纵比起实验 3 的操纵更加自然，也更加具有营销实践意义。第四，在之前的几个实验中，笔者对参与联名的初创品牌的专长介绍不清晰，可能会使消费者认为该初创品牌为低质量品牌。由于研究重点在于初创品牌（即强调品牌的新颖程度和较低的品牌觉知度），因此笔者也将排除这一因素对结果的潜在影响。第五，之前的几个实验都使用了来自北美的研究被试，而实验 5 将采用来自中国的研究被试，以检验是否研究假设的效应能同时在东方和西方文化背景下成立。在实验 5 中，笔者预测，若在介绍初创品牌产品时强调其品牌形象中的能力维度（vs.温暖维度），消费者在评估该品牌及其产品时也会更加关注其能力维度（vs.温暖维度）。在此情况下，与知名品牌联名（vs.不与知名品牌联名）所造成的对品牌能力感知的负面影响（vs.对品牌温暖感知的积极影响）将变得更加突出，从而降低（vs.提升）消费者对初创品牌独立开发产品的评价。

（一）实验方法

被试与实验设计：来自中国香港某高校的 128 名本科生（女

性占比为 67%,平均年龄为 20.74 岁)参加了本有偿行为实验。实验 5 采用 2(与知名品牌联名：是 vs.否)×2(消费者关注维度：能力维度 vs.温暖维度)的被试间设计。两个因素都会进行实验操纵。

实验步骤与测量：在实验 5 中,首先向被试呈现关于运动产品市场知名品牌的例子,然后让被试阅读有关新款运动产品的广告。与之前实验类似,不同组别(品牌联名组 vs.无品牌联名组)的被试将接收到不同的关于产品制造商的信息。接下来则向被试呈现第二则广告。在这一则广告中,被试将评估由初创品牌独立开发的一款新产品。但是这一次笔者将操纵该款独立研发产品的介绍,以使一半被试更关注初创品牌的能力维度,而另一半被试更关注初创品牌的温暖维度。在此基础上,被试将对该款产品进行最终评价。具体内容如下：

首先是品牌联名的操纵。先向所有被试呈现运动服装市场上的一些知名品牌名称,例如耐克、阿迪达斯、彪马(Puma)。同时,告知被试一些由初创品牌生产的运动服装也在进入市场。随后,向所有被试呈现一个虚构的初创品牌 Porvy 的介绍。该介绍指出,Porvy 是专注于生产健康领域智能设备的品牌。接下来,被试被随机分为两组,并被呈现不同的关于新款运动服的产品介绍信息。其中,品牌联名组的被试被告知 Porvy 与知名品牌阿迪达斯联名开发了一款新型运动服装"活力日"(Energetic-Day Sports Apparel)。而在无品牌联名组中,被试则被告知 Porvy 是该款新型运动服装唯一的制造商。接下来,所有被试再阅读其他关于这款产品的介绍(两个组被呈现的信息相同)。

消费者关注维度的操纵和对初创品牌独立开发产品的评价。在以上任务完成之后,被试进入第二则关于 Porvy 的广告。这则广告告诉被试 Porvy 还独立开发了自己的可穿戴智能健康监测仪。通过更改该款广告中强调的 Porvy 品牌形象,笔者操纵了被试在评价品牌时对品牌的关注维度(温暖维度 vs.能力维度)。具体而言,关注能力维度(vs.关注温暖维度)组中的被试被告知该款智能健康监测仪技术过硬(vs.值得信赖),如同一个能力优秀(vs.体贴可靠)的助手一样为消费者工作,凭借着卓越的实力(vs.无微不至的关照)来提升消费者的生活质量(详见本章附录 5-4)。通过强调相应的品牌形象,笔者让品牌温暖维度或者能力维度变得更加突出,从而使消费者在评价品牌时更愿意基于该维度形成自己的态度。接着,所有被试通过 7 点量表(1=不令人喜欢/7=令人喜欢,1=令人讨厌/7=令人愉快)来表达他们对这款智能健康监测仪的评价。最后,所有被试回答人口统计学相关问题并领取酬劳。

(二) 实验结果

通过相关分析发现,被试在因变量测量(消费者对初创品牌独立开发产品的态度)的两道题目上得分呈现显著的正相关($r=0.76$)。因此,笔者将被试在这两道题目上的得分计算平均值,作为因变量得分。接着,2(与知名品牌联名:是 vs.否)×2(消费者关注维度:能力维度 vs.温暖维度)的 ANOVA 分析表明,品牌联名和消费者关注维度的主效应均不显著(所有 p 值均大于 0.70)。更重要的是,品牌联名和消费者关注维度之间的交互作用在统计学上显著,$F(1, 124)=8.31$,$p=0.005$,$\eta_p^2=0.06$(如图 5-4)。随后,笔者通过 Planned Contrasts 进行了简单主效应分析。分析结果显示,若初创品牌强调自身品牌形象中的能力元素,消费者在评价该品牌时会更侧重品牌的能力维度。因此,在品牌联名组中的被试对初创品牌独立开发产品的评价($M = 4.80$)会显著低于那些在无品牌联名组中的被试的评价($M = 5.33$),$t(124) = -2.22$,$p = 0.028$。相反,若初创品牌强调自身品牌形象中的温暖元素,消费者在评价该品牌时会更倾侧重品牌的温暖维度。因此,在品牌联名组中的被试对初创品牌独立开发产品的评价($M = 5.36$)会在趋势上高于那些在无品牌联名组中的被试的评价,尽管这种差异呈现统计学上的边缘显著($M = 4.90$,$t(124) = 1.86$,$p = 0.065$)。因此,实验5的发现重复了实验3和实验4的结果,为假设3和假设4提供了进一步的实证支持。

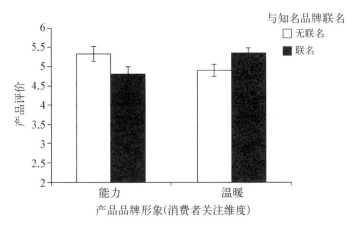

图 5-4 品牌联名如何影响消费者对初创品牌独立开发产品的影响——产品品牌形象(消费者关注维度)的调节作用(实验5)

(三)结果讨论

实验5采用了与实验4不同的实验范式,通过操纵品牌的产品介绍语来突出品牌形象中的温暖维度或是能力维度,并进而影响被试在评价品牌及其产品时的关注点。这一实验范式既贴合真实商业世界的情景,又为假设3和假设4提供了进一步的实证支持。纵观实验3到实验5,笔者对消费者关注维度的量化,从实验3中个体差异的测量,到实验4中直接通过指导语进行操纵,再到实验5中通过广告语语言的选择进行引导。这些发现也为假设3和假设4提供了不同范式下的实证支持。

此外,通过收集东亚被试的数据,实验5的结果证明无论是东方还是西方文化下的被试,无论是来自高校的学生样本还是更具代表性和分布性的成年样本,都会出现类似的品牌联名与消费者关注维度的交互效应。同时,这三个实验横跨食物、电子产品、运动产品这三个类别,具有一定的覆盖面和代表性。这些表明,本章研究发现的效应具有良好的外部效度。

通过采用品牌跨界联名的研究场景,并强调参与联名品牌各自的专长,实验5也证明了笔者的实验假设是针对"初创品牌"而不是"劣质品牌",从而排除了其他混淆解释。

第四节 关于本章实证研究的综合讨论

一、研究发现的总结

大众(甚至是很多管理从业者)往往持有这样的观点:与知名品牌进行联名总是会为初创品牌带来收益。然而,已往有关该问题的研究却呈现了彼此矛盾的发现(Cunha, Forehand, and Angle 2015; Washburn, Till, and Priluck 2000)。在本章研究中,笔者试图基于消费者推论和品牌人格的相关理论来整合已往研究中不一致的发现。具体来说,笔者假设与知名品牌进行联名会对消费者对一个初创品牌能力高低的判断产生负面影响,对消费者对该初创品牌温暖程度的判断产生正面影响(假设1和假设2)。基于这一假设,如果消费者在评价一个品牌时更多地关注其能力维度(vs.温暖维度),那么他们会对与知名品牌进行联名的初创品牌抱有消极(vs.积极)的评价(假设3和假设4)。

通过六个行为实验,笔者为上述实验假设提供了充足的实证支持。其中,实验1A、实验1B、实验2分别通过组间设计和混合设计的方法,为假设1和假设2提供了实证支持。接下来,实验3、实验4、实验5则测量(实验3)或操纵(实验4和实验5)了消费者在评价初创品牌时的关注维度,从而为假设3和假设4提供了实证支持。值得注意的是,为了强化本章实验的内部效度和外部效度,这六个行为实验同时考虑了在研究样本选择上的多样性(既有中国被试也有美国被试)、研究情景的多样性(来自相同产业的品牌联名与跨界联名)、实验品牌涉及类别的多样性(食物品牌、运动品牌、电子设备品牌、汽车品牌)、实验范式选择上的多样性(测量与操纵消费者的关注维度)、因变量测量上的多样性(对温暖和能力感知的分开测量和混合测量,测量消费者对初创品牌及其独立开发产品的态度)。因此,本章实验的论证过程尽量做到了严谨,且结论具有良好的可推广性。

二、本章研究的理论贡献与实践意义

本章研究对品牌心理学的多个领域(例如品牌人格、品牌知觉、品牌联名)均具有理论贡献。就"与知名品牌联名是否一直对初创品牌有利"这一问题,已往研究提供了不一致的发现(Cunha, Forehand, and Angle 2015;Washburn, Till, and Priluck 2000)。为了整合这些看似矛盾的发现,笔者结合消费者推论和品牌人格这两套理论体系,指出同样的品牌联名行为可能导致对品牌的两个维度截然不同的推论与感知。这一研究框架不但界定了一个可以整合过去发现的有效调节变量,也为分析品牌联名的影响和作用提供了新颖的视角。具体而言,已往研究主要是从记忆和学习理论的角度来探索品牌联名的作用(Anderson and Bower 1973; Keller 1993; Washburn, Till, and Priluck 2000)。例如支持品牌联名正向作用的研究主要是基于关联学习理论(Anderson and Bower 1973)。这一理论指出,当两个品牌联名时,消费者对其中一个品牌的评价可以转移到另一个品牌上。这是因为消费者将这两个合作品牌视为一个整体,并在其记忆网络中建立了这两个品牌之间的关联。而那些支持品牌联名负向作用的研究主要是基于适应学习理论(Cunha, Forehand, and Angle 2015)。这一理论认为,获知品牌联名信息的消费者往往会计算和评估联名合作中的哪个品牌具有更多的贡献(Cunha, Forehand, and Angle 2015; Van Osselaer and Janiszewski 2001)。本章研究提出的基于初创品牌品牌维度的推断,既是一种创新的解释,也与这两种学习理论形成了共鸣。

一方面,消费者对能力维度进行推论的过程与 Cunha 等人(2015)提出的适应学习有关。由于能力维度反映了一个品牌决定发展方向和产出成果的概率(Bandura 1989),因此关注品牌的能力维度可能会使消费者更倾向于比较参与联名的每个品牌和联名成果之间的关联,而这更接近适应性学习过程(Cunha, Janiszewski, and Laran 2008; Kruschke 2001)。此外,Cunha 等人(2015)也指出,适应性学习过程发生时,消费者往往没有将两个联名品牌视为统一的整体,而是将这两个联名品牌视为两个独立部分。由于能力维度的其中一个指标就是独立性(Wojciszke and

Abele 2008),因此在评价初创品牌时侧重能力维度也更容易造成类似的效果,即将两个联名品牌分开进行独立的考虑。

另一方面,消费者对温暖维度进行推论的过程也和关联学习理论(Anderson and Bower 1973)有关。由于温暖维度指向合作关系,因此当消费者关注品牌的温暖维度时,他们会更关心两个联名品牌之间的关系和链接(Helgeson 1994)。而关注两个联名品牌之间的关联就意味着消费者会更容易注意到初创品牌的社会资本(能吸引到知名品牌进行合作),并进而推断知名品牌的品牌资产已经传递给了初创品牌(Keller 1993; Washburn, Till, and Priluck 2000)。因此,本章研究的结果既可以整合已往研究中不一致的发现,又可以从一定程度上揭示关联学习/适应学习和品牌温暖/品牌能力推论的内在联系。

本章研究也为初创品牌或创业公司的品牌战略提供了管理实践上的启示。在竞争激烈的市场中,初创品牌或创业公司需要建立自己的品牌知名度才能生存,已领跑市场的知名品牌则希望继续保持其创新动力并挖掘新的增量市场。因此,初创品牌与市场知名品牌的联名更接近于双赢策略。然而,本章研究却通过实证数据发现,初创品牌的管理者在选择与知名品牌联名以及在构建自己的品牌形象时需要万分谨慎。具体而言,初创品牌在与一个知名品牌合作时,过分强调该初创品牌的能力维度可能会适得其反。更值得注意的是,这种负面效应甚至可以扩散到影响消费者对该初创品牌旗下其他产品的判断。而如果初创品牌选择强调自身品牌形象中温暖的一面,则更容易从与知名品牌的联名合作中获益。因此,本章研究的发现有利于品牌管理者选择适合自己的品牌定位和品牌联名战略,具有很强的营销实践意义。

三、本章研究的不足之处和未来展望

本章研究表明,与知名品牌进行联名可能对消费者对初创品牌能力高低的判断产生负面影响。但一个有趣的理论问题是:是否存在边界条件,使得这种品牌联名反而增加消费者对初创品牌的能力感知?从理论上推断,有几种潜在的调节变量可能产生作用。首先,品牌联名的类型可能是一个潜在的调节变量。本章研究的主要研究情景是两个处于相似或者相同行业内的品牌之间的联名,例如可口可乐和初创果汁饮料品牌 Suja 之间的联名(Kell 2015),迪士尼和初创玩具品牌 Sphero 之间的联名(Roberts 2015)。在这种情况下,消费者更有可能根据互补性原理对初创品牌的能力进行推断。这是因为这两个来自同样产业的品牌在能力维度上直接可比,并且知名品牌更容易被消费者感知为具有较高能力,所以导致了本章研究中揭示的互补推论效应。尽管本章研究的实验5对跨界联名进行了初步探索并也得到了支持性的结论,但获得这种结果的一个可能是运动服装品牌和健康监控设备还是存在一定的产业相似性(都和消费者的健康行为有关)。因而未来的研究可以探讨,当这两个品牌处在完全不相关的产业时,是否还能观察到对初创品牌能力的补偿性推断效应。例如美国最大的连锁药店之一沃尔格林(Walgreens)与一家初创品牌 Pager 合作,在移动平台上链接患者和附近的可用医疗服务(Pozin 2015)。在这种情况下,消费者无法直接比较这两个联名品牌的能力差异。与初创品牌单独提供相同服务的情况相比,与知名品牌的联名可能会使消费者推断初创品牌在自己的领域内具有强大的实力,因此才吸引了其他行业的知名品牌。

其次,未来研究可以检验联名产出的产品类型的调节作用。

本章研究中的所有品牌联名产品均隶属于知名品牌的专长领域。在这种情况下,消费者可能无法直接意识到初创品牌在品牌联名关系中所做的贡献。尽管实验 5 明确告知被试初创品牌的专长(专注于开发与健康相关的智能设备),可以在某种程度上减轻这种担忧,但是联名制造的产品在视觉上依然容易被消费者感知为属于服装类(也就是隶属于知名品牌的专长范围)。基于以上讨论,笔者假设,初创品牌一旦与知名品牌联名制造一个隶属于前者专长的产品,消费者就可能推断这次的品牌联名是由初创品牌领导,或者至少初创品牌为该联名做出了决定性的贡献。在这种情况下,消费者可能会更容易推断初创品牌具有较高能力。

再次,正如笔者之前所讨论的,未来研究可以探讨品牌感知与学习理论之间的关联。例如,当消费者更加重视品牌的能力维度时,他们似乎更倾向于采用个体分析的信息加工模式(Fiske, Cuddy, and Glick 2007),因此更加依赖于适应学习策略。相反,当消费者更加重视品牌的温暖维度时,他们似乎更倾向于采用整体分析的信息加工模式(Abele and Wojciszke 2007)。未来研究可以探索这种关联如何影响消费者对其他品牌策略的反应,例如品牌延伸、品牌赞助、品牌捆绑策略。

最后,本章主要集中在研究品牌联名如何影响消费者对初创品牌的知觉。未来研究可以探索这种品牌联名战略如何影响消费者对知名品牌的态度。一个可能的预测是,与初创品牌联名可以同时提升消费者对该知名品牌的能力和温暖的评价。这是因为这种合作一方面表明知名品牌正在扩大自身规模并愿意吸收新的知识和技能,另一方面也展现了知名品牌对初创品牌的帮扶。当然,这样的预测是否存在反转,还需要更多的实证数据来验证。

附　录

附录 5-1　实验 1A 和实验 1B 的研究材料（中文翻译版）

品牌联名组：

一个初创零食品牌"休闲时光"最近与哈根达斯一起合作开发了一款新的冰激凌——夏日梦幻冰激凌。以下是关于这款新冰激凌的介绍。

无品牌联名组：

一个初创零食品牌"休闲时光"最近开发了一款新的冰激凌——夏日梦幻冰激凌。以下是关于这款新冰激凌的介绍。

附录 5-2　实验 3 和实验 4 中采用的研究材料（中文翻译版）

品牌联名组：

一个初创食品品牌"晨光食品"最近与家乐氏一起合作开发了一款新的高膳食纤维早餐麦片——快乐日子早餐麦片。以下是关于这款高膳食纤维早餐麦片的介绍。

无品牌联名组：

一个初创食品品牌"晨光食品"最近开发了一款新的高膳食纤维早餐麦片——快乐日子早餐麦片。以下是关于这款高膳食纤维早餐麦片的介绍。

附录 5-3　实验 4 中初创品牌独立开发产品（豆浆）的研究材料（中文翻译版）

食品品牌"晨光食品"也独立开发了自己的豆浆产品——清晨豆浆。以下是关于这款豆浆的介绍：

名称：清晨豆浆

制造商：晨光食品

产品描述：

（1）富含蛋白质、维生素与矿物质；

（2）精选完全有机的大豆；

（3）不含酵母成分+低脂肪；

（4）每包 8 盎司，共 24 包（总计 192 盎司）。

附录 5-4　实验 5 中对初创品牌独立开发产品的产品形象的操纵（中文翻译版）

产品形象操纵——强调能力导向：

产品描述：Allyn 健康监测仪就像一个能力和技能卓越的助手那样为您工作。它可以帮助您监测您的活动和健康状况。它具有令人舒适的设计，运行也没有太多噪声，还能提供快速的反馈。Allyn 健康监测仪可以实时追踪您的血压、体温、睡眠质量和心率。Allyn 健康监测仪可以通过它无与伦比的能力提升您的生活质量。

产品形象操纵——强调温暖导向：

产品描述：Allyn 健康监测仪就像一个体贴和值得信赖的助手那样为您工作。它可以帮助您监测您的活动和健康状况。它具有令人舒适的设计，运行也没有太多噪声，还能提供快速的反馈。

Allyn健康监测仪可以实时追踪您的血压、体温、睡眠质量和心率。Allyn健康监测仪可以通过它无与伦比的关怀和贴心合作提升您的生活质量。

第六章

全书总结与未来研究方向

消费者行为学领域的许多研究结果表明,在信息不透明或者信息缺失的情况下,消费者将利用已有的信息,通过自身的背景知识或者各种认知工具建立逻辑链接,从而推断出有关产品、品牌或者其他未知信息(Bellezza, Gino, and Keinan 2014; Bellezza, Paharia, and Keinan 2017; Ross and Creyer 1992)。例如,消费者可能会基于品牌信息(Jiang, Gorn, Galli, and Chattopadhyay 2016)、产品的直接属性和看似无关的描述(Chernev 2007; Chernev and Blair 2015; Hamilton and Chernev 2013; Smith, Newman, and Dhar 2016)、产品制造者的特点(Reich, Kupor, and Smith 2018)、产品消费者的特点(Cheng, Mukhopadhyay, and Williams 2020)、个体主观感受(Miele and Molden 2010)、口碑传播(Grewal and Stephen 2019; He and Bond 2015)做出各种推断。这些研究发现从消费者推论的起源、机制、制约因素、后续结果等角度为这个领域构建了一个庞大的研究框架(Hastie 1983; Kruglanski and Orehek 2007; Crolic, Zheng, Hoegg, and Alba 2019)。尽管关于消费者推论的研究已经持续了数十年,但是这个领域的研究问题依然层出不穷。首先,已往研究呈现了大量的消费者形成推论的过程机制(例如启发式、内隐理论、经典条件反射)。然而这些研究往往基于一个前提,即作为线索的信息和推论目标多为抽象的或者语义上的概念(例如质量是否良好,产品是否健康),少有对更具体的实际感官体验的推断(Cunha, Forehand, and Angle 2015; Kardes, Posavac, and Cronley 2004)。即便是对产品感官体验进行推断的研究,也大多数集中在味觉和视觉这两个层面(Raghunathan, Naylor, and

Hoyer 2006；Rahnev，Maniscalco，Graves，Huang，De Lange，and Lau 2011；Schuldt and Hannahan 2013），而对于触觉、听觉、嗅觉的研究相对较少（Asutay and Västfjäll 2012；Lee and Schwarz 2012；Streit，Shockley，and Riley 2007）。与判断抽象概念所需的路径（基于语义关联）不同，对于具体感官体验的判断涉及不同的机制（基于机体反应），探究这一问题可以为消费者推论的研究提供全新的路径和理论模型。

其次，已往关于消费者推论的研究工作主要集中于对单个属性的推理，例如对一个缺失的产品属性的推理（Kivetz and Simonson 2000；Puzakova，Kwak，and Taylor 2013；Simmons and Lynch 1991），或仅是对目标（例如消费者、产品、品牌）的整体评估（Samper and Schwartz 2013；Spiller，Reinholtz，and Maglio 2020；Zhu，Bagchi，and Hock 2019）。近年来才有部分研究开始关注消费者如何基于同一组信息对品牌或产品的多个维度做出不同的推断（Peng，Cui，Chung，and Zheng 2020；Wang，Mao，Li，and Liu 2017）。例如，Peng 等人（2020）发现长相漂亮的个体会被观察者认为在社交能力上更强，但是在认知能力上更弱。由于在生活中往往需要对目标的多个维度同时进行推断和考虑，因此这一研究领域亟待进一步的挖掘。

同时，已往关于品牌信息如何影响消费者推论的研究主要关注品牌自身属性，例如品牌资产（McClure，Li，Tomlin，Cypert，Montague，and Montague 2004；Rubio，Oubiña，and Villaseñor 2014）、品牌人格（Puzakova，Kwak，and Taylor 2013）、品牌形象（Batra and Homer 2004；Lude and Prügl 2018）、品牌价位（Almenberg and Dreber 2011）对消费者产品推论的影响和作用，少有人探讨品牌的行动和战略对消费者推论的影响（Plassmann，

O'doherty, Shiv, and Rangel 2008)。在现实生活中,消费者往往是基于品牌战略相关信息(例如品牌联名、品牌延伸、独特的促销模式或是对其他品牌的并购)来对品牌和旗下产品进行推断,而这也成为亟须填补的研究空白。

正是基于以上问题,本书着眼于品牌联名战略,通过两个大型实证研究探讨了品牌联名如何影响消费者对产品感官属性的推断以及品牌联名如何改变消费者对初创品牌品牌人格的推断。具体来说,第四章的实证研究发现,当个体对某种价值观感受到较高(vs.较低)的重要性时,目标产品与传递该价值观的品牌进行联名会增加(vs.减少)消费者对这种产品重量的估计。通过调节模型,该研究发现这是因为感知价值观的重要性激活了消费者在持有产品时的机体反应(例如感受到更多的肌肉紧张)。消费者将这种机体反应作为推论的线索,从而导致了物理重量判断的变化。这一研究表明,对感官体验(例如重量体验)进行推断时,个体更多依赖于做决策时的机体状态。而这种机体状态是否被激活,以及激活后是否被用于最终感官推断,则取决于一系列的调节变量。可以说,这一研究首次探讨了品牌联名战略对于消费者感官体验的影响。

第五章的实证研究则发现,与知名品牌进行联名的决定可能会导致消费者对初创品牌的两个品牌人格维度(温暖 vs.能力)产生截然不同的推断结果。这一研究对于品牌战略与消费者推论都具有极强的理论意义和现实意义。一是本章研究发现对多个目标(或者对一个目标的多个维度)进行推论时,消费者并不一定只会采用完全一致的推论模式。事实上,对于两个正交的维度,消费者甚至可能会采用两套不同的推论体系(同化推论 vs 补偿推论)。二是本章研究发现品牌联名这一战略本身可能会造成截然不同的推断结果。而当消费者的注意力被引导到某个维度时,他们对品牌和旗下产品的总体偏好都可能发生逆转。这也揭示了品牌联名战略可能借由消费者推论带来的双刃剑效应。这一研究不仅解决了相关的理论问题,还就如何更有效地定位品牌或产品提供了具体的营销策略。

品牌联名和消费者推论都是具有广袤前景的研究领域(Mishra, Singh, Fang, and Yin 2017; Uleman, Adil Saribay, and Gonzalez 2008)。尽管已有研究取得了丰硕的成果,但是未来研究还可以探索许多可能性。在本章接下来的部分,笔者将从消费者推论和品牌联名两个角度分别讨论未来可能的研究方向。

第一节　从消费者推论角度探讨未来可能的研究方向

在本节中,笔者将首先探讨如何在未来研究中丰富消费者推论的理论体系。在此基础上,笔者将讨论如何从新视角研究品牌联名对消费者推论的影响。笔者总结了五个潜在的研究方向:

第一,大多数有关消费者推论的研究都集中在探索消费者如何对其他产品、品牌或人物(消费者、制造商)进行推断。未来的研究可以探究品牌因素是否会影响消费者的自我推断。已往关于自我推断的研究已经得出了丰富的研究结果。例如,在电脑游戏或者在线教育软件中采用拟人化的虚拟助手会导致用户推断自己缺乏自主性或者能力,从而导致他们产生更差的使用体验(Kim, Chen, and Zhang 2016; Kim, Zhang, and Park 2018)。当个体感觉到被他人观察时,他们会推断自己的行动和决策更具有影响力(Steinmetz,Xu,and Fishbach 2016)。而在网上分享信息,会导致消费者推断自己具有更多的主观知识(Zheng,Ward,and Broniarczyk 2017)。当品牌执行某种战略时,品牌的消费者也有可能根据这些信息进行关于自我的推断。品牌心理学相关研究指出,消费者往往会购买和自己身份认同相符合的产品(Kirmani 2009;Reed II 2004;Simonson,Carmon,Dhar,and Drolet 2001),或者通过购买品牌产品去彰显自己想要展示给他人的自我特征(Berger and Ward 2010;Erdem,Swait,and Valenzuela 2006;Wang and Griskevicius 2014)。那么一个值得探索的问题是:品牌 A 选择与品牌 B 联名,对于品牌 A 之前的消费者的自我感知会产生什么影响?一方面,品牌 A 与品牌 B 的联名可以从一定程度上丰富原有品牌的品牌资产和品牌形象,从而可能丰富品牌 A 原有消费者的自我推论与自我感知(Meyvis and Janiszewski 2004;Monga and John 2010;Swaminathan,Page,and Gürhan-Canli 2007)。另一方面,品牌联名却也有很大可能会稀释品牌 A 原有的品牌精髓(Brand essence),增加品牌 A 原有消费者的矛盾感(Pullig,Simmons,and Netemeyer 2006;Sood and Keller 2012;Brown,Kozinets,and Sherry 2003)。因此品牌联名对于消费者自我推论的影响和可能机制有待进一步探索,这也可以拓展我们对品牌联名后续影响的探究。

第二,大量关于消费者推论的研究都建立在一个前提假设上,即消费者进行推断是因为他们没有得到足够的信息(Haws,Reczek,and Sample 2017;Kwan,Dai,and Wyer 2017;Walters and Hershfield 2020;Zane,Smith,and Reczek 2020)。但是在现代社会中,消费者面临着另一个挑战,即"信息爆炸"。消费者可能面临的问题是,可用于作为推论线索的信息处在过载状态(Information overload),抑或是作为线索的信息看上去彼此矛盾。其一,重复接触大量同质化信息可能会改变消费者进行推理的方式。例如,关于视觉信息呈现的研究发现,尽管人们认为增加产品呈现的图片数会有助于消费者做出选择,但是实验结果却显示这种信息的过度呈现反而会模糊消费者对不同产品选择之间差异的感知,从而导致选择困难(Jia, Shiv, and Rao 2014)。同样,当消费者反复思考或者心理模拟产品的味觉体验时,也会造成消费者的餍足感,反而影响到偏好和实际消费(Morewedge, Huh, and Vosgerau 2010)。其二,当呈现的线索和信息彼此存在不一致和矛盾时,消费者如何检验并整合这些线索并最后形成推断?目前关于该研究方向的题目尚比较稀缺(Jun, Meng, and Johar 2017; Miyazaki, Grewal, and Goodstein 2005; West and Broniarczyk 1998)。而正如笔者在本书开头讲到的喜茶案例,在品牌联名的研究情景中也存在特定品牌与多种不同风格品牌分别(异时或同时)联名的情况。在这种情况下,消费者如何对联名产品以及参与联名的品牌进行推断,就取决于他们如何选择和整合这些复杂的、多元化的甚至彼此矛盾的信息。这也为未来关于品牌联名影响消费者推论的研究提供了一个有趣的研究方向。

第三,已往研究主要讨论了两种推论模式:同化推论和互补推论(Cunha and Shulman 2011; Chernev 2005a, 2005b; Chernev and Blair 2015; Chernev and Carpenter 2001; Wilcox, Roggeveen, and Grewal 2011)。例如,从价格推断质量、从保修期长短推断产品质量,都属于同化推论(被推断目标和线索之间呈现正相关关系)(Beckwith and Lehmann 1975; Kupor and Laurin 2020; Yan and Sengupta 2011)。研究人员也发现了互补推论的证据,也就是说已

有线索和被推断目标呈现互相补偿或者负相关的关系(Newman, Gorlin, and Dhar 2014; Peng, Cui, Chung, and Zheng 2020; Yan and Muthukrishnan 2014)。例如,Yan 和 Muthukrishnan(2014)的研究发现,博彩机构设立安慰奖,会降低消费者对自己能够得到大奖的概率的推断。这是因为消费者存在一种内隐的假设,即得到安慰奖和得到大奖属于互相补偿的事件。一旦博彩机构开始强调安慰奖,消费者就更容易反过来认为得到大奖的可能性被稀释了。而在本书的研究中,笔者发现同样的品牌联名信息也可以造成类似于补偿推论的效果(推断初创品牌在温暖维度上得分升高,但是在能力维度上得分降低)。未来的研究可以探索两个方面:其一,其他品牌战略是否也可以在一定情景中导致消费者做出补偿推论?其二,在品牌信息和品牌战略相同的情况下,哪些因素决定消费者推论模式的选择(何时会做出同化推论,何时又会做出补偿推论)?探索这两个方面的问题可以进一步深化对品牌与消费者推论之间的联系的了解。

第四,尽管目前对同化推论的研究要远远多于对补偿推论的研究,但是在前者的研究领域中依然存在一些研究空白。已往关于同化推论的研究的基本范式是:消费者先被直接或者间接引导向某一个线索,然后再通过这个线索对未知信息进行推断(Huang and Kwong 2016; Jiang, Adaval, Steinhart and Wyer 2014; Kim and Labroo 2011; Labroo and Kim 2009)。例如 Shen 等人(2010)的研究先激发消费者感知的信息加工困难度(Processing difficulty),再考察消费者如何依靠这一线索去推断自己对广告的喜爱程度。然而在现实生活中,消费者往往会面临多个产品或者目标同时呈现的情况。例如本书探讨的品牌联名,就是两个品牌(品牌 A 和品牌 B)信息同时呈现给消费者的情景。根据关联学习理论,两个联名品牌的品牌资产和品牌形象可以彼此转移和扩散到对方身上（Anderson and Bower 1973；Broniarczyk and Alba 1994；Miller and Allen 2012；Sjödin, and Törn 2006）。那么一个有趣的研究问题是：这种合作模式下，两个参与者对彼此的影响程度是否一致？或者说，消费者在评价这两个参与联名的品牌时，会主要以哪一个作为参照标准？已往研究指出，当两个品牌进行联名时，品牌资产相对较少（或者品牌觉知相对较弱势）的品牌会更容易受到影响（Aaker and Keller 1990；Boush and Loken 1991；Broniarczyk and Alba 1994；Leuthesser, Kohli, and Suri 2003；Levin and Levin 2000；Simonin and Ruth 1998；Washburn, Till, and Priluck 2000）。例如，Washburn等人（2000）发现，对于品牌资产较多的品牌来说，无论与之联名的品牌具有较多品牌资产还是较少品牌资产，都不会对这个品牌本身的品牌资产造成显著影响。但有趣的是，对于品牌资产较少的品牌来说，无论是和品牌资产较少的品牌合作还是和品牌资产较多的品牌合作，都会对自身的品牌资产造成明显影响。Simonin和Ruth（1998）发现，消费者对品牌联名效果的总体比较，主要取决于合作方中相对强势（例如品牌资产更多、品牌知名度更好）的品牌。Leuthesser等人（2003）也指出，即便是品牌联名以失败而告终，相对不知名的品牌也更容易被归罪为失败的主要责任方。

如果将以上的研究情景进行拓展，考察两个品牌资产差异不大的品牌各自推出一个新品进行绑定促销（这也是一种广义上的品牌联名）的情形，那么消费者对这两种产品各自的体验又会如何被品牌联名影响？笔者与香港大学贾轼副教授的一个项目就考察了这个问题。具体来说，我们设计了一个产品体验的实验情景。在这个情景中，我们告知实验被试一个本地零食品牌（生产果冻豆)和一个本地玩具品牌(生产小型毛绒玩具)的相关信息。我们特地告知实验被试,这两个品牌都是本地的新品牌(以控制两个品牌的知名度和品牌资产)。接下来,我们告知被试现在这两个品牌旗下各有一款产品。尽管被试都被要求对这两种产品进行体验和判断,但是他们被随机分配到了四个组。在这四个组中,向被试呈现的产品组合以及相关的描述信息各有不同。首先,我们在挑选用于每个组的产品时,采用了"高低搭配"的方法。具体来说,我们先在同一个被试库中招募和主实验近似的实验被试进行了独立前测,挑选出了被试认为口感较好和较差的果冻豆,也挑选出了触感较好和较差的毛绒玩具。接下来,在第一组和第二组中,我们向被试呈现较好的玩具与较差的果冻豆的组合,在第三组和第四组中,我们则向被试呈现较差的玩具与较好的果冻豆的组合。同时,第一组和第三组中的被试均被告知这两个品牌正在进行绑定促销,他们现在看到的是一个套餐组合。第二组和第四组中的被试则被简单告知他们需要对这两个品牌各自的产品进行体验和评价。具体的实验设计模式如表6-1所示。

表6-1 实验设计与分组(2×2组间设计)

	好玩具+差零食	差玩具+好零食
品牌联名(绑定促销)	第一组	第三组
不联名(独立评价)	第二组	第四组

我们首先对比了第一组和第二组(较好玩具和较差零食),数据分析的结果显示,当较好的玩具和较差的零食被联名在一起时,相对于不联名的组,消费者对玩具的体验显著下降,但是他们对零食的体验却没有显著上升。而在对比第三组和第四组(较差玩具和较好零食)时,数据分析的结果显示,相比于不联名组,联名情况

下消费者对零食的体验显著下降,但是对玩具的体验却没有显著改变。这一研究显示了两个重要的结果:其一,当联名品牌各自的资产没有太大差别时,个体会依照产品的具体体验来进行判断;其二,当消费者判断联名中的两个产品时,他们的判断更容易受到体验较差的产品的影响(也就是说以体验较差的产品作为判断的参照依据)。笔者随后又在多个品牌联名场景中重复了这一结果(例如电影品牌与食物品牌的联名,抑或是两个食物品牌的联名)。这一系列研究的结论和已往依据品牌知名度或者其他品牌资产进行判断的研究不同。在那些研究中,品牌资产或者知名度相对占优的联名参与者会主导消费者对品牌联名效果和每个品牌的具体评价。笔者据此指出,在语义和抽象概念层面上对品牌联名进行判断的机制不同于依据具体产品体验的判断。在依照具体体验进行判断时,较差的体验会更容易被实验被试选择为判断的参照点(Reference point)。笔者认为,这是由于较差的体验更容易被视为损失(Loss),而较好的体验更容易被视为获益(Gain)。根据前景理论(Prospect theory)(Gneezy, Gneezy, and Lauga 2014; Hoch and Loewenstein 1991; Tversky and Kahneman 1992; Barberis 2013),消费者的普遍趋势是规避损失(Loss aversive)。因此当损失和获得规格相同(例如损失1美元 vs.得到1美元)时,前者带来的对消费者的效用影响大于后者。笔者的这一研究则将其扩展到品牌联名的情景中,这也丰富了相关研究(Brough and Chernev 2012; Chernev 2011; Chernev and Gal 2010; Chernev, Hamilton, and Gal 2011)。关于品牌联名中判断参照点的选择还可以出现多种形式:一是除开以较差体验的参与品牌作为参照点之外,还有哪些品牌或者产品信息可能导致消费者选择其作为参照点(例如品牌历史、品牌CEO信息)(Bronnenberg, Dhar, and Dubé 2009;

Gorn, Jiang, and Johar 2008)?二是当涉及多种感官通道的体验（例如同时有听觉和味觉效果,Cornil and Chandon 2016)时,哪种感官通道更有可能被选为参照点?探索这类问题有助于将品牌联名、消费者推论这两个领域和行为决策论甚至认知科学有机结合,从而进一步丰富相关的研究领域。

第五,本书的研究探讨了品牌联名对消费者产品重量体验的影响。在未来的研究中,还可以探讨产品评价与体验的其他方面。产品的感官体验涉及视觉、味觉、听觉、触觉和嗅觉（Haase and Wiedmann 2018；Hultén 2011；Petit, Velasco, and Spence 2019),重量体验属于触觉体验（Jha, Balaji, Peck, Oakley, and Deitz 2020；Luangrath, Peck and Gustafsson 2020；Pereira et al. 2007；Ringler, Sirianni, Gustafsson, and Peck 2019；Shapiro and Spence 2002)。触觉体验还包括质地感知（Streicher and Estes 2016),例如柔软还是坚韧（Imschloss and Kuehnl 2019)、粗糙还是光滑（Wang, Zhu, and Handy 2016),甚至包括咀嚼过程中口腔的触感（Biswas, Szocs, Krishna, and Lehmann 2014)。研究者也指出,产品的触觉也会反向作用于对品牌定位的感知和判断,证明了两者之间更复杂的联系（Serhal, Pantin-Sohier, and Peck 2018)。因此,探讨品牌行动和品牌战略对产品其他触觉感知的影响具有极强的理论和现实意义。此外,在味觉领域,当前的研究主要探讨的是一次性的体验,例如一次性品尝时的味觉感知（Djordjevic, Zatorre, and Jones-Gotman 2004；Elder and Krishna 2010)。但是在生活中,消费往往涉及对产品和服务重复的体验、消费和使用（Chugani, Irwin and Redden 2015；Redden 2008；Su, Jiang, Chen, and DeWall 2017)。那么,品牌联名是否会改变这些场景中的产品评价?其中一个值得研究的点就是品牌联名是否会改变消费者随时间变化的体验效用。一系列的研究表明,重复消费会导致消费者满意感的下降,即餍足感(Hasegawa, Terui, and Allenby, 2012; Sevilla and Redden 2014)。对于商家而言,增加产品体验的新鲜感,降低消费者产生餍足感的速度,对于增强品牌忠诚度、减少顾客流失,具有重要的作用(McAlister 1982; Sevilla, Zhang, and Kahn 2016)。有研究指出,可以通过增加观点的多元化(Jung, Gonzalez, and Critcher 2020)、主观感知到的品类多样性(Galak, Redden, and Kruger 2009; Redden 2008)以及产品的稀缺性(Redden, Haws, and Chen 2017; Sevilla and Redden 2014)来延缓产生餍足感的过程。而品牌联名战略也有可能从品牌定位、品牌资产等角度改变消费者对产品的感知。这些因素何时以及如何影响消费者对联名产品的持续消费体验,是很值得探究的问题。

第二节　从品牌联名角度探讨未来可能的研究方向

在本书的研究中,笔者探讨了消费者在决策时关注的维度(温暖维度 vs.能力维度)以及感知到的价值观重要性对于他们评价品牌联名的影响。这些研究的本质是从个体在信息加工模式上的差异入手。而从这一角度入手的相关研究,有的探讨了消费者其他信息加工模式(关联寻找式 vs.特征映射式)如何影响他们对品牌联名的判断(Swaminathan, Gürhan-Canli, Kubat, and Hayran 2015),有的从消费者的内隐信念入手,发现消费者对品牌人格可塑性的信念会影响他们对品牌延伸的态度(Yorkston, Nunes, and

Matta 2010)。近年来,这一类研究进一步延伸到消费者自身的生活经历,探讨他们生活中的转折事件如何塑造他们的思维模式,并进而影响对品牌延伸的评价(Su, Monga, and Jiang 2021)。除开这些个体差异因素,未来的研究也可以放眼更宏观的变量,探讨诸如文化与社会规范等因素如何影响消费者对品牌联名的态度。

在以下部分,笔者从消费者个体差异因素、消费者与品牌的关系因素和文化因素这三个角度整理和概括了相关概念和潜在的研究假设。

一、消费者个体差异因素对品牌联名偏好的影响

在这一部分,笔者为大家总结了一些在社会心理学和消费行为学中常用的个体差异因素,例如消费者自我概念、消费者的情绪与信息加工模式、消费者的人口学变量信息。

(一) 消费者自我概念

近年来消费者行为学研究开始探讨消费者自我身份的多样性(Identity multiplicity)和冲突性(Identifty conflict)对其决策判断的影响。Rifkin 和 Etkin(2019)发现个体在生活中往往具有多种自我身份认知,例如会在表达自我偏好时表现出更多元化的特征。而这种自我身份的多样性表达会影响其决策行为。品牌联名本身也是对品牌过去人格的扩展,那么是否激发消费者感知自我身份的多样性,会提高他们对品牌跨界联名的接受度?

与之相关的另一种自我概念,即自我身份冲突性,则与消费者自我概念的清晰度(Self-concept clarity)有关(Adam, Obodaru, Lu, Maddux, and Galinsky 2018; Campbell, Trapnell, Heine, Katz, Lavallee, and Lehman 1996; Jiang, Chen, and Sedikides 2020)。自

我概念清晰度指的是个体自我概念中的成分和属性是否被明确定义,各个成分和属性是否彼此之间存在内部一致性,以及是否能被整合进一个完整的、定义清楚的自我框架中(Campbell 1990;Campbell, Assanand, and Di Paula 2003;Campbell and Lavalle 1993)。当个体感觉到较低的自我概念清晰度时,结合其他的自我概念相关的心理学研究,可能会采取两种路径(Jiang, Zhan, and Rucker 2014;Rucker and Galinsky 2008;Rucker, Hu, and Galinsky 2014)。第一种是同化机制(Assimilative effects):个体会依照自己当时所处的状态,做出和当时状态一致的反应。例如,处于低自尊状态的消费者,即便面临糟糕的服务也不会选择更换服务商。因为低自尊使他们更倾向于忍耐以规避风险,切换服务商可能会给他们带来更多的不确定性和风险(Consiglio and Osselaer 2019)。第二种是补偿机制(Compensatory effects):个体会采取与现有状态相反的行动来弥补自己受损的自我价值,从而使自我价值恢复到正常的水平和状态。同样以自尊相关的消费者研究为例,有学者发现,处于低自尊状态的消费者会通过购买增强自我价值的产品来进行应对(Stuppy, Mead, and Van Osselaer 2020)。与之类似,目前关于自我概念清晰度的研究也呈现出同化机制和补偿机制这两种效应。有学者发现处于较低自我清晰度状态下的个体会相应采用被动和消极的应对手段,例如拒绝接受现实(Smith, Wethington, and Zhan 1996)。有学者则发现,当个体处于低自我清晰度状态时,他们会主动追求那些口碑上更两极分化(代表了消费者爱恨分明的态度更明确)的产品,来增强自我确定感(Rozenkrants, Wheeler, and Shiv 2017)。而笔者认为自我概念的清晰度也可能影响消费者对品牌联名的接受度,但是这其中的关系方向存在两种可能。由于品牌联名可能会模糊和稀释原有品牌的品牌人格概念(稀释效应),当个体处于低自我概念清晰度的状态时,补偿机制可能使他们对品牌联名的接受度更低,但是同化机制则不会产生如此显著的影响。研究这个问题可以同时丰富关于品牌联名和自我概念清晰度的研究。

除开自我概念的结构之外,关于自我概念的研究还包括自我概念的广度。例如,有学者发现当个体感受到自己的身份具有更大的广度(上海大学学生 vs.上海大学某学院某系学生)时,他们会认为自己具有更多的主观知识,从而在选择产品时集中选择功能更高级的产品(Ding, Wan, and Xu 2017)。近年来,有学者从自我概念的本地化和全球化程度进行了划分,提出了本地化身份认同(Local identity)和全球化身份认同(Global identity)这两个概念(Gao, Zhang, and Mittal 2017; Yang, Sun, Lalwani, and Janakiraman 2019)。其中,本地化身份认同指的是个体对本地社群的归属感和认同感。这种身份认同得到增强时,个体会更加信任和尊奉本地的传统,对本地的事件会更关心,与本地社群的其他成员会产生更强的社会连接(Reed II, Forehand, Puntoni, and Warlop 2012; Tu, Khare, and Zhang 2012)。而那些具有全球化身份认同的个体,则更关注全球化,以世界公民自居,相信地球村概念,没有明确的本地和非本地的界限(Arnett 2002; Gao, Mittal, and Zhang 2020; Zhang and Khare 2009)。相对于持全球化身份认同的个体,那些持本地化身份认同的个体更在意事物之间的差异化,对区别组内和组外成员的线索更敏感(Mussweiler 2001, 2003; Yang, Sun, Lalwani, and Janakiraman 2019)。由于品牌联名也涉及两个相似或者互补的品牌的合作,因此未来的研究可以探讨消费者的本地化(vs.全球化)身份认同是否会影响到他们对不同类型品牌联名的态度。根据上述推理,笔者推测持本地化身份认同的消费者会更偏好两个相似品牌之间的联名,而持全球化身份认同的消费者则更偏好两个互补品牌之间的联名。

(二)消费者的情绪与信息加工模式

关于情绪影响消费者决策的研究已经持续了数十年(George and Dane 2016;Lerner, Li, Valdesolo, and Kassam 2015),而关于情绪启动如何影响品牌相关决策的研究则相对较少(Chen, Yeh, and Huan 2014;Wen, Qin, and Liu 2019)。例如,已往研究主要集中在情绪启动如何增强消费者和品牌之间的联系(Heath, Brandt, and Nairn 2006;Proksch, Orth, and Cornwell 2015),如何影响品牌的购买价值(Ding and Tseng 2015;Tsai 2005),而关于情绪如何影响消费者对品牌联名的态度的研究则相对较少(Abosag, Roper, and Hind 2012)。例如,相关研究探索了情绪对于品牌延伸的影响(Barone, Miniard, and Romeo 2000)。这类研究结果显示,当延伸品牌和母品牌之间为中等程度相似(相对于完全不相似和极其相似)时,积极情绪会提升消费者对延伸品牌的态度。而 Barone 和 Miniard(2002)在后续研究中进一步探讨了当母品牌本身评价较差时,情绪是否会对此类品牌的延伸品牌产生不同影响。结果发现当母品牌本身不被消费者喜欢时,无论是该品牌做何种相似程度的延伸,情绪启动都不会改变消费者对该品牌的延伸品牌的看法。Barone(2005)还发现,除开母品牌本身的评价,消费者在做决策时的卷入度(Involvement)也会调节情绪对品牌延伸评价的影响。以上这些关于情绪影响品牌判断的研究都是基于消费者在不同情绪下会采纳不同的信息加工过程这一角度来进行探究的,也由此激发了学者直接从具体信息加工模式对这一领域进行研究的动力(Monga and Gürhan-Canli 2012;Monga and John 2007, 2010)。

例如,Kim 和 John(2008)发现当个体处于高解释水平(High construal level)状态,也就是思维模式更加抽象时,他们会更在意延伸品牌和母品牌之间的匹配度。母品牌与延伸品牌之间的相似度越高,消费者越容易采取积极态度。同样,学者发现增加图片和比较信息有助于使消费者采用具体而不是抽象的思维来分析品牌延伸。在这种情况下,消费者会更多关注品牌质量而不是延伸品牌与母品牌的匹配度,从而增加消费者对延伸品牌的好感(Meyvis, Goldsmith and Dhar 2012)。Monga 和 Gürhan-Canli(2012)则发现激发求偶思维(Mating-mindset)可以引发男性消费者关系寻求的信息加工模式,从而增加其对延伸品牌的接受度。

然而值得注意的是,上述研究都是在考察消费者对品牌延伸的态度而不是对品牌联名的态度。品牌联名与品牌延伸不同:其一,品牌延伸看重母品牌和延伸品牌之间的相似性,但是品牌联名相对而言更看重参与双方或者多方之间的互补性(Park, Jun, and Shocker 1996; Swaminathan, Gürhan-Canli, Kubat, and Hayran 2015)。其二,在品牌延伸中,母品牌与延伸品牌之间的关系其实是类似于父母与子女的关系。然而在品牌联名中,参与联名的各方之间其实属于类似于夫妻的联姻关系(Cao and Yan 2017; Van der Lans, Van den Bergh, and Dieleman 2014; Zhang and Sood 2002)。这也使得在品牌延伸领域被研究过的消费者信息加工模式,也许会在品牌联名上产生不同的效果。举例来说,解释水平理论(Construal level theory)指出,高解释水平的个体更看重长期利益,也更愿意采用抽象的思维模式(Cho, Khan, and Dhar 2013; Fujita, Trope, Liberman, and Levin-Sagi 2006; Wiesenfeld, Reyt, Brockner, and Trope 2017; Xu, Jiang, and Dhar 2013)。Fujita 和 Carnevale(2012)指出,高解释水平可以有效减少短期的和当下的诱惑对消费者的吸引力,使之更多考虑长远目标。而一系列研究(Cho, Khan, and Dhar 2013; Xu, Jiang, and Dhar 2013)都发现,高解释水平可以很好地帮助消费者去理解和比较不同选项之间差异较大的事物,从而减少决策的困难度。基于此,笔者推断,相比于低解释水平的消费者,具有高解释水平的消费者更能接受两个不相似(或者互补)品牌之间的联名,因为他们更能找到事物之间的联系,更能为两个不相似的品牌的联名找到合理的归因,并且更愿意关注长远的发展结果。而互补品牌之间的联名相比于相似品牌之间的联名,在长远意义上会带来更多整体效用上的提升(增加互补的品牌资产,扩大现有的消费群体)。综合以上两点,在品牌联名的情景下,解释水平对消费者判断产生的影响也许会不同于品牌延伸的情景。

(三)消费者的人口学变量信息

已往研究指出,人口学变量也会塑造消费者的信息加工模式。例如,Smith 和 Trope(2006)发现发挥社会地位因素的作用会让个体拥有更多抽象思维。Mehta 和 Zhu(2016)的研究却发现,如果让消费者临时感到资源匮乏(具有较低的社会经济地位),则会增加消费者的创造性思维。而根据前文的讨论,抽象的思维模式和高度的创造力(更加多元和灵活的视角)都有益于增加消费者对品牌联名的接受度。此外,来自社会心理学领域的证据显示,性别因素和年龄因素也会在很大程度上改变消费者的信息加工模式(Darley and Smith 1995; Cole and Balasubramanian 1993; Wang and Cole 2016)。例如,Darley 和 Smith(1995)发现,女性是更全面的信息考虑者,她们会整合所有主观和客观的线索信息进行判断。相对而言,男性则更依赖于启发式和选择式的信息加工。在这种情况下,女性可能会更愿意整合细节信息来合理化品牌联名的动机,因此可能会对品牌联名具有更高的接受度。同时,有研究进一步指出,年轻的个体具有更高的促进定向(Promotion-focus),更关注如何扩大事物的收益;而年老的个体具有更高的预防定向(Prevention focus),更关注如何减少潜在的风险(Lockwood,Chasteen, and Wong 2005)。由于相似品牌之间的联名相比品牌跨界来说风险更少(但是收益也更少),因此笔者推断年老的消费群体相比年轻的消费群体会更偏好属性相似(vs.互补)的品牌之间的联名。总的来说,探讨个体差异如何调节消费者对品牌联名的态度,有助于品牌方思考如何针对不同人群精准投放联名广告。

二、消费者与品牌的关系因素对品牌联名偏好的影响

这一部分主要讨论消费者感知到的与品牌之间的关系如何影响其对品牌联名的态度。具体来说,讨论消费者自我—品牌的联系强度(Self-brand connection)、品牌依恋(Brand attachment)、品牌拟人化(Brand anthropomorphism)、消费者—品牌关系规范(Relationship norm)这些概念各自的定义、理论和相关研究假设。

(一)消费者自我—品牌的联系强度

研究者指出,自我—品牌联系强度反映了消费者感知到的品牌与自我系统融合和关联的程度(Aron, Aron, Tudor, and Nelson 1991;Song, Huang, and Li 2017)。品牌可以被消费者整合进自己的自我系统中(Ferraro, Kirmani, and Matherly 2013),而这种整合是通过品牌属性和自我概念之间的相似性和关联建立来实现(Escalas and Bettman 2000, 2003;Wang and John 2019)。例如,当消费者的同类群体(In-group members)也使用这个品牌,抑或是这

个品牌本身传递的意义和形象与消费者想要实现的形象相贴合时,消费者可以感受到更强的自我—品牌连接(Chaplin and John 2005; Escalas 1998; Escalas and Bettman 2005; White and Dahl 2007)。那些具有较强的自我—品牌连接的消费者,有更大的动机去维护品牌的形象(Fournier 1998; Harrigan, Evers, Miles, and Daly 2018)。这是因为对于具有较强的自我—品牌连接的消费者,品牌的失败也就意味着自我的失败,这会动摇消费者的自我价值,降低其自尊水平(Gaustad, Samuelsen, Warlop, and Fitzsimons 2018; Lisjak, Lee, and Gardner, 2012; Cheng, White, and Chaplin 2012; Swaminathan, Page, and Gürhan-Canli 2007)。因此,消费者维护品牌,加强对品牌的积极态度,也是对自我价值的修复和巩固(Cheng, White, and Chaplin 2012; Escalas and Bettman 2009)。例如,当面对品牌的负面信息时,那些具有较强的自我—品牌连接的消费者会选择去淡化和反驳这样的负面信息(Sprott, Czellar, and Spangenberg 2009; Swaminathan, Page, and Gürhan-Canli 2007)。

(二)品牌依恋

研究者指出,当自我—品牌连接程度较强时,消费者会将自己的自我概念投射到品牌中,并建立更强的品牌依恋(Park, MacInnis, Priester, Eisingerich, and Iacobucci 2010)。品牌依恋是基于社会心理学中的依恋理论(Attachment theory)提出的概念(Bretherton 1992; Mikulincer, Shaver, and Pereg 2003)。它指的是消费者个人与品牌之间的亲密程度(Huang, Huang, and Wyer 2018; Jahn, Gaus, and Kiessling 2012; MacInnis and Folkes 2017; Pieters 2013; Thomson, MacInnis, and Park 2005)。当消费者有较强的品牌依恋时,他们对品牌会更忠诚,并乐意付出更多关心

(Malär, Krohmer, Hoyer, and Nyffenegger 2011；Park, Eisingerich, and Park 2013)。基于此,研究者指出那些自我—品牌连接程度较强的消费者会更倾向于关心品牌的行动和品牌的象征意义。而对于那些自我—品牌连接程度较弱的消费者,品牌的形象和行为并不能成为他们自我价值的体现(Ferraro, Kirmani, and Matherly 2013；Rindfleisch, Burroughs, and Wong 2009)。这样的消费者也不会对品牌产生太强的依恋,对品牌会抱有更加宽松和灵活的态度和观点。以上这些理论发现也引出了一个值得深入探讨的问题：一方面,由于具有较弱自我—品牌连接度的消费者对品牌的观点更加灵活,他们因而可能对品牌的联名(尤其是跨界联名)具有更高的包容度。另一方面,由于具有较强自我—品牌连接度的消费者对品牌更具有忠诚感,也使得其可能对品牌的行动给予更多合理化的归因和支持。因此,很有可能存在一个调节变量,使得在某些情况下较强的自我—品牌连接度会增加消费者对品牌联名的支持,而在另外的情况下则出现相反的结果。其中一个可能的变量就是消费者对品牌联名做出判断的阶段。有研究指出,决策和购买往往涉及多个阶段(Xu and Wyer 2007；Zhu, Billeter, and Inman 2012),例如购买(使用前)阶段和使用阶段(Goodman and Irmak 2013)。基于此,若向消费者呈现品牌跨界联名的相关信息,具有较弱自我—品牌连接度的消费者相比于具有较强自我—品牌连接度的消费者更容易接受品牌联名,因为其在态度上更具有灵活性。然而当真正进入使用阶段后,具有较强自我—品牌连接度的消费者相对于具有较弱自我—品牌连接度的消费者更容易对品牌联名的结果进行合理化,进而会更倾向于对具体的使用和体验结果进行积极评价。研究这一问题可以系统阐释消费者自我—品牌连接度对品牌联名评价的影响和作用,也可以通过决策阶段这一全新的角度对相关研究领域进行拓展。

（三）品牌拟人化

消费者与品牌之间关系的建立，不仅需要将品牌整合入消费者自我系统，也涉及消费者以何种形式看待自身和品牌的关系。拟人化（Anthropomorphism）研究为我们看待消费者与品牌之间的关系提供了一种全新的视角（Aggarwal and McGill 2012；Epley, Waytz, and Cacioppo 2007；Waytz, Epley, and Cacioppo 2010；Waytz, Morewedge, Epley, Monteleone, Gao, and Cacioppo 2010）。拟人化被定义为将事物感知为具有人类的特征和性质（Epley, Akalis, Waytz, and Cacioppo 2008；Epley, Waytz, Akalis, and Cacioppo 2008；Waytz, Cacioppo, and Epley 2010）。拟人化可以发端于事物本身的特征。例如，事物在视觉上、声音上乃至行动上的表现使得观察者更容易将事物视为近似于人类的存在（Caruso, Burns, and Converse 2016；Cowan, Branigan, Obregón, Bugis, and Beale 2015；Kim and McGill 2011）。同时，拟人化也可以来自观察者在自身信念、动机与需求状态下的知觉偏差（Bartz, Tchalova, and Fenerci 2016；Chen, Sengupta, and Adaval 2018；Chen, Wan, and Levy 2017；Kwok, Crone, Ardern, and Norberg 2018；Mourey, Olson, and Yoon 2017）。当事物被拟人化之后，观察者也会把该事物看作人的相关图式（Human schema），这也意味着他们会把和其他人进行社会交往和对他人进行社会判断的模式也运用到与该事物打交道的过程中（Aggarwal and McGill 2007；Chen, Chen, and Yang 2020；Touré-Tillery and McGill 2015）。例如，当消费者将自身持有的产品拟人化之后，他们会更容易想到自身和该产品之间的情感联系，进而减少他们置换和弃置该产品的意愿（Chandler and Schwarz 2010)。当人们将大自然拟人化之后,人们会对大自然产生更多的共情,进而也会增加保护大自然的意愿(Tam,Lee, and Chao 2013)。

与之类似,品牌拟人化也会改变消费者感知的自身与品牌的关系。例如,Aggarwal 和 McGill(2012)发现,品牌拟人化会激发消费者与之进行社会交流和互动的意愿。当这个拟人化的品牌像一个受欢迎的伙伴时,消费者会不自觉地做出与这个品牌的精神相一致的行为。相反,当这个拟人化的品牌像一个不受欢迎的伙伴时,消费者会尽可能让自己的行为表现和该品牌的精神区别开来。Puzakvoa 和 Aggarwal(2018)发现,当消费者具有追求独特性的目的时,将品牌包装成一个独特的人物会损害消费者自我感知的独特性,进而降低他们对该品牌的喜爱。除此之外,品牌拟人化相关研究发现,拟人化的品牌更容易被消费者感知为具有自己的意图(Intention)和意志(Will),这也会影响他们对自身和品牌关系的判断。例如,当品牌方发生错误行为时,拟人化的品牌会更容易使消费者认为这种错误是品牌方刻意造成的(Puzakova,Kwak,and Rocereto 2013)。因为拟人化的品牌被认为像人一样具有自由意志,所以更容易被认为是这种错误行为的主导者。同理,相关研究也发现当品牌存在涨价现象时,拟人化品牌的涨价会更容易激发消费者的不公平感,因为消费者会感到自己是在被他人剥削(Kwak,Puzakova,and Rocereto 2015)。

Aggarwal 和 Mcgill(2007)的研究也指出,当消费者对拟人化品牌进行判断时,他们会期望拟人化品牌的视觉呈现和行为模式都更接近于人类的模式。例如,当品牌被拟人化时,消费者会更倾向于认为该品牌的产品像人一样具有本质的成分(Human essence)。在这样的情况下,消费者会倾向于将该品牌/产品旗下的所有属性整合进一个完整的框架中进行理解,而不是将该品牌/产品的每个属性分别进行独立的考虑(Huang, Wong, and Wan 2020)。基于以上讨论,品牌拟人化可能从以下两个方面对品牌联名的效果产生影响:

其一,由于品牌拟人化之后消费者会采用社会知觉和判断的方式来判断品牌(Golossenko, Pillai, and Aroean 2020; Kniazeva and Belk 2010),因此品牌联名的行为会更容易被消费者以"联姻"(Marriage)这种人类社会的活动模式进行解读,这也使得社会科学中与该领域相关的研究能够提供一些全新的视角。例如,当消费者将品牌进行拟人化,并将品牌联名感知为品牌之间的联姻时,他们对品牌联名中的伴侣选择(选择相似的还是互补的)具有何种偏好? 已往研究指出,在婚姻或者亲密关系中,伴侣之间的相似性要比互补性重要,这也被称为"相似性—吸引力"原理(Bouchard and McGue 1981; Dijkstra and Bareldes 2008; Klohnen and Luo 2003; Luo and Klohnen 2005; White 1980)。因此,与品牌联名更偏好互补型联名的一般结果不同,品牌拟人化反而会增加消费者对相似型联名的偏好。而现有的研究往往只讨论品牌联名的开始,却很少讨论品牌联名的终结。当消费者将品牌进行拟人化时,品牌联名的终结更接近于两个品牌之间的分手和离异。在这样的情况下,将品牌拟人化也许会让消费者高估品牌联名结束对参与品牌带来的伤害。

其二,品牌拟人化会使得消费者认为品牌具有自身的统一精神和内核(Haslam, Bastian, and Bissett 2004; Prentice and Miller 2007; Rangel and Keller 2011)。在这种情况下,品牌联名对于原有品牌的内核是补充还是稀释,将直接决定消费者对联名的态度。一般来说,初创品牌与成熟的知名品牌进行合作会给初创品牌带来收益(例如知名品牌品牌资产和消费者群体的转移)。然而由于拟人化增强了消费者对初创品牌的品牌内核的重视(Huang, Wong, and Wan 2020),也使得他们更容易把注意力集中在品牌的自主性和自由意志上(Hur, Koo, and Hofmann 2015; Kim and McGill 2018; May and Monga 2014; Puzakova, Kwak, and Rocereto 2013)。因此,相比于非拟人化情形而言,将初创品牌进行拟人化可能会在总体上减少消费者对初创品牌与知名品牌联名的评价。已往研究也指出,拟人化有多种类型,例如强调智力上的拟人化或者强调情感上的拟人化(Eddy, Gallup, and Povinelli 1993)。这些拟人化类型是否可以调节消费者对品牌联名的态度,也是值得进一步探索的问题。

(四)消费者—品牌关系规范

对于关系规范的研究最初起源于社会心理学(Batson 1993; Clark 1986; Clark and Mills 1993),后逐渐成为服务科学领域的重要概念(Aggarwal and Law 2005; Clark, Mills, and Powell 1986; Johnson and Grimm 2010)。学者指出,社会交往中存在两种类型的关系规范(Clark, Dubash, and Mills 1998; Clark and Mills 1979; Williamson, Clark, Pegalis, and Behan 1996):一种为共享关系规范(Communal relationship norm),另一种则是交换关系规范(Exchange relationship norm)。共享关系规范指的是关系双方互相给予社会支持(Buunk, Doosje, Jans, and Hopstaken 1993; Clark, Mills and Powell 1986; Hughes and Snell 1990; Mills and Clark 1986)。具体而言,在共享关系中,一方给予另一方支持和帮助往往是出于对对方真诚的关心,希望能够真切地满足对方的需要(Clark 1984; Kim and Sung 2016)。而在这段关系中,他们也希望

对方能给自己以同样的关怀和支持。这种关系规范常见于家庭关系(父母与子女之间,兄弟姐妹之间)、爱情关系、亲密的朋友关系(Clark 1986; Clark and Mills 1979; Miller, Akiyama, and Kapadia 2017)。Aggarwal(2004)指出,共享关系规范并不意味着关系中的双方不寻求互惠互利。相反,这种关系规范强调的是人们在交往中不以利益平等为首要考虑,而是寻求一种长期的互相关心和互相支持的状态。与之相对应,交换关系规范则不同(Bartz and Lydon 2008; Clark and Mills 1993; Lemay and Clark 2008)。在交换关系中,一方给予另一方帮助的同时,是明确期望另一方能够给予同等条件的补偿或者回馈。而作为帮助的接受方感受到的更多是亏欠,并希望能够予以相应的补偿。这种关系常见于商业交易中,因为涉及公平交易和减少剥削与负债的期待(Aggarwal and Larrick 2012; Clark and Waddell 1985; Williamson and Clark 1989)。Aggarwal(2004)专门整理了这两种关系规范的十种对比特征,如表6-2所示。

表6-2 交换关系规范与共享关系规范特征对比

交换关系规范	共享关系规范
在接受利益时,应该立即予以偿还	在接受利益时,并不需要立即予以偿还
在接受利益时,应该给予等价的回报	在接收利益时,等价回报并不是必需的
在给予他人帮助后,更可能要求偿还	在给予他人帮助后,并不迫切要求偿还
在合作任务中,更愿意计较自己与他人各自的付出和产出	在合作任务中,较少计较自己与他人各自的付出和产出

第六章 全书总结与未来研究方向

(续表)

交换关系规范	共享关系规范
在分配奖励时,更愿意采取"按劳分配"的原则	在分配奖励时更愿意采取"按需分配"的原则
较少主动帮助他人	较多主动帮助他人
较少向他人寻求帮助	较多向他人寻求帮助
相比于非金钱的帮助,更偏好在金钱上的帮助	相比于金钱的帮助,更偏好非金钱的帮助
较少去追踪和关心他人的需求	较多去追踪和关心他人的需求
对他人的情绪状态关心和回应较少	对他人的情绪状态关心和回应较多

营销学者指出,类似于人与人之间的关系规范,人和品牌之间的关系规范也符合这两个维度的描述(Aggarwal 2004;Aggarwal and Zhang 2006;Wan, Hui, and Wyer 2011)。在消费者评价品牌时,这种与品牌之间的关系规范也会影响他们的信息加工和决策过程。例如,Aggarwal 和 Law(2005)发现,当共享关系规范被激活时,消费者更倾向于通过高解释水平(抽象思维)的信息加工模式来评价品牌。Aggarwal(2004)的研究指出,当消费者持有的关系规范(共享关系规范 vs.交换关系规范)和品牌的行为匹配时,消费者会对品牌持更积极的态度。例如,为服务收取费用虽然不符合共享关系规范,但是符合交换关系规范,因此那些持交换关系规范的人会对品牌收费行为采取相对宽容的态度。研究者也指出,在品牌面临服务失败的情况下,消费者与品牌之间的关系规范和消费者认为的事故责任方会共同影响他们对品牌的态度(Wan, Hui, and Wyer 2011)。Aggarwal 和 Larrick(2012)则发现,消费者

与品牌之间的关系规范会影响他们对该品牌分配公平性的评价。此外,Aggarwal 和 Zhang(2006)探讨了关系规范对风险偏好的影响,他们的研究发现,比起那些被激活交换关系规范的消费者,被激活共享关系规范的消费者会展现出更强的损失厌恶感(Loss aversion),因为他们和产品/品牌之间建立了更强的情感依恋。

基于以上讨论,笔者认为消费者与品牌的关系规范至少可以从两个方面影响他们对品牌联名的态度:当消费者感知到自身和某品牌之间是处于共享关系时,消费者对品牌会产生较强的情感依恋(Aggarwal and Zhang 2006)。因此,该品牌与其他品牌(尤其是存在较大差异的品牌)的联名更容易被消费者感知为对这段关系的破坏和背叛,进而降低消费者对该联名行动的评价。相反,当消费者感知到自身和某品牌之间是处于交换关系时,消费者会更加关心能否在品牌上得到更有价值的回报。在这种情况下,进行跨界品牌联名反而能增加消费者对联名行动的评价。此外,研究者也可以探索在初创品牌与知名品牌联名时,消费者持有的关系规范如何影响他们对初创品牌的看法。由于交换关系规范强调的是公平对等的交易(Chen, Bolton, Ng, Lee, and Wang 2017; Grote and Clark 1998),因此在初创品牌和知名品牌联名时,持交换关系规范的消费者更容易认为初创品牌也同样具有潜力(所以才能吸引到知名品牌与之进行合作)。若消费者持共享关系规范,情况则可能相反。因为这样的消费者会倾向于认为是知名品牌非常友爱才促成了这样的联名合作,这样反而会进一步增强消费者对知名品牌的好感。

三、文化因素对品牌联名偏好的影响

文化心理学的研究探索了文化元素对消费者决策和行为的影

响（Gelfand 2019；Kacen and Lee 2002；Lee 2000；McCracken 1986；Parker and Tavassoli 2000；Torelli 2006）。例如，学者发现不同文化背景的消费者会有不同的自我建构（Cross，Bacon，and Morris 2000；Singelis and Sharkey 1995）：一种是彼此独立的自我建构（Independent self-construal），另一种是互相依靠的自我建构（Interdependent self-construal）。相比于互相依靠的自我，建构独立自我的消费者更愿意尝试和使用新产品（Ma，Yang，and Mourali 2014）。Lalwani 和 Shavitt（2013）则发现处于互相依靠文化背景的消费者更愿意用价格来推断产品质量。而 Zhang 和 Shrum（2009）发现，在追求独立（vs.互相依靠）的文化氛围中，消费者更可能出现冲动消费。

在品牌研究领域，营销学者也探讨了文化因素对品牌偏好的影响。例如，文化心理学相关研究区别了两种文化下的信息加工模式（Foard and Kemler 1984；Hossain 2018；Krishna，Zhou，and Zhang 2008；Latour and Deighton 2019；McElroy and Seta 2003）：整体加工（Holistic processing）与分析加工（Analytic processing）。整体加工被认为与东亚文化相关，更关注场景中的客体与其所处场景之间的关系。分析加工被认为与西方文化相关，会将场景中的客体单独剥离出来进行考虑（Choi，Koo，and Choi 2007；Nisbett and Miyamoto 2005；Nisbett，Peng，Choi，and Norenzayan 2001）。Monga 和 John（2007）的研究显示，东方文化（以整体加工为主）相比于西方文化（以分析加工为主），会使消费者感受到更强的延伸品牌和母品牌之间的匹配性，进而增加其对品牌延伸的接受度。Monga 和 John（2010）则发现对功能性产品而言，整体加工有助于消费者增加对相对较远的品牌延伸的喜爱程度。

在文化的氛围和规范层面，Triandis（1996）提出了文化的紧—

松划分（Tightness-looseness distinction）。在"紧"的文化中，社会和文化规范被清晰地定义，文化中的个体也更难容忍偏离文化规范的行为。而在"松"的文化中则意味着文化规范相对模糊，文化中的个体对偏离文化规范的行为也有更高的容忍度（Gelfand 2012；Gelfand et al., 2011；Gunia, Brett, Nandkeolyar, and Kamdar 2011；Harrington and Gelfand 2014；Pelto 1968；Triandis 2004）。关于这种文化划分模式如何影响消费者行为，营销学者也进行了相应的探究。例如，Torelli 和 Rodas（2017）探讨了文化松紧度和品牌心理学的关系。他们认为品牌精神的稀释效应（Brand dillution）更容易在"紧"文化中出现。同时，"紧"文化中的群体对品牌失败（Brand failure）也会更加难以容忍。这都是因为"紧"文化中的消费者对违反社会规范的行为具有更强的惩罚意愿（Chua, Roth, and Lemoine 2015；Gelfand, Li, and Gordon 2017；Li, Gordon, and Gelfand 2017）。Gupta 和 Hagtvedt（2021）则发现，文化松紧度会影响消费者对品牌标识物理位置的看法。这也为关于文化对品牌偏好的影响研究提供了新的视角。

除了在自我概念、信息加工模式与社会规范上的差别，跨文化研究的学者还从其他维度对文化进行了划分，其中以 Hofstede 等学者的文化维度理论最为出名。根据这一理论，文化上的价值观可以通过五个维度来体现（Hofstede 2003；Hofstede and Bond 1984；Soares, Farhangmehr, and Shoham 2007；Yoo, Donthu, and Lenartowicz 2011），分别是权力距离（Power distance）、不确定性规避（Uncertainty avoidance）、集体主义与个人主义（Collectivism and individualism）、男性化与女性化（Masculinity and femininity）、长期导向和短期导向（Long-term orientation and short-term orientation）。下面笔者将分别讨论这五种文化价值维度如何与品牌联名产生新的研究问题。

(一)权力距离

文化研究者指出,关于权力距离的信念(Power distance belief)反映了在一种文化中的个体对社会和文化中权力结构的看法(Gao, Li, Liu, and Fang 2018;Winterich, Gangwar, and Grewal 2018;Zhang, Winterich, and Mittal 2010;Oyserman 2006)。对权力距离的信念越强,就意味着个体越能接受在社会中权力、财富、地位分配上的不平等(Hofstede 1984,2001)。值得注意的是,对权力距离的信念和个体实际拥有的权力是彼此独立的两个概念(Han, Lalwani, and Duhachek 2017;Oyserman 2006;Wang, Wang, Fang, and Jiang 2018;Xu, Bolton, and Winterich 2021)。同时,对权力距离的信念也和实际上的社会分配公平彼此独立。例如,在权力距离信念上得分较低的美国,便依然存在大量的社会不公平的情况(Tsui, Enderle, and Jiang 2018;Yan, Keh, and Wang 2019;Zhang, Winterich, and Mittal 2010)。因此,对权力距离的信念更多是个体自身的观念而不是客观情况,反映的是他们如何感知和解读社会的阶层和平等问题(Jain and Jain 2018;Jain and Lee 2020;Lalwani and Wang 2019;Smith and Hume 2005;Vitell, Nwachukwu, and Barnes 1993)。

近年来,营销学者探讨了权力距离信念对消费者行为的作用(Shavitt and Barnes 2019)。Lalwani 和 Forcum(2016)发现,当个体抱有更强的权力距离信念时,他们更愿意用价格来推论产品的质量。这是因为这样的消费者有更强烈的需求去寻找事物中的结构(Need for structure)。这种结构化思维使人们更愿意对事物进行从高到低的排序。同时,价格又是一种帮助进行快速排序的信息,因此更容易受到这类消费者的青睐,进而成为他们判断质量的首选标准。其他学者也从消费者价格敏感性的角度探讨了权力距离信念的作用(Lee, Lalwani, and Wang 2020)。他们的研究结果显示,具有较强权力距离信念的消费者,因为更追求认知闭合(渴望快速实现决策),所以更容易接受初始的价格,而不是寻找更便宜的价格,表现出较低的价格敏感度。除了对价格与金钱相关的决策进行研究外,研究者也探讨了权力距离信念对消费者地位消费(Status consumption)的影响。例如,Kim 和 Zhang(2014)发现,抱有较强权力距离信念的消费者更偏好购买可以彰显社会地位的产品。有学者进一步发现,这种效应也受到在场的其他消费者的社会地位的调节(Gao, Winterich, and Zhang 2016)。同时,消费者的权力距离信念和自身实际地位还会共同影响他们在国家品牌(National brand)和自有品牌(Private brand)之间的相对偏好(Wang, Torelli, and Lalwani 2020)。

近年来,除了品牌偏好外,研究者也探讨了权力距离信念如何影响消费者对公司产品和广告的态度。例如,最新的研究显示,具有相对较弱的权力距离信念的消费者更偏好用户设计的产品。相反,具有较强的权力距离信念的消费者更偏好设计师设计的产品(Paharia and Swaminathan 2019;Song, Jung, and Zhang 2021)。在广告学领域,研究者发现,名人代言的广告会对具有较强的权力距离信念的消费者产生更强的吸引力(Winterich, Gangwar, and Grewal 2018)。与之相关的是,在一个最新发表的研究中,研究团队发现那些具有较强权力距离信念的个体相比于具有较弱权力距离信念的个体,更容易被基于认知角度的广告说服(Tu, Kwon, and Gao 2021)。这也进一步说明了强权力距离信念与理性决策模式息息相关。

该领域研究的另一个热门问题是权力距离信念对消费者其他决策行为的影响。一系列研究探索了这一文化差异如何影响消费者的亲社会行为。例如,Winterich 和 Zhang(2014)发现,较强的权力距离信念会减少消费者对他人的责任感,进而降低他们参与慈善捐赠的意愿。Han 等人(2017)发现,这种效应取决于捐赠人自身的权力地位。而在消费者自我控制领域,Zhang 等人(2010)研究发现具有较强权力距离信念的消费者具有更强的自我控制能力,会使自己更少陷入冲动消费的泥潭中。

而在本书中,笔者认为消费者对权力距离的信念也会影响他们对品牌联名的判断。具体而言,已往研究指出具有较强的权力距离信念的消费者更容易接受权力和阶层的划分。Ordabayeva 和 Fernandes(2018)发现,具有较强权力距离信念的人更希望品牌在产品的阶层性上展现差异化(纵向差异化),而不是在产品口味上展现差异化(横向差异化)。Goenka 和 Thomas(2020)也发现,具有较强权力距离信念的个体更容易在观念上认可炫耀式的、彰显地位的消费模式。与之相似的是,研究者也指出,由于具有较强权力距离信念的个体更渴望维持阶层的稳定,因此激活阶层维持的目标(Status-maintenance goal)更容易让这类人追求奢侈品消费(Kim,Park,and Dubois 2018)。由于选择品牌联名对象这一行为本身便隐含一定的阶层性,同时可能使消费者感知到这种阶层性,进而影响消费者对品牌联名的评价,因此探究权力距离信念对于不同品牌联名策略评价的影响具有直接的营销实践意义。具体来说,品牌联名可能发生在具有类似地位的品牌之间(例如大品牌和大品牌之间的联名),也有可能发生在具有不同地位的品牌之间(例如大品牌和初创品牌之间的联名)。由于人们普遍对阶层逆转持相对保守和谨慎的态度(Xie,Ho,Meier,and Zhou 2017),因此强权力距离信念会进一步促使消费者接受阶层和地位的稳定性。也就是说,具有较强权力距离信念的消费者对具有地位差异的品牌联名应该会持更负面的态度。当初创品牌和知名大牌进行合作时(即参与联名的品牌之间存在地位差异的时候),强权力距离信念可能会影响消费者对参与联名的各个品牌的评价。具体来说,和知名品牌联名有助于提升初创品牌的地位,因此具有较强权力距离信念的消费者会对初创品牌更加看好。但是对于知名品牌来说,由于其和初创品牌的合作类似于屈尊低就(即放弃了自己的高地位),因此具有较强权力距离信念的消费者可能会降低对知名品牌的评价。同理,哪怕是品牌本身的知名度近乎相同,如果一个品牌走的是高端奢侈路线,而另一个品牌走的是亲民大众化路线,那么对于具有较强权力距离信念的消费者来说,这样的品牌融合路线也模糊了阶层的边界,让其难以接受。此外,尽管在品牌联名中彼此互补的品牌的联名比起彼此相似的品牌的联名可以提供更高的效用,但是对于具有较强权力距离信念的消费者而言,相似品牌之间的联名更符合同阶层品牌和同类品牌内部的整合,而互补品牌之间的联名则可能涉及不同阶层、不同类型的整合,具有更多的不确定性。在这种情况下,强权力距离信念反而会降低消费者对互补型品牌联名的评价。

(二) 不确定性规避

在文化心理学研究中,不确定性规避指个体会更偏好熟悉的、规律的结构,并尽可能增强对不可控因素的控制感(Hofstede 2001; Merkin 2006; Minkov and Hofstede 2014; Shane 1995)。相反,那些不确定性规避倾向较弱的个体更有勇气尝试新事物,追求风险,对不可控的因素也更加泰然(Reimann, Lünemann, and

Chase 2008)。与不确定性规避相关的动机因素在社会心理学领域得到广泛关注和研究,例如趋近—回避动机(Approach motivation/Avoidance motivation)(Elliot and Covington 2001; Elliot and Thrash 2002; Roth and Cohen 1986)、促进定向—预防定向(Promotion focus/Prevention focus; Crowe and Higgins 1997; Higgins 1998; Liberman, Idson, Camacho and Higgins 1999)、风险寻求—规避动机(Risk seeking/Risk avoidance)(Scholer, Zou, Fujita, Stroessner, and Higgins 2010; Zaleskiewicz 2001; Zhang, Hou, and Li 2020)、控制感寻求(Need for control)(Greenaway, Storrs, Philipp, Louis, Hornsey, and Vohs 2015; Leotti, Iyengar, and Ochsner 2010; Nowicki and Duke 1974; Phillips and Gully 1997)、对于结构感的需求(Need for structure)(Freund, Kruglanski, and Shpitzajzen 1985; Neuberg and Newsom 1993; Schaller, Boyd, Yohannes, and O'Brien 1995)和对于新奇的寻求(Novelty seeking)(Bardo, Donohew, and Harrington 1996; Hirschman 1980; Lee and Crompton 1992)。关于不确定性规避的消费者行为学研究主要见于以下几个方面。

1. 不确定性规避的前置因素

已往研究从个人因素、信息因素、社会关系因素、环境因素等方面探讨了消费者不确定性规避形成的机理。例如在个人因素方面,学者发现资源稀缺度和社会经济地位的变化可能会影响消费者的冒险精神(Anderson and Galinsky 2006; Fan, Li, and Jiang 2019; Haushofer and Fehr 2014)。而个体感知到的压力等情绪因素也会影响其对不确定的规避倾向(Cheung and Mikels 2011; Druckman and McDermott 2008; Jordan, Sivanathan, and Galinsky 2011)。近年来,研究者进一步发现,个体的政治观念也有可能对金融决策上的不确定性偏好产生影响(Han, Jung, Mittal, Zyung, and Adam 2019)。

在社会关系因素领域,已往研究发现社会关系的剥夺(例如社会排斥)会影响人们在金融上的冒险行为(Duclos, Wan, and Jiang 2013)。在浪漫关系中风险寻求和风险规避也是主要的研究课题(Henderson et al. 2005; Winterheld and Simpson 2011)。有的研究则比较了个体的自我建构(互相依靠 vs.独立)以及决策目标(为他人决策 vs.为自己决策)对不确定性规避的影响(Mandel 2003; Stone, Yates, and Caruthers 2002)。

在信息因素上,已往研究显示,信息呈现的清晰度和全面度也会对消费者的风险决策产生影响(Huang, Wu, and Shi 2018; Song and Schwarz 2009)。此外,学者们也探讨了环境因素对消费者风险偏好的影响。例如研究显示,拥挤的环境中,个体决策会更加趋于保守(Maeng, Tanner, and Soman 2013)。而当环境中的威胁性因素(例如传染病)凸显时,消费者也会更加谨慎(Navarrete and Fessler 2006; Neuberg, Kenrick, and Schaller 2011)。

综上,尽管不确定性规避具有文化属性,但是由于其和风险寻求与规避的动机相关联,这种动机也可能被消费者的长期因素(例如人口学变量)和临时因素(例如身处某种特殊环境)所激活。

2. 不确定性规避的结果影响

营销学领域的研究者主要探讨不确定性规避对消费者决策的影响。例如,很多文献探讨了对于不确定性规避程度不同的消费者,该如何设置广告信息才能匹配其个人偏好,从而增加广告说服力(Aaker and Lee 2006; Avnet and Higgins 2006; Cesario, Grant and Higgins 2004; Cesario, Higgins, and Scholer 2008; Lee and Aaker 2004)。有研究则探讨了这种对不确定性的偏好如何与其他因素(例如时间)共同影响消费者的动机(Kees, Burton, and Tangari, 2010; Keller 2006; Kim, Rao and Lee 2009; Mogilner, Aaker, and Pennington 2008)。还有研究探讨了消费者的这一趋势对其信息加工方式的影响(Jain, Lindsey, Agrawal, and Maheswaran 2007; Wan, Hong, and Sternthal 2009; Yoon, Sarial-Abi, and Gürhan-Canli 2012; Zhou and Pham 2004)。近年来,更多的研究开始探讨规避不确定性的动机如何影响消费者对产品和服务的偏好(Chen, Lee, and Yap 2017; Cutright and Samper 2014; Jia, Khan, and Litt 2015; Su, Jiang, Chen, and Dewall 2017)。

值得注意的是,关于不确定性规避和品牌偏好的研究目前较少见于营销类学术期刊(Beck, Rahinel, and Bleier 2020; Hamerman and Johar 2013)。例如,研究发现当消费者寻求更多的结构化时,他们对那些与母品牌不匹配的延伸品牌会抱有更负面的态度(Cutright, Bettman, and Fitzsimons 2013)。Hamerman 和 Johar(2013)则发现当个体寻求控制感时,消费者会更容易在品牌偏好上展现迷信的态度。在不同市场份额的品牌的选择上,研究者发现那些希望重建控制感、规避不确定性的消费者更偏好市场上的领军品牌(Beck, Rahinel, and Bleier 2020)。这些研究为我们初步揭示了不确定性规避和品牌选择中的心理学机制。基于这些研究,笔者认为可以从以下几个方面去探讨不确定性规避与品牌联名的研究问题。第一,不确定性规避倾向越强,消费者应该越发追求安全和低风险。那么当成熟的知名品牌选择和初创品牌合作时,消费者可能会持有更悲观的态度。第二,不确定性规避倾向越强,消费者可能反而会更支持品牌与多个其他品牌同时进行联名。尽管与多个品牌进行联名可能会造成品牌稀释效应,但是与多个品牌形成联名也意味着风险的分散("不把鸡蛋都放在一个篮子里"),这对于那些希望减轻潜在风险的消费者来说也会更有吸引力。第三,由于品牌的跨界合作(相对于相近行业合作)可能带来更多潜在的冲突,因此对于希望规避不确定性风险的消费者来说可能并不是一个充满吸引力的选项。探索这些要素也有助于从风险偏好的角度来理解消费者对品牌联名的偏好和态度。

(三)集体主义与个人主义

集体主义(Collectivism)和个人主义(Individualism)是文化心理学中被广泛探讨的研究主题(Greenfield 2000;Oyserman, Coon, and Kemmelmeier 2002;Suh 2002;Gelfand, Triandis, and Chan 1996;Triandis and Suh 2002)。Triandis(1989)指出,西欧、北欧与北美的文化更接近于个人主义文化,而亚洲、非洲和南美的文化则更接近于集体主义文化。在个人主义文化中,个体更强调的是独立的、个人化的自我。而在集体主义文化中,个体更强调的是在集体中的自我,抑或是在他人眼中的自我(Triandis 2001)。研究者指出,集体主义意味着个体与群体(例如家庭、单位、组织、国家)中的其他成员互相依赖、互相支持,并将集体的目标与行为规范放在最优先级(Hui and Villareal 1989;Singelis, Triandis, Bhawuk, and Gelfand 1995;Mills and Clark 1982)。这也意味着集体主义文化中的人们是以关系维护为目标的(Oyserman and Lee 2008;Triandis and Gelfand 1998;Triandis, McCusker, and Hui 1990)。相反,个体主义文化中的人们更加追求自由和自主性,会将他们自己与群体内的其他人独立和区别开来(Hui and Triandis 1986;Schwartz and Bilsky 1990;Triandis, Bontempo, Villareal, Asai, and Lucca 1988;Wagner 1995)。在这种情况下,个体文化主义中的人们会将自己的个人目标(而不是集体目标)和个人的态度、价值观放在首位（Brewer and Chen 2007；Chen, Chen, and Meindl 1998；Singelis, Bond, Sharkey, and Lai 1999；Singelis, Triandis, Bhawuk, and Gelfand 1995；Wagner and Moch 1986）。

关于集体主义和个人主义对消费者行为的影响研究涉及消费者决策与判断的多个方面和多个阶段。Aaker 和 Williams（1998）发现，在广告中的情绪号召对不同文化中的消费者有不同影响。具体来说，他们将情绪号召分为两种主要类型，即关注自我型和关注他人型。关注自我型的情绪包含骄傲（Pride）与快乐（Happiness），而关注他人型的情绪则包含共情（Empathy）与平静（Peacefulness）。他们的研究结果显示，对于个人主义文化中的消费者，在广告中采用关注自我型的情绪号召会增加广告的说服力。而对于集体主义文化中的消费者，在广告中采用关注他人型的情绪号召效果更好。此外，Aaker 和 Maheswaran（1997）指出，处于集体主义文化中的消费者在决策时会更看重他人意见，而不是具体产品的属性信息。在 Spassova 和 Lee（2013）的研究中，他们发现文化甚至可以改变消费者的信息加工抽象程度。具体来说，个人主义文化（vs.集体主义文化）中的消费者会更加倾向采用抽象（vs.具体）的信息加工模式，也会更容易把发生在未来的事件感知为更遥远（vs.更靠近）的事件。而当消费者需要在选择集中进行选择时，集体主义文化中的消费者更倾向于选择中庸的选项（Briley, Morris, and Simonson 2000）。Zhang 和 Shrum（2009）则探讨了购买数量这一变量，揭示了个人主义文化对冲动消费意愿产生影响的作用机制。Hong 和 Chang（2015）则发现，个人主义文化中的消费者会倾向于通过产品的感性元素（例如外形设计的美感）来评价产品，而集体主义文化中的消费者则会倾向于通过产品的理性元素（例如处理器速度和内存大小）来决定对产品的购买意愿。在最新发表的研究中,研究者也发现相比于个人主义文化中的个体,集体主义文化中的个体在疫情的风险感知和心理调整等方面的表现具有很大差异(Germani, Buratta, Delvecchio, and Mazzeschi 2020)。

除开消费者对产品的偏好之外,已有研究也探讨了不同文化如何影响消费者与服务商之间的关系。例如,研究者探讨了消费者对服务失败的反应(Chan, Wan, and Sin 2009)。结果显示在集体主义文化中,消费者对和社会因素相关的失败的服务更加反感。相反,在个人主义文化中,消费者对和非社会因素相关的失败的服务更加反感。有学者把目光投向定价研究领域(Chen, Bolton, Ng, Lee, and Wang 2018),发现集体主义文化中的消费者相较于个人主义文化中的消费者,更容易认为商家的不对称定价(当生产成本上升时,商家上调价格;但是当生产成本下降时,商家却维持价格不变,而不是下调价格)是不公平的行为。

对于个体主义/集体主义文化与品牌消费行为之间的联系,研究者也进行了一系列探索。例如 Escalas 和 Bettman(2005)发现,处于个人主义文化中的消费者有更强的将自己与他人进行区别的动机。在这种情况下,当一个品牌的品牌形象和自己不想与之产生关联的人相一致时,个人主义文化中的消费者会对该品牌持更负面的态度。有研究者进一步发现,消费者与品牌之间的连接(Self-brand connection)类型受到消费者自身文化特性的影响(Swaminathan, Page, and Gürhan-Canli 2007)。譬如,集体主义文化中的消费者和品牌更容易形成集体层面上的联系(例如消费者所属群体和品牌原产国之间的联系),而个人主义文化中的消费者和品牌更容易形成个体层面上的联系(例如消费者个人的自我概念和品牌精神之间的联系)。

基于以上讨论,笔者认为集体主义和个人主义文化也会塑造消费者对品牌联名的态度和偏好。首先,与个人主义文化不同,集体主义文化中的消费者更尊重组内群体的准则和价值观。在这种情况下,品牌联名可能更要考虑品牌价值观的整合。具体而言,当两个具有不同(甚至是稍显矛盾)品牌形象和价值观的品牌选择联名时,对于个人主义文化中的消费者而言,这是一种高自由度和高自主性的信号,而且持有这样的产品更能帮助个人主义文化中的消费者彰显自己的独特和个性。因此,个人主义文化会使消费者更喜欢此类品牌联名。然而,对于集体主义文化中的消费者而言,这种联名代表的是准则的不一致性和价值观的混乱。可以说,集体主义文化反而会降低消费者对此类品牌联名的好感度。此外,已往关于品牌联名的实证研究较少考察跨国联名(例如中国的联想和美国的IBM)的案例。由于集体主义文化更多是强调组内的凝聚力和身份认同,因此这种跨国的品牌联名必须要考虑海外品牌的原产国效应(Country-of-origin effect)。如果海外品牌的原产国和消费者自身所处的集体存在价值观或者其他方面的冲突,那么集体主义文化会降低消费者对此类品牌联名的喜爱。同时,本土品牌自身的文化属性和品牌形象也有可能影响集体主义文化中消费者对跨国联名的态度。具体来说,如果本土品牌是怀旧品牌(Nostalgic brand),或者是反映本国文化精髓(Cultural essence)的品牌,那么与海外品牌的联名会加重集体主义文化中消费者对品牌精髓流失的担忧。由此可推知,该类型的品牌联名会降低集体主义文化中的消费者对参与合作的本土品牌的偏好和喜爱。

(四)男性化与女性化

文化心理学的研究者指出,男性化和女性化代表了社会对性别角色的态度(Coltrane 1988;Hofstede 1980;McSweeney 2002;Miller 1994)。其中男性化指代的是一个社会在多大程度上期待男性是强势的、有野心的、竞争性强的(从而获得更多物质上的成功)。在男性化的文化背景下,社会中的个体会更尊重那些更大、更强、更快的事物,并且要求女性主要从事与物质成功无关的工作(例如照顾儿童和弱小)。相反,女性化文化代表的是男性和女性在性别角色上的相对平等(De Mooij and Hofstede 2002,2011)。具体而言,女性化文化中的男性和女性都不应该过度展现野心和竞争性。同时,女性化的文化意味着人们会更看重彼此之间的合作关系,关怀弱小并关注生活质量,并且男性和女性的社会角色应该是有重叠的(Hofstede 1983,1996;Huang and Crotts 2019;Vitell,Nwachukwu,and Barnes 1993)。例如在女性化的文化中,男性也会从事家务,参与购物(De Mooij and Hofstede 2010)。管理学学者进一步提炼出了两种文化的差别:在男性化文化中人们最看重的是成功与成就,而在女性化文化中人们更看重的是合作与关怀(Franke,Hofstede,and Bond 1991;Markus,Crane,Bernstein,and Siladi,1982;Obeidat,Shannak,and Al-Jarrah 2012)。

过去关于男性化和女性化的营销研究主要见于关于社会知觉和消费者推论的研究,尤其是关于刻板印象(Stereotype)的研究。例如,营销学者发现,相比于女性而言,男性更不倾向于接受环保产品(Eco-friendly products)。产生这一现象的原因是环保产品在刻板印象上和女性化相关联。因此,使用环保产品会被男性消费者认为将损害他们自己的男子气概(Brough,Wilkie,Ma,Isaac,and Gal 2016)。研究者也探讨了不同文化下广告内容对男性和女性消费者的影响(Nelson,Brunel,Supphellen,and Manchanda 2006),结果显示,在男性化的文化中男性更容易被利己主义的慈善捐赠广告说服,而女性则更容易被利他主义的慈善捐赠广告说服。相较之下,在女性化文化中(男性和女性的性别角色差异缩小甚至反转)这一趋势出现了反转。Yan(2016)则发现,在消费者心目中数字也和性别存在联系。具体而言,精确的数字(Precise number)被认为更加男性化,而整十、整百类型的数字(Round number)则更容易被认为女性化。当企业面临失败时,人们对男性领导者和女性领导者的态度也有所差异(Montgomery and Cowen 2020)。其中,当企业失败是由道德上(vs.能力上)的错误造成时,女性领导者相比于男性领导者更无法被大众原谅。但是当企业失败是由能力上(vs.道德上)的错误引起时,男性领导者相较于女性领导者会迎来更多的批评。Cowen 和 Montgomery(2020)则发现,当企业服务失败时,女性领导者更适合采用最诚挚的道歉(Unqualified apology,指不期待任何原谅的道歉),而对于男性领导来说,道歉方式则不会带来太大的差异。

在品牌研究领域,已往研究主要探讨了品牌的性别维度(Lieven, Grohmann, Herrmann, Landwehr, and Van Tilburg 2014; Machado, Vacas-de-Carvalho, Azar, André, and Dos Santos 2019)。例如,Grohmann(2009)界定了品牌性别维度的定义,并开发了相关测量工具。在其论文中,一系列的形容词被用于分别描述品牌的男性化维度和女性化维度。其中,男性化维度的形容词包括:冒险的、侵略性的、勇敢的、无畏的、主导的、强健的;女性化维度的形容词包括:情感细腻的、脆弱的、优雅的、敏感的、甜美的、温柔的。研究者也探讨了消费者对品牌性别感知的形成机制。其中,有学者探讨了品牌设计上的元素对品牌性别感知的影响(Aspara and Van Den Bergh 2014; Lieven, Grohmann, Herrmann, Landwehr, and Van Tilburg 2015; Pang and Ding 2021)。例如,当品牌的标识更加厚重并多角时,消费者会更倾向于认为该品牌更男性化;而当品牌的标识更加苗条和圆滑(少角)时,消费者会认为该品牌更女性化。同时,学者也发现了色彩对品牌性别感知的影响(Hess and Melnyk 2016;Machado, Fonseca, and Martins 2020)。例如,粉色时常与女性知觉联系在一起,而深蓝色则主要和男性知觉联系在一起。

值得注意的是,以上的品牌研究更多是品牌自身如何被感知为男性化或者女性化,却少有研究探讨男性化和女性化的文化氛围对于品牌评价和偏好的影响。尤其是在品牌联名领域,目前的研究更是空白。根据以上讨论,可以在未来的研究中将文化的男性化和女性化与品牌的男性或者女性特征结合起来。例如,在男性化的文化中,个体预期男性会在社会中拥有更高权力和更高的主导性,而女性相对则处于从属性和支持性的地位(An and Kim 2007;Constantinople 1973;Yoo, Donthu, and Lenartowicz 2011)。那么当两个品牌进行联名时,相对强势的品牌更容易被感知为男性化,而相对弱势的品牌则更容易被感知为女性化,进而对基于顾客的品牌资产造成不同的影响(Lieven, Grohmann, Herrmann, Landwehr, and Van Tilburg 2014)。当一个形象相对男性化的品牌和形象相对女性化的品牌进行联名合作时,形象男性化的品牌会对形象女性化的品牌造成对比效果(Hsee and Zhang 2010;Muller and Butera 2007;Zheng, Baskin, and Peng 2018),这也会使形象女性化的品牌的品牌刻板印象更加深刻。在这种情况下,男性化的文化会导致人们更加低估形象女性化的品牌的作用。因此在男性化的文化中,联名合作的品牌最好应该在品牌形象上属于同一性别(男性化品牌与男性化品牌合作,或者女性化品牌与女性化品牌联名)。此外,由于女性化文化中男性和女性有更多的社会角色交集,因此当具有不同品牌性别的品牌进行合作时,消费者会更容易产生关联学习效应,认为双方在品牌资产上存在大量的相似性与共享性。探讨这些问题有助于厘清品牌性别与品牌联名之间的关系,具有深刻的理论和实践意义。

（五）长期导向和短期导向

与其他维度不同,长期导向和短期导向属于时间坐标上的维度(Hofstede and Minkov 2010; Lumpkin and Brigham 2011; Mosakowski and Earley 2000)。关于时间的决策是人一生中总要面对的问题。关于时间的态度在很大程度上决定了人们如何看待不同时刻(过去、现在、将来),如何衡量、估计与分配这一稀缺资源,以及如何制定生活中的目标和计划(Bearden, Money, and Nevins 2006; Bond 2004; Hofstede 1980; Spears, Lin, and Mowen 2000; Spector, Cooper, and Sparks 2001)。不同文化中的人在时间观念上往往存在一定的差异。例如,文化研究者区分了两种类型的文化：单一时间文化(Monochronic)与多元时间文化(Polychronic)。其中,单一时间文化中的个体会把每一件事的时间和顺序都设定好,在一段时间内只集中完成一件事；多元时间文化中的个体对时间则没有这么多的限定,更容易同时在一段时间内进行多项任务(Bluedorn, Kaufman, and Lane 1992; Hall 1993; Lindquist and Kaufman-Scarborough 2007; Widyanti and Regamalela 2019)。在时间相关决策上的长期导向和短期导向则是一种在生活中更加常见的区分模式(Hofstede 2001; Prelec and Loewenstein 1998; Robertson and Hoffman 2000)。长期导向指的是个体在看待时间时采用更加整体的观点,将过去到现在的长期阶段均考虑在内。短期指向则指的是个体在看待时间时采用局部化的观点,重点关注现在和相对较短的阶段(Lumpkin, Brigham, and Moss 2010; Nevins, Bearden, and Money 2007; Ryu, Park, and Min 2007; Wang and Bansal 2012)。值得注意的是,这样的概念其实反映了个体在进行时间决策时考虑的跨度与范围,而不仅仅是单纯地关注未来或者关注过去(Bearden, Money, and Nevins 2006; Flammer and Bansal 2017; Hassan, Shiu, and Walsh 2011)。正因如此,那些持有长期导向的个体或者组织(例如公司)被认为更加注意制定计划、尊重传统,以及通过持续不断的努力和坚持来收获长期的利益(Arli and Tjiptono 2014; Cannon, Doney, Mullen, and Petersen 2010; Memili, Fang, Koc, Yildirim-Öktem and Sonmez 2018; Wang, Siu, and Barnes 2008)。

在消费者行为学领域,已往关于长期导向和短期导向的研究主要探讨了这一时间观念形成的原因,以及这一时间观念对消费决策可能造成的影响(Hoch and Loewenstein 1991; Loewenstein and Prelec 1992; Loewenstein and Thaler 1989; Muraven 2010; Thaler and Shefrin 1981)。其中最有影响力的研究当属跨期选择(Intertemporal choice)和消费者自我控制(Self-control)。跨期选择反映了人们会分析不同决策在几个时间点各自造成的成本和收益,并在权衡取舍后作出最终决定(Berns, Laibson, and Loewenstein 2007; Kable and Glimcher 2007; Loewenstein 1988)。经典的跨期选择范式包含即时收益和长期收益之间的权衡取舍(Hardisty and Weber 2009)。例如,参加实验的消费者可以选择现在得到120美元的报酬抑或是三个月后得到200美元的报酬。这两个选项之间存在权衡取舍,消费者可以选择得到即时但较少的报酬,也可以选择付出更长的等待,但是收获较多的报酬(Joshi and Fast 2013; Lempert, Johnson, and Phelps 2016; Xu, González-Vallejo, and Vincent 2020)。

已往研究从消费者个人因素和信息设计因素探讨了在什么情况下消费者更愿意耐心等待(Amasino, Sullivan, Kranton, and Huettel 2019; Reeck, Wall, and Johnson 2017)。例如,Joshi 和 Fast(2013)发现权力地位高的个体更倾向于长期导向,会耐心等待更优的结果。一些社会心理学家探索了年龄对于个体形成长期导向或短期导向的影响(Green, Myerson, Lichtman, Rosen, and Fry 1996; Green, Myerson, and Ostaszewski 1999; Löckenhoff, O'Donoghue, and Dunning 2011)。有研究者则从消费者的自我概念入手,提出了自我概念的连续性(Self continuity)这一概念。根据这一理论,当个体感觉自己的自我概念是连续的(而不是在每一个阶段彼此独立)时,他们更倾向于长期导向,展现出更低的时间折扣、更高的未来计划性(例如储蓄)、更强的道德观念(Bartels and Rips 2010; Bartels and Urminsky 2011; Ersner-Hershfield, Wimmer, and Knutson 2009; Hershfield 2011; Hershfield, Cohen, and Thompson 2012; Hershfield et al. 2011; Urminsky 2017)。研究者也指出,当个体习惯采用抽象思维时,他们更容易倾向于长期导向(Fujita 2008; Fujita and Carnevale 2012; Fujita and Han 2009; Fujita and Roberts 2010; Fujita, Trope, Liberman, and Levin-Sagi 2006)。

在个人因素之外,研究者也试图从信息呈现的形式或者框架来探讨什么时候人们会倾向于长期导向或短期导向(Liu, Heath, and Onculer 2020; Read, Olivola, Hardisty 2017)。例如 Hardisty 和 Pfeffer(2017)发现,操纵未来选项和即时选项的相对不确定会逆转人们的长期导向和短期导向。有研究进一步发现,对于正面事件(例如收获)和负面事件(例如损失),人们具有不同的时间折扣(Molouki, Hardisty, and Caruso 2019)。此外,对于时间采用不同的表征(例如采用间隔或是具体日期,采用水平或是垂直呈现)都可能会改变人们的跨期选择(Berns, Laibson, and Loewenstein 2007; May 2017; Read, Frederick, Orsel, and Rahman 2005; Romero, Craig, and Kumar 2019; Zauberman, Kim, Malkoc, and Bettman 2009)。

另一个与长期/短期导向相关的概念是自我控制(Ballard, Kim, Liatsis, Aydogan, Cohen, and McClure, 2017; Kable 2014)。自我控制被定义为放弃即时可得的诱惑以保证长远利益的达成(Baumeister 2002; Fishbach and Shah 2006; Fishbach and Trope 2005; Hare, Camerer, and Rangel 2009; Hofmann, Friese, and Strack 2009)。童年时期的自我控制被认为可以有效预测个体在成年后的健康、财务和公共安全状况(Moffitt et al., 2011)。自我控制被认为和更好的适应能力、更好的生理与心理健康状态、更优秀的学业成绩和更好的人际关系挂钩(King and Gaerlan 2014; Tangney, Baumeister, and Boone 2004; Will Crescioni et al. 2011)。这也反映了长期导向(即更多关注整体和未来的利益)对个体带来的积极作用(Figlio, Giuliano, Özek, and Sapienza 2019; Strömbäck, Lind, Skagerlund, Västfjäll, and Tinghög 2017)。值得注意的是,那些倾向于长期导向(例如更多自我控制)的个体,往往在社会上也是更容易被他人尊重的。例如,社会心理学家发现,当个体更多展现自我控制时,他们在人际交往中更容易为他人所信任(Righetti and Finkenauer 2011)。

尽管关于长期/短期导向的研究已经成果丰硕,但是长期/短期导向的文化如何影响消费者对品牌的态度却少有人研究。在本书中,笔者认为,这一时间意义上的文化维度也会影响消费者对品牌联名的态度。已往研究将品牌联名比喻为联姻关系,消费者在判断品牌联名时会更容易使用和思考婚姻关系相近的思维模式来进行判断。由于前文提到过的相似性吸引原则(构建长期关系更需要双方相似而不是存在差异)(Wetzel and Insko 1982),在属性或者地位上相似的两个品牌进行联名可能会更受到倾向于长期导向的消费者的喜爱。相反,当消费者倾向于短期导向时,差异化带来的互补性会让属性和地位不同的品牌之间的联名更具有吸引力。另一种不同的观点则认为,由于品牌联名涉及资源整合,因此从长期发展来看,具有互补性的品牌联名更具有前景,而相似性强的品牌之间的联名则会造成重复和冗余。因此长期导向和短期导向如何影响消费者对品牌联名的态度还值得深入研究。通过以上讨论,笔者认为一个潜在的调节变量是消费者如何理解品牌之间的联名关系。具体而言,当消费者从共有关系(Communal relationship)的角度去理解品牌联名时,长期导向文化中的消费者会更容易接受相似性强的品牌联名。然而,当消费者从交换关系(Exchange relationship)的角度去理解品牌联名时,长期导向文化会让消费者更偏好互补性品牌之间的联名。未来的研究也可以探讨其他调节变量在其中产生的作用。

总的来说,本章总结了全书的内容,并且分别从消费者推论与品牌联名角度对可以拓展的研究方向进行了综合的讨论。这些问题有待学者们进一步挖掘和探索。

参 考 文 献

Aaker, David A., and Kevin Lane Keller. "Consumer evaluations of brand extensions." *Journal of Marketing* 54, no. 1 (1990): 27-41.

Aaker, Jennifer L. "Dimensions of brand personality." *Journal of Marketing Research* 34, no.3(1997): 347-356.

Aaker, Jennifer L., and Angela Y. Lee. "Understanding regulatory fit." *Journal of Marketing Research* 43, no.1(2006): 15-19.

Aaker, Jennifer L., and Durairaj Maheswaran. "The effect of cultural orientation on persuasion." *Journal of Consumer Research* 24, no.3(1997): 315-328.

Aaker, Jennifer, Kathleen D. Vohs, and Cassie Mogilner. "Nonprofits are seen as warm and for-profits as competent: Firm stereotypes matter." *Journal of Consumer Research* 37, no. 2 (2010): 224-237.

Aaker, Jennifer L., and Patti Williams. "Empathy versus pride: The influence of emotional appeals across cultures." *Journal of Consumer Research* 25, no.3(1998): 241-261.

Abele, Andrea E., and Bogdan Wojciszke. "Agency and communion from the perspective of self versus others." *Journal of Personality* and *Social Psychology* 93, no.5(2007): 751−763.

Abele, Andrea E., and Bogdan Wojciszke. "Communal and agentic content in social cognition: A dual perspective model." In *Advances in Experimental Social Psychology*, vol.50, pp.195−255. Academic Press, 2014.

Abele, Andrea E., Mirjam Uchronski, Caterina Suitner, and Bogdan Wojciszke. "Towards an operationalization of the fundamental dimensions of agency and communion: Trait content ratings in five countries considering valence and frequency of word occurrence." *European Journal of Social Psychology* 38, no.7 (2008): 1202−1217.

Abosag, Ibrahim, Stuart Roper, and Daniel Hind. "Examining the relationship between brand emotion and brand extension among supporters of professional football clubs." *European Journal of Marketing* 46, no.9(2012): 1233−1251.

Ackerman, Joshua M., Christopher C. Nocera, and John A. Bargh. "Incidental haptic sensations influence social judgments and decisions." *Science* 328, no.5986(2010): 1712−1715.

Adam, Hajo, Otilia Obodaru, Jackson G. Lu, William W. Maddux, and Adam D. Galinsky. "The shortest path to oneself leads around the world: Living abroad increases self-concept clarity." *Organizational Behavior and Human Decision Processes* 145 (2018): 16−29.

Aggarwal, Pankaj. "The effects of brand relationship norms on consumer attitudes and behavior." *Journal of Consumer Research* 31, no.1(2004): 87−101.

Aggarwal, Pankaj, and Ann L. McGill. "Is that car smiling at me? Schema congruity as a basis for evaluating anthropomorphized products." *Journal of Consumer Research* 34, no. 4 (2007): 468–479.

Aggarwal, Pankaj, and Ann L. McGill. "When brands seem human, do humans act like brands? Automatic behavioral priming effects of brand anthropomorphism." *Journal of Consumer Research* 39, no.2(2012): 307–323.

Aggarwal, Pankaj, and Meng Zhang. "The moderating effect of relationship norm salience on consumers' loss aversion." *Journal of Consumer Research* 33, no.3(2006): 413–419.

Aggarwal, Pankaj, and Min Zhao. "Seeing the big picture: The effect of height on the level of construal." *Journal of Marketing Research* 52, no.1(2015): 120–133.

Aggarwal, Pankaj, and Richard P. Larrick. "When consumers care about being treated fairly: The interaction of relationship norms and fairness norms." *Journal of Consumer Psychology* 22, no.1 (2012): 114–127.

Aggarwal, Pankaj, and Sharmistha Law. "Role of relationship norms in processing brand information." *Journal of Consumer Research* 32, no.3(2005): 453–464.

Ahn, Hongmin, and Yongjun Sung. "A two-dimensional approach to between-partner fit in co-branding evaluations." *Journal of Brand Management* 19, no.5(2012): 414–424.

Ahuvia, Aaron C. "Beyond the extended self: Loved objects and consumers' identity narratives." *Journal of Consumer Research*

32, no.1(2005): 171-184.

Ajzen, Icek. "Intuitive Theories of Events and the Effects of Base—Rate Information on Prediction." *Journal of Personality and Social Psychology* 35, no.5(1977): 303-314.

Albert, Noel, Dwight Merunka, and Pierre Valette-Florence. "When consumers love their brands: Exploring the concept and its dimensions." *Journal of Business Research* 61, no.10 (2008): 1062-1075.

Allen, Michael W., Richa Gupta, and Arnaud Monnier. "The interactive effect of cultural symbols and human values on taste evaluation." *Journal of Consumer Research* 35, no.2 (2008): 294-308.

Allison, Ralph I., and Kenneth P. Uhl. "Influence of beer brand identification on taste perception." *Journal of Marketing Research* 1, no.3(1964): 36-39.

Almenberg, Johan, and Anna Dreber. "When does the price affect the taste? Results from a wine experiment." *Journal of Wine Economics* 6, no.1(2011): 111-121.

Alvarez, Claudio, and Susan Fournier. "Brand flings: When great brand relationships are not made to last." *Consumer-Brand Relationships: Theory and Practice*(2012): 74-96.

Amasino, Dianna R., Nicolette J. Sullivan, Rachel E. Kranton, and Scott A. Huettel. "Amount and time exert independent influences on intertemporal choice." *Nature Human Behaviour* 3, no.4 (2019): 383-392.

Amos, Clinton, Gary Holmes, and David Strutton. "Exploring the relationship between celebrity endorser effects and advertising effectiveness: A quantitative synthesis of effect size." *International Journal of Advertising* 27, no.2(2008): 209–234.

An, Daechun, and Sanghoon Kim. "Relating Hofstede's masculinity dimension to gender role portrayals in advertising: A cross-cultural comparison of web advertisements." *International Marketing Review* 24, no.2(2007): 181–207.

Anderson, Cameron, and Adam D. Galinsky. "Power, optimism, and risk-taking." *European Journal of Social Psychology* 36, no.4 (2006): 511–536.

Anderson, John R. "A spreading activation theory of memory." *Journal of Verbal Learning and Verbal Behavior* 22, no.3(1983): 261–295.

Anderson, John R., and Gordon H. Bower. *Human Associative Memory*. Oxford: Winston, 1973.

Aniss, A. M., S. C. Gandevia, and R. J. Milne. "Changes in perceived heaviness and motor commands produced by cutaneous reflexes in man." *The Journal of Physiology* 397, no.1(1988): 113–126.

Arli, Denni, and Fandy Tjiptono. "The end of religion? Examining the role of religiousness, materialism, and long-term orientation on consumer ethics in Indonesia." *Journal of Business Ethics* 123, no.3(2014): 385–400.

Arnett, Jeffrey. "The psychology of globalization." *American Psychologist* 57, no.10(2002): 774–783.

Aron, Arthur, Elaine Aron, Michael Tudor, and Greg Nelson. "Close relationships as including other in the self." *Journal of Personality and Social Psychology* 60, no.2(1991): 241-253.

Asch, Solomon E. "Forming impressions of personality." *The Journal of Abnormal and Social Psychology* 41, no.3(1946): 258-290.

Aspara, Jaakko, and Bram Van Den Bergh. "Naturally designed for masculinity vs. femininity? Prenatal testosterone predicts male consumers' choices of gender-imaged products." *International Journal of Research in Marketing* 31, no.1(2014): 117-121.

Asutay, Erkin, and Daniel Västfjäll. "Perception of loudness is influenced by emotion." *PloS One* 7, no.6(2012): e38660.

Avnet, Tamar, and E. Tory Higgins. "How regulatory fit affects value in consumer choices and opinions." *Journal of Marketing Research* 43, no.1(2006): 1-10.

Bakan, David. "The duality of human existence." Chicago: Rand McNally.1966.

Balcetis, Emily, and David Dunning. "See what you want to see: Motivational influences on visual perception." *Journal of Personality and Social Psychology* 91, no.4(2006): 612-625.

Ballard, Ian C., Bokyung Kim, Anthony Liatsis, Gökhan Aydogan, Jonathan D. Cohen, and Samuel M. McClure. "More is meaningful: the magnitude effect in intertemporal choice depends on self-control." *Psychological Science* 28, no.10(2017): 1443-1454.

Bandura, Albert. "Human agency in social cognitive theory." *American Psychologist* 44(1989): 1175-1184.

Banović, Marija, Magda Aguiar Fontes, Maria Madalena Barreira, and Klaus G. Grunert. "Impact of product familiarity on beef quality perception." *Agribusiness* 28, no.2(2012): 157-172.

Bar, Varda, Yaffa Brosh, and Cary Sneider. "Weight, mass, and gravity: Threshold concepts in learning science." *Science Educator* 25, no.1(2016): 22-34.

Barberis, Nicholas C. "Thirty years of prospect theory in economics: A review and assessment." *Journal of Economic Perspectives* 27, no.1(2013): 173-196.

Bardo, Michael T., R. L. Donohew, and Nancy G. Harrington. "Psychobiology of novelty seeking and drug seeking behavior." *Behavioural Brain Research* 77, no.1-2(1996): 23-43.

Barham, Elizabeth. "Towards a theory of values-based labeling." *Agriculture and Human Values* 19, no.4(2002): 349-360.

Barone, Michael J. "The interactive effects of mood and involvement on brand extension evaluations." *Journal of Consumer Psychology* 15, no.3(2005): 263-270.

Barone, Michael J., and Paul W. Miniard. "Mood and brand extension judgments: Asymmetric effects for desirable versus undesirable brands." *Journal of Consumer Psychology* 12, no.4(2002): 283-290.

Barone, Michael J., Paul W. Miniard, and Jean B. Romeo. "The influence of positive mood on brand extension evaluations." *Journal of Consumer Research* 26, no.4(2000): 386-400.

Barsalou, Lawrence W. "Perceptual symbol systems." *Behavioral and Brain Sciences* 22, no.4(1999): 577-660.

Barsalou, Lawrence. "Grounded cognition." *Annual Review of*

Psychology 59(2008): 617-645.

Barsalou, Lawrence W. "Grounded cognition: Past, present, and future." *Topics in Cognitive Science* 2, no.4(2010): 716-724.

Bartels, Daniel, and Lance Rips. "Psychological connectedness and intertemporal choice." *Journal of Experimental Psychology: General* 139, no.1(2010): 49-69.

Bartels, Daniel M., and Oleg Urminsky. "On intertemporal selfishness: How the perceived instability of identity underlies impatient consumption." *Journal of Consumer Research* 38, no.1 (2011): 182-198.

Bartz, Jennifer A., and John E. Lydon. "Relationship-specific attachment, risk regulation, and communal norm adherence in close relationships." *Journal of Experimental Social Psychology* 44, no.3(2008): 655-663.

Bartz, Jennifer A., Kristina Tchalova, and Can Fenerci. "Reminders of social connection can attenuate anthropomorphism: A replication and extension of Epley, Akalis, Waytz, and Cacioppo (2008)." *Psychological Science* 27, no.12(2016): 1644-1650.

Batra, Rajeev, Aaron Ahuvia, and Richard P. Bagozzi. "Brand love." *Journal of Marketing* 76, no.2(2012): 1-16.

Batra, Rajeev, and Pamela Miles Homer. "The situational impact of brand image beliefs." *Journal of Consumer Psychology* 14, no.3 (2004): 318-330.

Batson, C. Daniel. "Communal and exchange relationships: What is the difference?." *Personality and Social Psychology Bulletin* 19, no.6(1993): 677-683.

Baumeister, Roy F. "Yielding to temptation: Self-control failure, impulsive purchasing, and consumer behavior." *Journal of Consumer Research* 28, no.4(2002): 670–676.

Baumgarth, Carsten. "Evaluations of co-brands and spill-over effects: Further empirical results." *Journal of Marketing Communications* 10, no.2(2004): 115–131.

Bearden, William O., R. Bruce Money, and Jennifer L. Nevins. "A measure of long-term orientation: Development and validation." *Journal of the Academy of Marketing Science* 34, no.3(2006): 456–467.

Beck, Joshua T., Ryan Rahinel, and Alexander Bleier. "Company worth keeping: Personal control and preferences for brand leaders." *Journal of Consumer Research* 46, no.5(2020): 871–886.

Beckwith, Neil E., and Donald R. Lehmann. "The importance of halo effects in multi-attribute attitude models." *Journal of Marketing Research* 12, no.3(1975): 265–275.

Bellezza, Silvia, Francesca Gino, and Anat Keinan. "The red sneakers effect: Inferring status and competence from signals of nonconformity." *Journal of Consumer Research* 41, no.1(2014): 35–54.

Bellezza, Silvia, Neeru Paharia, and Anat Keinan. "Conspicuous consumption of time: When busyness and lack of leisure time become a status symbol." *Journal of Consumer Research* 44, no.1 (2017): 118–138.

Benedetti, Fabrizio, Helen S. Mayberg, Tor D. Wager, Christian S.

Stohler, and Jon-Kar Zubieta. "Neurobiological mechanisms of the placebo effect." *Journal of Neuroscience* 25, no.45(2005): 10390-10402.

Berger, Jonah, Michaela Draganska, and Itamar Simonson. "The influence of product variety on brand perception and choice." *Marketing Science* 26, no.4(2007): 460-472.

Berger, Jonah, and Morgan Ward. "Subtle signals of inconspicuous consumption." *Journal of Consumer Research* 37, no.4(2010): 555-569.

Bergkvist, Lars, and Kris Qiang Zhou. "Celebrity endorsements: a literature review and research agenda." *International Journal of Advertising* 35, no.4(2016): 642-663.

Berns, Gregory S. "Price, placebo, and the brain." *Journal of Marketing Research* 42, no.4(2005): 399-400.

Berns, Gregory S., David Laibson, and George Loewenstein. "Intertemporal choice-toward an integrative framework." *Trends in Cognitive Sciences* 11, no.11(2007): 482-488.

Besson, Theo, Fanny Lalot, Nicolas Bochard, Valentin Flaudias, and Oulmann Zerhouni. "The calories underestimation of 'organic' food: Exploring the impact of implicit evaluations." *Appetite* 137 (2019): 134-144.

Bettman, James R., Deborah Roedder John, and Carol A. Scott. "Covariation assessment by consumers." *Journal of Consumer Research* 13, no.3(1986): 316-326.

Bhattacharjee, Amit, Jonah Berger, and Geeta Menon. "When identity marketing backfires: Consumer agency in identity

expression." *Journal of Consumer Research* 41, no.2 (2014):
294-309.

Bienenfeld, Laura, William Frishman, and Stephen P. Glasser. "The placebo effect in cardiovascular disease." *American Heart Journal* 132, no.6(1996): 1207-1221.

Biswas, Dipayan, Courtney Szocs, Aradhna Krishna, and Donald R. Lehmann. "Something to chew on: the effects of oral haptics on mastication, orosensory perception, and calorie estimation." *Journal of Consumer Research* 41, no.2(2014): 261-273.

Blackett, Tom, and Nick Russell. "What is co-branding?." in *Co-Branding*, pp.1-21. Palgrave Macmillan, London, 1999.

Blanco, Fernando. "Positive and negative implications of the causal illusion." *Consciousness and Cognition* 50(2017): 56-68.

Bluedorn, Allen C., Carol Felker Kaufman, and Paul M. Lane. "How many things do you like to do at once? An introduction to monochronic and polychronic time." *Academy of Management Perspectives* 6, no.4(1992): 17-26.

Bond, Michael Harris. "Culture and aggression-From context to coercion." *Personality and Social Psychology Review* 8, no.1 (2004): 62-78.

Bouchard, Thomas J., and Matthew McGue. "Familial studies of intelligence: A review." *Science* 212, no.4498(1981): 1055-1059.

Boush, David M., and Barbara Loken. "A process-tracing study of brand extension evaluation." *Journal of Marketing Research* 28, no.1(1991): 16-28.

Bretherton, Inge. "The origins of attachment theory: John Bowlby and Mary Ainsworth." *Developmental Psychology* 28, no.5 (1992): 759–775.

Brewer, Marilynn, and Ya-Ru Chen. "Where (Who) are collectives in collectivism? Toward conceptual clarification of individualism and collectivism." *Psychological Review* 114, no. 1 (2007): 133–151.

Briley, Donnel A., Michael W. Morris, and Itamar Simonson. "Reasons as carriers of culture: Dynamic versus dispositional models of cultural influence on decision making." *Journal of Consumer Research* 27, no.2 (2000): 157–178.

Broniarczyk, Susan M., and Joseph W. Alba. "The role of consumers' intuitions in inference making." *Journal of Consumer Research* 21, no.3 (1994): 393–407.

Broniarczyk, Susan M., and Joseph W. Alba. "Theory versus data in prediction and correlation tasks." *Organizational Behavior and Human Decision Processes* 57, no.1 (1994): 117–139.

Bronnenberg, Bart J., Sanjay K. Dhar, and Jean-Pierre H. Dubé. "Brand history, geography, and the persistence of brand shares." *Journal of Political Economy* 117, no.1 (2009): 87–115.

Brough, Aaron R., and Alexander Chernev. "When opposites detract: Categorical reasoning and subtractive valuations of product combinations." *Journal of Consumer Research* 39, no.2 (2012): 399–414.

Brough, Aaron R., James EB Wilkie, Jingjing Ma, Mathew S. Isaac, and David Gal. "Is eco-friendly unmanly? The green-feminine stereotype and its effect on sustainable consumption." *Journal of Consumer Research* 43, no.4(2016): 567-582.

Brown, Stephen, Robert V. Kozinets, and John F. Sherry Jr. "Teaching old brands new tricks: Retro branding and the revival of brand meaning." *Journal of Marketing* 67, no. 3 (2003): 19-33.

Bruner, Jerome S. "On perceptual readiness." *Psychological Review* 64, no.2(1957): 123-152.

Buunk, Bram, Bert Doosje, Liesbeth Jans, and Liliane Hopstaken. "Perceived reciprocity, social support, and stress at work: The role of exchange and communal orientation." *Journal of Personality and Social Psychology* 65, no.4(1993): 801-811.

Cacioppo, John T., Richard E. Petty, and Katherine J. Morris. "Semantic, evaluative, and self-referent processing: Memory, cognitive effort, and somatovisceral activity." *Psychophysiology* 22, no.4(1985): 371-384.

Cai, Fengyan, Zhiyong Yang, Robert S. Wyer Jr, and Alison Jing Xu. "The interactive effects of bitter flavor and mood on the decision to spend or save money." *Journal of Experimental Social Psychology* 70(2017): 48-58.

Cameron, James E. "A three-factor model of social identity." *Self and Identity* 3, no.3(2004): 239-262.

Campbell, Jennifer. "Self-esteem and clarity of the self-concept." *Journal of Personality and Social Psychology* 59, no.3(1990): 538-549.

Campbell, Jennifer D., Sunaina Assanand, and Adam Di Paula. "The structure of the self-concept and its relation to psychological adjustment." *Journal of Personality* 71, no.1(2003): 115-140.

Campbell, Jennifer D., and Loraine F. Lavallee. "Who am I? The role of self-concept confusion in understanding the behavior of people with low self-esteem." in *Self-Esteem*, pp. 3-20. Springer, Boston, MA, 1993.

Campbell, Jennifer, Paul Trapnell, Steven Heine, Ilana Katz, Loraine Lavallee, and Darrin Lehman. "Self-concept clarity: Measurement, personality correlates, and cultural boundaries." *Journal of Personality and Social Psychology* 70, no.1(1996): 141-156.

Cannon, Joseph P., Patricia M. Doney, Michael R. Mullen, and Kenneth J. Petersen. "Building long-term orientation in buyer-supplier relationships: The moderating role of culture." *Journal of Operations Management* 28, no.6(2010): 506-521.

Cao, Zixia, and Ruiliang Yan. "Does brand partnership create a happy marriage? The role of brand value on brand alliance outcomes of partners." *Industrial Marketing Management* 67 (2017): 148-157.

Carson, Robert C. "Interaction concepts of personality," Chicago: Aldine, 1969.

Caruso, Eugene M., Zachary C. Burns, and Benjamin A. Converse. "Slow motion increases perceived intent." *Proceedings of the National Academy of Sciences* 113, no.33(2016): 9250-9255.

Cesario, Joseph, Heidi Grant, and E. Higgins. "Regulatory fit and persuasion: Transfer from 'feeling right.'" *Journal of Personality and Social Psychology* 86, no.3(2004): 388 – 404.

Cesario, Joseph, E. Tory Higgins, and Abigail A. Scholer. "Regulatory fit and persuasion: Basic principles and remaining questions." *Social and Personality Psychology Compass* 2, no.1 (2008): 444 – 463.

Chaiken, Shelly. "Communicator physical attractiveness and persuasion." *Journal of Personality and Social Psychology* 37, no.8(1979): 1387 – 1397.

Chaiken, Shelly, and Durairaj Maheswaran. "Heuristic processing can bias systematic processing: Effects of source credibility, argument ambiguity, and task importance on attitude judgment." *Journal of Personality and Social Psychology* 66, no.3(1994): 460 – 473.

Chan, Haksin, Lisa C. Wan, and Leo YM Sin. "The contrasting effects of culture on consumer tolerance: Interpersonal face and impersonal fate." *Journal of Consumer Research* 36, no.2 (2009): 292 – 304.

Chandler, Jesse J., David Reinhard, and Norbert Schwarz. "To judge a book by its weight you need to know its content: Knowledge moderates the use of embodied cues." *Journal of Experimental Social Psychology* 48, no.4(2012): 948 – 952.

Chandler, Jesse, and Norbert Schwarz. "Use does not wear ragged the fabric of friendship: Thinking of objects as alive makes people less willing to replace them." *Journal of Consumer Psychology* 20, no.2(2010): 138 – 145.

Chandon, Pierre, and Brian Wansink. "The biasing health halos of fast-food restaurant health claims: lower calorie estimates and higher side-dish consumption intentions." *Journal of Consumer Research* 34, no.3(2007): 301-314.

Chandon, Pierre, and Nailya Ordabayeva. "Supersize in one dimension, downsize in three dimensions: Effects of spatial dimensionality on size perceptions and preferences." *Journal of Marketing Research* 46, no.6(2009): 739-753.

Chandon, Pierre. "Note on measuring brand awareness, brand image, brand equity and brand value." *Fontainebleau: Insead*, 2003.

Chang, Wei-Lun. "Roadmap of co-branding positions and strategies." *The Journal of American Academy of Business* 15, no.1(2009): 77-84.

Chaplin, Lan Nguyen, and Deborah Roedder John. "The development of self-brand connections in children and adolescents." *Journal of Consumer Research* 32, no.1(2005): 119-129.

Chen, Chao C., Xiao-Ping Chen, and James R. Meindl. "How can cooperation be fostered? The cultural effects of individualism-collectivism." *Academy of Management Review* 23, no.2(1998): 285-304.

Chen, Charlene Y., Leonard Lee, and Andy J. Yap. "Control deprivation motivates acquisition of utilitarian products." *Journal of Consumer Research* 43, no.6(2017): 1031-1047.

Chen, Fangyuan, Rocky Peng Chen, and Li Yang. "When sadness comes alive, Will it be less painful? The effects of anthropomorphic thinking on sadness regulation and consumption." *Journal of Consumer Psychology* 30, no.2(2020): 277-295.

Chen, Fangyuan, Jaideep Sengupta, and Rashmi Adaval. "Does endowing a product with life make one Feel more alive? The effect of product anthropomorphism on consumer vitality." *Journal of the Association for Consumer Research* 3, no.4(2018): 503 - 513.

Chen, Haipeng, Lisa E. Bolton, Sharon Ng, Dongwon Lee, and Dian Wang. "Culture, relationship norms, and dual entitlement." *Journal of Consumer Research* 45, no.1(2018): 1 - 20.

Chen, Hung-Bin, Shih-Shuo Yeh, and Tzung-Cheng Huan. "Nostalgic emotion, experiential value, brand image, and consumption intentions of customers of nostalgic-themed restaurants." *Journal of Business Research* 67, no.3(2014): 354 - 360.

Chen, Rocky Peng, Echo Wen Wan, and Eric Levy. "The effect of social exclusion on consumer preference for anthropomorphized brands." *Journal of Consumer Psychology* 27, no.1(2017): 23 - 34.

Cheng, Andria. "'Fair trade' becomes a fashion trend," https://www.wsj.com/articles/fair-trade-becomes-a-fashion-trend - 1436307440, 2015.

Cheng, Shirley YY, Tiffany Barnett White, and Lan Nguyen Chaplin. "The effects of self-brand connections on responses to brand failure: A new look at the consumer-brand relationship." *Journal of Consumer Psychology* 22, no.2(2012): 280 - 288.

Cheng, Yimin, Anirban Mukhopadhyay, and Patti Williams. "Smiling signals intrinsic motivation." *Journal of Consumer Research* 46, no.5(2020): 915 - 935.

Chernev, Alexander. "Context effects without a context: Attribute balance as a reason for choice." *Journal of Consumer Research* 32, no.2(2005): 213-223.

Chernev, Alexander. "Feature complementarity and assortment in choice." *Journal of Consumer Research* 31, no.4(2005): 748-759.

Chernev, Alexander. "Jack of all trades or master of one? Product differentiation and compensatory reasoning in consumer choice." *Journal of Consumer Research* 33, no.4(2007): 430-444.

Chernev, Alexander. "The dieter's paradox." *Journal of Consumer Psychology* 21, no.2(2011): 178-183.

Chernev, Alexander, and David Gal. "Categorization effects in value judgments: Averaging bias in evaluating combinations of vices and virtues." *Journal of Marketing Research* 47, no.4(2010): 738-747.

Chernev, Alexander, and Gregory S. Carpenter. "The role of market efficiency intuitions in consumer choice: A case of compensatory inferences." *Journal of Marketing Research* 38, no.3(2001): 349-361.

Chernev, Alexander, Ryan Hamilton, and David Gal. "Competing for consumer identity: Limits to self-expression and the perils of lifestyle branding." *Journal of Marketing* 75, no.3(2011): 66-82.

Chernev, Alexander, and Sean Blair. "Doing well by doing good: The benevolent halo of corporate social responsibility." *Journal of Consumer Research* 41, no.6(2015): 1412-1425.

Cheung, Elaine, and Joseph Mikels. "I'm feeling lucky: The

relationship between affect and risk-seeking in the framing effect." *Emotion* 11, no.4(2011): 852-859.

Chiaburu, Dan S., Sophia V. Marinova, and Audrey S. Lim. "Helping and proactive extra-role behaviors: The influence of motives, goal orientation, and social context." *Personality and Individual Differences* 43, no.8(2007): 2282-2293.

Cho, Eunice Kim, Uzma Khan, and Ravi Dhar. "Comparing apples to apples or apples to oranges: The role of mental representation in choice difficulty." *Journal of Marketing Research* 50, no.4 (2013): 505-516.

Choi, Incheol, Minkyung Koo, and Jong An Choi. "Individual differences in analytic versus holistic thinking." *Personality and Social Psychology Bulletin* 33, no.5(2007): 691-705.

Choi, Sejung Marina, and Nora J. Rifon. "It is a match: The impact of congruence between celebrity image and consumer ideal self on endorsement effectiveness." *Psychology & Marketing* 29, no.9 (2012): 639-650.

Chua, Roy YJ, Yannig Roth, and Jean-François Lemoine. "The impact of culture on creativity: How cultural tightness and cultural distance affect global innovation crowdsourcing work." *Administrative Science Quarterly* 60, no.2(2015): 189-227.

Chugani, Sunaina K., Julie R. Irwin, and Joseph P. Redden. "Happily ever after: The effect of identity-consistency on product satiation." *Journal of Consumer Research* 42, no.4(2015): 564-577.

Cian, Luca, Chiara Longoni, and Aradhna Krishna. "Advertising a desired change: When process simulation fosters (vs. hinders) credibility and persuasion." *Journal of Marketing Research* 57, no.3(2020): 489 – 508.

Cislak, Aleksandra, and Bogdan Wojciszke. "Agency and communion are inferred from actions serving interests of self or others." *European Journal of Social Psychology* 38, no.7(2008): 1103 – 1110.

Clark, Margaret S. "Evidence for the effectiveness of manipulations of communal and exchange relationships." *Personality and Social Psychology Bulletin* 12, no.4(1986): 414 – 425.

Clark, Margaret S. "Record keeping in two types of relationships." *Journal of Personality and Social Psychology* 47, no.3 (1984): 549 – 557.

Clark, Margaret S., and Barbara Waddell. "Perceptions of exploitation in communal and exchange relationships." *Journal of Social and Personal Relationships* 2, no.4(1985): 403 – 418.

Clark, Margaret S., and Judson Mills. "Interpersonal attraction in exchange and communal relationships." *Journal of Personality and Social Psychology* 37, no.1(1979): 12 – 24.

Clark, Margaret S., and Judson Mills. "The difference between communal and exchange relationships: What it is and is not." *Personality and Social Psychology Bulletin* 19, no.6 (1993): 684 – 691.

Clark, Margaret S., Judson Mills, and Martha Powell. "Keeping track of needs in communal and exchange relationships." *Journal of Personality and Social Psychology* 51, no.2(1986): 333 – 338.

Clark, Margaret S., Parastu Dubash, and Judson Mills. "Interest in another's consideration of one's needs in communal and exchange relationships." *Journal of Experimental Social Psychology* 34, no. 3(1998): 246-264.

Clifton, Jim. http://www.gallup.com/businessjournal/180431/american-entrepreneurship-dead-alive.aspx, 2015.

Colagiuri, Ben, Lieven A. Schenk, Michael D. Kessler, Susan G. Dorsey, and Luana Colloca. "The placebo effect: from concepts to genes." *Neuroscience* 307(2015): 171-190.

Cole, Catherine A., and Siva K. Balasubramanian. "Age differences in consumers' search for information: Public policy implications." *Journal of Consumer Research* 20, no.1(1993): 157-169.

Collins, Allan, and Elizabeth Loftus. "A spreading-activation theory of semantic processing." *Psychological Review* 82, no.6(1975): 407-428.

Coltrane, Scott. "Father-child relationships and the status of women: A cross-cultural study." *American Journal of Sociology* 93, no.5 (1988): 1060-1095.

Consiglio, Irene, and Stijn MJ Van Osselaer. "The devil you know: Self-esteem and switching responses to poor service." *Journal of Consumer Research* 46, no.3(2019): 590-605.

Constantinople, Anne. "Masculinity-femininity: An exception to a famous dictum?." *Psychological Bulletin* 80, no. 5 (1973): 389-407.

Conway, Michael, M. Pizzamiglio, and Lauren Mount. "Status, communality, and agency: Implications for stereotypes of gender and other groups." *Journal of Personality and Social Psychology* 71, no.1(1996): 25 – 38.

Cooper, William. "Ubiquitous halo." *Psychological Bulletin* 90, no.2 (1981): 218 – 244.

Cornil, Yann, and Pierre Chandon. "Pleasure as a substitute for size: How multisensory imagery can make people happier with smaller food portions." *Journal of Marketing Research* 53, no.5(2016): 847 – 864.

Cornil, Yann, Pierre Chandon, and Aradhna Krishna. "Does red bull give wings to vodka? Placebo effects of marketing labels on perceived intoxication and risky attitudes and behaviors." *Journal of Consumer Psychology* 27, no.4(2017): 456 – 465.

Cowan, Benjamin R., Holly P. Branigan, Mateo Obregón, Enas Bugis, and Russell Beale. "Voice anthropomorphism, interlocutor modelling and alignment effects on syntactic choices in human-computer dialogue." *International Journal of Human-Computer Studies* 83(2015): 27 – 42.

Cowen, Amanda, and Nicole Montgomery. "To be or not to be sorry? How CEO gender impacts the effectiveness of organizational apologies." *Journal of Applied Psychology* 105, no.2(2020): 196 – 208.

Crolic, Cammy, Yanmei Zheng, JoAndrea Hoegg, and Joseph W. Alba. "The influence of product aesthetics on consumer inference making." *Journal of the Association for Consumer Research* 4, no.4(2019): 398 – 408.

Cronley, Maria L., Steven S. Posavac, Tracy Meyer, Frank R.

Kardes, and James J. Kellaris. "A selective hypothesis testing perspective on price-quality inference and inference-based choice." *Journal of Consumer Psychology* 15, no. 2 (2005): 159–169.

Cross, Susan, Pamela Bacon, and Michael Morris. "The relational-interdependent self-construal and relationships." *Journal of Personality and Social Psychology* 78, no.4(2000): 791–808.

Crowe, Ellen, and E. Tory Higgins. "Regulatory focus and strategic inclinations: Promotion and prevention in decision-making." *Organizational Behavior and Human Decision Processes* 69, no.2 (1997): 117–132.

Cuddy, Amy JC, Susan T. Fiske, and Peter Glick. "When professionals become mothers, warmth doesn't cut the ice." *Journal of Social Issues* 60, no.4(2004): 701–718.

Cunha Jr, Marcus, Chris Janiszewski, and Juliano Laran. "Protection of prior learning in complex consumer learning environments." *Journal of Consumer Research* 34, no.6(2008): 850–864.

Cunha Jr, Marcus, and Jeffrey D. Shulman. "Assimilation and contrast in price evaluations." *Journal of Consumer Research* 37, no.5(2011): 822–835.

Cunha Jr, Marcus, and Juliano Laran. "Asymmetries in the sequential learning of brand associations: Implications for the early entrant advantage." *Journal of Consumer Research* 35, no.5 (2009): 788–799.

Cunha Jr, Marcus, Mark R. Forehand, and Justin W. Angle. "Riding coattails: When co-branding helps versus hurts less-known brands." *Journal of Consumer Research* 41, no.5(2015): 1284 – 1300.

Cutright, Keisha M., and Adriana Samper. "Doing it the hard way: How low control drives preferences for high-effort products and services." *Journal of Consumer Research* 41, no.3(2014): 730 – 745.

Cutright, Keisha M., James R. Bettman, and Gavan J. Fitzsimons. "Putting brands in their place: How a lack of control keeps brands contained." *Journal of Marketing Research* 50, no. 3 (2013): 365 – 377.

Dacin, Peter A., and Daniel C. Smith. "The effect of brand portfolio characteristics on consumer evaluations of brand extensions." *Journal of Marketing Research* 31, no.2(1994): 229 – 242.

Dai, Xianchi, and Christopher K. Hsee. "Wish versus worry: Ownership effects on motivated judgment." *Journal of Marketing Research* 50, no.2(2013): 207 – 215.

Darley, William K., and Robert E. Smith. "Gender differences in information processing strategies: An empirical test of the selectivity model in advertising response." *Journal of Advertising* 24, no.1(1995): 41 – 56.

Dalton, Amy N., and Li Huang. "Motivated forgetting in response to social identity threat." *Journal of Consumer Research* 40, no.6 (2014): 1017 – 1038.

De Mooij, Marieke, and Geert Hofstede. "Convergence and divergence in consumer behavior: implications for international retailing." *Journal of Retailing* 78, no.1(2002): 61 – 69.

De Mooij, Marieke, and Geert Hofstede. "Cross-cultural consumer behavior: A review of research findings." *Journal of International Consumer Marketing* 23, no.3-4(2011): 181-192.

De Mooij, Marieke, and Geert Hofstede. "The Hofstede model: Applications to global branding and advertising strategy and research." *International Journal of Advertising* 29, no.1(2010): 85-110.

De Morree, Helma M., Christoph Klein, and Samuele M. Marcora. "Perception of effort reflects central motor command during movement execution." *Psychophysiology* 49, no.9(2012): 1242-1253.

Decety, Jean, and Julie Grèzes. "The power of simulation: Imagining one's own and other's behavior." *Brain Research* 1079, no.1 (2006): 4-14.

Demanet, Jelle, Frederick Verbruggen, Baptist Liefooghe, and André Vandierendonck. "Voluntary task switching under load: Contribution of top-down and bottom-up factors in goal-directed behavior." *Psychonomic Bulletin & Review* 17, no.3 (2010): 387-393.

Deng, Xiaoyan, and Barbara E. Kahn. "Is your product on the right side? The 'location effect' on perceived product heaviness and package evaluation." *Journal of Marketing Research* 46, no.6 (2009): 725-738.

Denke, Claudia, Michael Rotte, Hans-Jochen Heinze, and Michael Schaefer. "Lying and the subsequent desire for toothpaste: activity in the somatosensory cortex predicts embodiment of the moral-purity metaphor." *Cerebral Cortex* 26, no.2(2016): 477 - 484.

Desai, Kalpesh Kaushik, and Kevin Lane Keller. "The effects of ingredient branding strategies on host brand extendibility." *Journal of Marketing* 66, no.1(2002): 73 - 93.

Deval, Hélène, Susan P. Mantel, Frank R. Kardes, and Steven S. Posavac. "How naive theories drive opposing inferences from the same information." *Journal of Consumer Research* 39, no. 6 (2013): 1185 - 1201.

Dick, Alan, Dipankar Chakravarti, and Gabriel Biehal. "Memory-based inferences during consumer choice." *Journal of Consumer Research* 17, no.1(1990): 82 - 93.

Diehl, Manfred, Stephanie K. Owen, and Lise M. Youngblade. "Agency and communion attributes in adults' spontaneous self-representations." *International Journal of Behavioral Development* 28, no.1(2004): 1 - 15.

Dijkstra, Pieternel, and Dick PH Barelds. "Do people know what they want: A similar or complementary partner?." *Evolutionary Psychology* 6, no.4(2008): 595 - 602.

Ding, Cherng G., and Timmy H. Tseng. "On the relationships among brand experience, hedonic emotions, and brand equity." *European Journal of Marketing* 49, no.7 - 8(2015): 994 - 1015.

Ding, Ying, Echo Wen Wan, and Jing Xu. "The impact of identity breadth on consumer preference for advanced products." *Journal of Consumer Psychology* 27, no.2(2017): 231 - 244.

Djordjevic, Jelena, R. J. Zatorre, and M. Jones-Gotman. "Odor-induced changes in taste perception." *Experimental Brain Research* 159, no.3(2004): 405-408.

Druckman, James N., and Rose McDermott. "Emotion and the framing of risky choice." *Political Behavior* 30, no.3(2008): 297-321.

Dubois, David, Derek D. Rucker, and Adam D. Galinsky. "Dynamics of communicator and audience power: The persuasiveness of competence versus warmth." *Journal of Consumer Research* 43, no.1(2016): 68-85.

Duclos, Rod, Echo Wen Wan, and Yuwei Jiang. "Show me the honey! Effects of social exclusion on financial risk-taking." *Journal of Consumer Research* 40, no.1(2013): 122-135.

Duffy, Elizabeth. "The concept of energy mobilization." *Psychological Review* 58, no.1(1951): 30-40.

Dufner, Michael, Daniel Leising, and Jochen E. Gebauer. "Which basic rules underlie social judgments? Agency follows a zero-sum principle and communion follows a non-zero-sum principle." *Personality and Social Psychology Bulletin* 42, no.5(2016): 677-687.

Dunn, Lea, and JoAndrea Hoegg. "The impact of fear on emotional brand attachment." *Journal of Consumer Research* 41, no.1(2014): 152-168.

Dunning, David, and Emily Balcetis. "Wishful seeing: How preferences shape visual perception." *Current Directions in Psychological Science* 22, no.1(2013): 33-37.

Durante, Federica, Courtney Bearns Tablante, and Susan T. Fiske.

"Poor but warm, rich but cold (and competent): Social classes in the stereotype content model." *Journal of Social Issues* 73, no. 1 (2017): 138–157.

Dwivedi, Abhishek, Bill Merrilees, and Arthur Sweeney. "Brand extension feedback effects: A holistic framework." *Journal of Brand Management* 17, no.5 (2010): 328–342.

Eddy, Timothy J., Gordon G. Gallup Jr, and Daniel J. Povinelli. "Attribution of cognitive states to animals: anthropomorphism in comparative perspective." *Journal of Social Issues* 49, no. 1 (1993): 87–101.

Eisend, Martin, and Tobias Langner. "Immediate and delayed advertising effects of celebrity endorsers' attractiveness and expertise." *International Journal of Advertising* 29, no.4 (2010): 527–546.

Elder, Ryan S., and Aradhna Krishna. "The effects of advertising copy on sensory thoughts and perceived taste." *Journal of Consumer Research* 36, no.5 (2010): 748–756.

Elder, Ryan S. and Aradhna Krishna (2012), "The 'visual depiction effect' in advertising: Facilitating embodied mental simulation through product orientation." *Journal of Consumer Research*, 38 (6), 988–1003.

Elliot, Andrew J., and Martin V. Covington. "Approach and avoidance motivation." *Educational Psychology Review* 13, no.2 (2001): 73–92.

Elliot, Andrew, and Todd Thrash. "Approach-avoidance motivation in personality: Approach and avoidance temperaments and goals."

Journal of Personality and Social Psychology 82, no.5 (2002): 804 - 818.

Epley, Nicholas, Adam Waytz, and John Cacioppo. "On seeing human: A three-factor theory of anthropomorphism." *Psychological Review* 114, no.4 (2007): 864 - 886.

Epley, Nicholas, Adam Waytz, Scott Akalis, and John T. Cacioppo. "When we need a human: Motivational determinants of anthropomorphism." *Social Cognition* 26, no.2 (2008): 143 - 155.

Epley, Nicholas, Scott Akalis, Adam Waytz, and John T. Cacioppo. "Creating social connection through inferential reproduction: Loneliness and perceived agency in gadgets, gods, and greyhounds." *Psychological Science* 19, no.2 (2008): 114 - 120.

Erdem, Tülin, Joffre Swait, and Ana Valenzuela. "Brands as signals: A cross-country validation study." *Journal of Marketing* 70, no.1 (2006): 34 - 49.

Erdogan, B. Zafer. "Celebrity endorsement: A literature review." *Journal of Marketing Management* 15, no.4 (1999): 291 - 314.

Ersner-Hershfield, Hal, G. Elliott Wimmer, and Brian Knutson. "Saving for the future self: Neural measures of future self-continuity predict temporal discounting." *Social Cognitive and Affective Neuroscience* 4, no.1 (2009): 85 - 92.

Escalas, Jennifer Edson. "Advertising narratives: What are they and how do they work." *Representing Consumers: Voices, Views, and Visions* 1 (1998): 267 - 289.

Escalas, Jennifer Edson. "Imagine yourself in the product: Mental simulation, narrative transportation, and persuasion." *Journal of Advertising* 33, no.2(2004): 37-48.

Escalas, Jennifer Edson. "Narrative processing: Building consumer connections to brands." *Journal of Consumer Psychology* 14, no.1-2(2004): 168-180.

Escalas, Jennifer Edson, and James R. Bettman. "Connecting with celebrities: Celebrity endorsement, brand meaning, and self-brand connections." *Journal of Marketing Research* 13, no.3 (2009): 339-348.

Escalas, Jennifer Edson, and James R. Bettman. "Self-construal, reference groups, and brand meaning." *Journal of Consumer Research* 32, no.3(2005): 378-389.

Escalas, Jennifer Edson and James R. Bettman, "Using narratives and autobiographical memories to discern motives," in *The Why of Consumption: Perspectives on Consumer Motives, Goals, and Desires*, ed. S. Ratneshwar, David Glen Mick, and Cynthia Huffman, New York: Routledge, 237-258, 2000

Escalas, Jennifer Edson, and James R. Bettman. "You are what they eat: The influence of reference groups on consumers' connections to brands." *Journal of Consumer Psychology* 13, no.3(2003): 339-348.

Fan, Linying, Xueni Li, and Yuwei Jiang. "Room for opportunity: Resource scarcity increases attractiveness of range marketing offers." *Journal of Consumer Research* 46, no.1(2019): 82-98.

Fang, Xiang, Surendra Singh, and Rohini Ahluwalia. "An examination of different explanations for the mere exposure effect." *Journal of Consumer Research* 34, no.1 (2007): 97 – 103.

Ferraro, Rosellina, Amna Kirmani, and Ted Matherly. "Look at me! Look at me! Conspicuous brand usage, self-brand connection, and dilution." *Journal of Marketing Research* 50, no.4 (2013): 477 – 488.

Figlio, David, Paola Giuliano, Umut Özek, and Paola Sapienza. "Long-term orientation and educational performance." *American Economic Journal: Economic Policy* 11, no.4 (2019): 272 – 309.

Fishbach, Ayelet, and James Shah. "Self-control in action: Implicit dispositions toward goals and away from temptations." *Journal of Personality and Social Psychology* 90, no.5 (2006): 820 – 832.

Fishbach, Ayelet, and Yaacov Trope. "The substitutability of external control and self-control." *Journal of Experimental Social Psychology* 41, no.3 (2005): 256 – 270.

Fishbein, Michael B. http://www.huffingtonpost.com/michael-b-fishbein/how-startups-and-large-co_b_3944433.html, 2013.

Fiske, Alan P., Shinobu Kitayama, Hazel R. Markus, and Richard E. Nisbett. "The cultural matrix of social psychology," in *The Handbook of Social Psychology*, 4th. ed., ed. Daniel T. Gilbert, Susan T. Fiske, and Gardner Lindzey, New York: McGraw-Hill, 915 – 981, 1998.

Fiske, Susan T., Amy JC. Cuddy, and Peter Glick. "Universal dimensions of social cognition: Warmth and competence." *Trends in Cognitive Sciences* 11, no.2 (2007): 77 – 83.

Fiske, Susan T., Amy JC. Cuddy, Peter Glick, and Jun Xu. "A model of (often mixed) stereotype content: Competence and warmth respectively follow from perceived status and competition." *Journal of Personality and Social Psychology* 82, no.6(2002): 878–902.

Fiske, Susan T., Juan Xu, Amy JC. Cuddy, and Peter Glick. "(Dis) respecting versus (dis) liking: Status and interdependence predict ambivalent stereotypes of competence and warmth." *Journal of Social Issues* 55, no.3(1999): 473–489.

Flammer, Caroline, and Pratima Bansal. "Does a long-term orientation create value? Evidence from a regression discontinuity." *Strategic Management Journal* 38, no.9(2017): 1827–1847.

Foard, Christopher, and Deborah Kemler. "Holistic and analytic modes of processing: The multiple determinants of perceptual analysis." *Journal of Experimental Psychology: General* 113, no.1(1984): 94–111.

Ford, Gary T., and Ruth Ann Smith. "Inferential beliefs in consumer evaluations: An assessment of alternative processing strategies." *Journal of Consumer Research* 14, no.3(1987): 363–371.

Fournier, Susan. "Consumers and their brands: Developing relationship theory in consumer research." *Journal of Consumer Research* 24, no.4(1998): 343–373.

Fournier, Susan M. "Lessons learned about consumers' relationships with their brands," in *Handbook of Brand Relationships*, ed. D. J. MacInnis, C. W. Park, and J. R. Priester, Armonk, NY: M. E. Sharpe, 5–23, 2009.

Fournier, Susan, and Claudio Alvarez. "Brands as relationship partners: Warmth, competence, and in-between." *Journal of Consumer Psychology* 22, no.2(2012): 177-185.

Franke, Richard H., Geert Hofstede, and Michael H. Bond. "Cultural roots of economic performance: A research notea." *Strategic Management Journal* 12, no. S1(1991): 165-173.

Freeman, John, and Jerome S. Engel. "Models of innovation: Startups and mature corporations." *California Management Review* 50, no. 1(2007): 94-119.

Freund, Tallie, Arie W. Kruglanski, and Avivit Shpitzajzen. "The freezing and unfreezing of impressional primacy: Effects of the need for structure and the fear of invalidity." *Personality and Social Psychology Bulletin* 11, no.4(1985): 479-487.

Fujita, Kentaro. "Seeing the forest beyond the trees: A construal-level approach to self-control." *Social and Personality Psychology Compass* 2, no.3(2008): 1475-1496.

Fujita, Kentaro, and H. Anna Han. "Moving beyond deliberative control of impulses: The effect of construal levels on evaluative associations in self-control conflicts." *Psychological Science* 20, no.7(2009): 799-804.

Fujita, Kentaro, and Jessica J. Carnevale. "Transcending temptation through abstraction: The role of construal level in self-control." *Current Directions in Psychological Science* 21, no. 4 (2012): 248-252.

Fujita, Kentaro, and Joseph C. Roberts. "Promoting prospective self-control through abstraction." *Journal of Experimental Social*

Psychology 46, no.6(2010): 1049-1054.

Fujita, Kentaro, Yaacov Trope, Nira Liberman, and Maya Levin-Sagi. "Construal levels and self-control." *Journal of Personality and Social Psychology* 90, no.3(2006): 351-367.

Galak, Jeff, Joseph P. Redden, and Justin Kruger. "Variety amnesia: Recalling past variety can accelerate recovery from satiation." *Journal of Consumer Research* 36, no.4(2009): 575-584.

Gallese, Vittorio. "Embodied simulation: From neurons to phenomenal experience." *Phenomenology and the Cognitive Sciences* 4, no.1(2005): 23-48.

Gallese, Vittorio, and Corrado Sinigaglia. "What is so special about embodied simulation?." *Trends in Cognitive Sciences* 15, no.11(2011): 512-519.

Gallese, Vittorio, and Fausto Caruana. "Embodied simulation: beyond the expression/experience dualism of emotions." *Trends in Cognitive Sciences* 20, no.6(2016): 397-398.

Gallese, Vittorio, and George Lakoff. "The brain's concepts: The role of the sensory-motor system in conceptual knowledge." *Cognitive Neuropsychology* 22, no.3-4(2005): 455-479.

Gandevia, Simon C. "Roles for perceived voluntary motor commands in motor control." *Trends in Neurosciences* 10, no.2(1987): 81-85.

Gandevia, Simon C. and Douglas I. McCloskey. "Effects of related sensory inputs on motor performances in man studied through changes in perceived heaviness." *The Journal of physiology* 272, no.3(1977): 653-672.

Gao, Baojun, Xiangge Li, Shan Liu, and Debin Fang. "How power distance affects online hotel ratings: The positive moderating roles of hotel chain and reviewers' travel experience." *Tourism Management* 65(2018): 176 – 186.

Gao, Huachao, Karen Page Winterich, and Yinlong Zhang. "All that glitters is not gold: How others' status influences the effect of power distance belief on status consumption." *Journal of Consumer Research* 43, no.2(2016): 265 – 281.

Gao, Huachao, Vikas Mittal, and Yinlong Zhang. "The differential effect of local-global identity among males and females: The case of price sensitivity." *Journal of Marketing Research* 57, no.1 (2020): 173 – 191.

Gao, Huachao, Yinlong Zhang, and Vikas Mittal. "How does local-global identity affect price sensitivity?." *Journal of Marketing* 81, no.3(2017): 62 – 79.

Gaustad, Tarje, Bendik M. Samuelsen, Luk Warlop, and Gavan J. Fitzsimons. "The perils of self-brand connections: Consumer response to changes in brand meaning." *Psychology & Marketing* 35, no.11(2018): 818 – 829.

Gebauer, Jochen E., Jenny Wagner, Constantine Sedikides, and Wiebke Neberich. "Agency-communion and self-esteem relations are moderated by culture, religiosity, age, and sex: Evidence for the "self-centrality breeds self-enhancement" principle." *Journal of Personality* 81, no.3(2013): 261 – 275.

Gelfand, Michele J. "Culture's constraints: International differences in the strength of social norms." *Current Directions in Psychological*

Science 21, no.6(2012): 420 – 424.

Gelfand, Michele J. "Universal and culture-specific patterns of tightness-looseness across the 31 Chinese provinces." *Proceedings of the National Academy of Sciences* 116, no.14(2019): 6522 – 6524.

Gelfand, Michele J., Harry C. Triandis, and Darius K-S. Chan. "Individualism versus collectivism or versus authoritarianism?." *European Journal of Social Psychology* 26, no.3(1996): 397 – 410.

Gelfand, Michele J., Jana L. Raver, Lisa Nishii, Lisa M. Leslie, Janetta Lun, Beng Chong Lim, Lili Duan et al. "Differences between tight and loose cultures: A 33 – nation study." *Science* 332, no.6033(2011): 1100 – 1104.

Gelfand, Michele J., Ren Li, and Sarah Gordon. "Tightness-looseness and consumer behavior: The road ahead." *Journal of Consumer Psychology* 27, no.3(2017): 405 – 407.

George, Jennifer M., and Erik Dane. "Affect, emotion, and decision making." *Organizational Behavior and Human Decision Processes* 136(2016): 47 – 55.

Germani, Alessandro, Livia Buratta, Elisa Delvecchio, and Claudia Mazzeschi. "Emerging adults and COVID – 19: the role of individualism-collectivism on perceived risks and psychological maladjustment." *International Journal of Environmental Research and Public Health* 17, no.10(2020): 1 – 15.

Gibbs, Raymond W., Jr. (2006), "Embodiment and cognitive science," New York: Cambridge University Press.

Gilovich, Thomas, Dale Griffin, and Daniel Kahneman, eds. (2002), "Heuristics and biases: The psychology of intuitive judgment," Cambridge: Cambridge University Press.

Gneezy, Ayelet, Uri Gneezy, and Dominique Olié Lauga. "A reference-dependent model of the price-quality heuristic." *Journal of Marketing Research* 51, no.2(2014): 153 - 164.

Goenka, Shreyans, and Manoj Thomas. "The malleable morality of conspicuous consumption." *Journal of Personality and Social Psychology* 118, no.3(2020): 562 - 583.

Golossenko, Artyom, Kishore Gopalakrishna Pillai, and Lukman Aroean. "Seeing brands as humans: Development and validation of a brand anthropomorphism scale." *International Journal of Research in Marketing* 37, no.4(2020): 737 - 755.

González, Julio, Alfonso Barros-Loscertales, Friedemann Pulvermüller, Vanessa Meseguer, Ana Sanjuán, Vicente Belloch, and César Ávila. "Reading cinnamon activates olfactory brain regions." *Neuroimage* 32, no.2(2006): 906 - 912.

Goodman, Joseph K., and Caglar Irmak. "Having versus consuming: failure to estimate usage frequency makes consumers prefer multifeature products." *Journal of Marketing Research* 50, no.1 (2013): 44 - 54.

Gorn, Gerald J., Yuwei Jiang, and Gita Venkataramani Johar. "Babyfaces, trait inferences, and company evaluations in a public relations crisis." *Journal of Consumer Research* 35, no.1 (2008): 36 - 49.

Green, Leonard, Joel Myerson, David Lichtman, Suzanne Rosen, and

Astrid Fry. "Temporal discounting in choice between delayed rewards: The role of age and income." *Psychology and Aging* 11, no.1(1996): 79–84.

Green, Leonard, Joel Myerson, and Pawel Ostaszewski. "Discounting of delayed rewards across the life span: age differences in individual discounting functions." *Behavioural Processes* 46, no.1 (1999): 89–96.

Greenaway, Katharine H., Katherine R. Storrs, Michael C. Philipp, Winnifred R. Louis, Matthew J. Hornsey, and Kathleen D. Vohs. "Loss of control stimulates approach motivation." *Journal of Experimental Social Psychology* 56(2015): 235–241.

Greenfield, Patricia M. "Three approaches to the psychology of culture: Where do they come from? Where can they go?." *Asian Journal of Social Psychology* 3, no.3(2000): 223–240.

Grewal, Lauren, and Andrew T. Stephen. "In mobile we trust: The effects of mobile versus nonmobile reviews on consumer purchase intentions." *Journal of Marketing Research* 56, no.5(2019): 791–808.

Grohmann, Bianca. "Gender dimensions of brand personality." *Journal of Marketing Research* 46, no.1(2009): 105–119.

Grote, Nancy K., and Margaret S. Clark. "Distributive justice norms and family work: What is perceived as ideal, what is applied, and what predicts perceived fairness?." *Social Justice Research* 11, no.3(1998): 243–269.

Guiltinan, Joseph P. "The price bundling of services: A normative framework." *Journal of Marketing* 51, no.2(1987): 74–85.

Gunasti, Kunter, and William T. Ross. "How inferences about missing attributes decrease the tendency to defer choice and increase purchase probability." *Journal of Consumer Research* 35, no.5(2009): 823–837.

Gunia, Brian, Jeanne Brett, Amit Nandkeolyar, and Dishan Kamdar. "Paying a Price: Culture, Trust, and Negotiation Consequences." *Journal of Applied Psychology* 96, no.4(2011): 774–789.

Gupta, Tanvi, and Henrik Hagtvedt. "Safe together, vulnerable apart: How interstitial space in text logos impacts brand attitudes in tight versus loose cultures." *Journal of Consumer Research* (2021): forthcoming.

Gürhan-Canli, Zeynep, and Durairaj Maheswaran. "The effects of extensions on brand name dilution and enhancement." *Journal of Marketing Research* 35, no.4(1998): 464–473.

Haase, Janina, and Klaus-Peter Wiedmann. "The sensory perception item set (SPI): An exploratory effort to develop a holistic scale for sensory marketing." *Psychology & Marketing* 35, no.10 (2018): 727–739.

Hadjicharalambous, Costas. "A unified framework for evaluating brand alliances and cobranding strategies: implications and future directions." *Academy of Marketing Studies Journal* 17, no.2 (2013): 13–26.

Hagtvedt, Henrik, and S. Adam Brasel. "Color saturation increases perceived product size." *Journal of Consumer Research* 44, no.2 (2017): 396–413.

Hall, Stuart. "Culture, community, nation." *Cultural Studies* 7, no.3

(1993): 349-363.

Hamerman, Eric J., and Gita V. Johar. "Conditioned superstition: Desire for control and consumer brand preferences." *Journal of Consumer Research* 40, no.3(2013): 428-443.

Hamilton, Ryan, and Alexander Chernev. "Low prices are just the beginning: Price image in retail management." *Journal of Marketing* 77, no.6(2013): 1-20.

Han, DaHee, Ashok K. Lalwani, and Adam Duhachek. "Power distance belief, power, and charitable giving." *Journal of Consumer Research* 44, no.1(2017): 182-195.

Han, Kyuhong, Jihye Jung, Vikas Mittal, Jinyong Daniel Zyung, and Hajo Adam. "Political identity and financial risk taking: Insights from social dominance orientation." *Journal of Marketing Research* 56, no.4(2019): 581-601.

Hardisty, David, and Elke Weber. "Discounting future green: Money versus the environment." *Journal of Experimental Psychology: General* 138, no.3(2009): 329-340.

Hardisty, David J., and Jeffrey Pfeffer. "Intertemporal uncertainty avoidance: When the future is uncertain, people prefer the present, and when the present is uncertain, people prefer the future." *Management Science* 63, no.2(2017): 519-527.

Hare, Todd A., Colin F. Camerer, and Antonio Rangel. "Self-control in decision-making involves modulation of the vmPFC valuation system." *Science* 324, no.5927(2009): 646-648.

Harrigan, Paul, Uwana Evers, Morgan P. Miles, and Tim Daly. "Customer engagement and the relationship between involvement, engagement, self-brand connection and brand usage intent." *Journal of Business Research* 88(2018): 388 – 396.

Harrington, Jesse R., and Michele J. Gelfand. "Tightness-looseness across the 50 united states." *Proceedings of the National Academy of Sciences* 111, no.22(2014): 7990 – 7995.

Hasegawa, Shohei, Nobuhiko Terui, and Greg M. Allenby. "Dynamic brand satiation." *Journal of Marketing Research* 49, no. 6 (2012): 842 – 853.

Haslam, Nick, Brock Bastian, and Melanie Bissett. "Essentialist beliefs about personality and their implications." *Personality and Social Psychology Bulletin* 30, no.12(2004): 1661 – 1673.

Hassan, Louise M., Edward Shiu, and Gianfranco Walsh. "A multi-country assessment of the long-term orientation scale." *International Marketing Review* 28, no.1(2011): 81 – 101.

Hastie, Reid. "Social inference." *Annual Review of Psychology* 34, no.1(1983): 511 – 542.

Haushofer, Johannes, and Ernst Fehr. "On the psychology of poverty." *Science* 344, no.6186(2014): 862 – 867.

Haws, Kelly L., Rebecca Walker Reczek, and Kevin L. Sample. "Healthy diets make empty wallets: The healthy = expensive intuition." *Journal of Consumer Research* 43, no.6(2017): 992 – 1007.

He, Stephen X., and Samuel D. Bond. "Why is the crowd divided? Attribution for dispersion in online word of mouth." *Journal of Consumer Research* 41, no.6(2015): 1509 – 1527.

Heath, Robert, David Brandt, and Agnes Nairn. "Brand relationships:

Strengthened by emotion, weakened by attention." *Journal of Advertising Research* 46, no.4(2006): 410-419.

Helgeson, Vicki. "Relation of agency and communion to well-being: Evidence and potential explanations." *Psychological Bulletin* 116, no.3(1994): 412-428.

Helgeson, Vicki S., and Heidi L. Fritz. "The implications of unmitigated agency and unmitigated communion for domains of problem behavior." *Journal of Personality* 68, no.6(2000): 1031-1057.

Helmig, Bernd, Jan-Alexander Huber, and Peter Leeflang. "Explaining behavioural intentions toward co-branded products." *Journal of Marketing Management* 23, no.3-4(2007): 285-304.

Henderson, Vani R., Michael Hennessy, Daniel W. Barrett, Brenda Curtis, Marci McCoy-Roth, Nicole Trentacoste, and Martin Fishbein. "When risky is attractive: sensation seeking and romantic partner selection." *Personality and Individual Differences* 38, no.2(2005): 311-325.

Herbert, Beate M., and Olga Pollatos. "The body in the mind: on the relationship between interoception and embodiment." *Topics in Cognitive Science* 4, no.4(2012): 692-704.

Hershfield, Hal E. "Future self-continuity: how conceptions of the future self transform intertemporal choice." *Annals of the New York Academy of Sciences* 1235, no.1(2011): 30-43.

Hershfield, Hal E., Daniel G. Goldstein, William F. Sharpe, Jesse Fox, Leo Yeykelis, Laura L. Carstensen, and Jeremy N.

Bailenson. "Increasing saving behavior through age-progressed renderings of the future self." *Journal of Marketing Research* 48, no. SPL (2011): S23 - S37.

Hershfield, Hal E., Taya R. Cohen, and Leigh Thompson. "Short horizons and tempting situations: Lack of continuity to our future selves leads to unethical decision making and behavior." *Organizational Behavior and Human Decision Processes* 117, no.2 (2012): 298 - 310.

Hess, Alexandra Claudia, and Valentyna Melnyk. "Pink or blue? The impact of gender cues on brand perceptions." *European Journal of Marketing* 50, no.9(2016): 1550 - 1574.

Higgins, E. Tory. "Knowledge activation: Accessibility, applicability, and salience," in *Social Psychology: Handbook of Basic Principles*, ed. E. Tory Higgins and Arie Kruglanski, New York: Guilford, 133 - 168, 1996.

Higgins, E. Tory. "Promotion and prevention: Regulatory focus as a motivational principle." in *Advances in Experimental Social Psychology*, vol.30, pp.1 - 46. Academic Press, 1998.

Hirschman, Elizabeth C. "Innovativeness, novelty seeking, and consumer creativity." *Journal of Consumer Research* 7, no.3 (1980): 283 - 295.

Hitlin, Steven. "Values as the core of personal identity: Drawing links between two theories of self." *Social Psychology Quarterly* (2003): 118 - 137.

Hoch, Stephen J., and George F. Loewenstein. "Time-inconsistent preferences and consumer self-control." *Journal of Consumer*

Research 17, no.4(1991): 492-507.

Hoegg, JoAndrea, and Joseph W. Alba. "Taste perception: More than meets the tongue." *Journal of Consumer Research* 33, no.4 (2007): 490-498.

Hofmann, Wilhelm, Malte Friese, and Fritz Strack. "Impulse and self-control from a dual-systems perspective." *Perspectives on Psychological Science* 4, no.2(2009): 162-176.

Hofstede, Geert. "Cultural dimensions in management and planning." *Asia Pacific Journal of Management* 1, no.2(1984): 81-99.

Hofstede, Geert. "Culture and organizations." *International Studies of Management & Organization* 10, no.4(1980): 15-41.

Hofstede, Geert. "Culture's recent consequences: Using dimension scores in theory and research." *International Journal of Cross Cultural Management* 1, no.1(2001): 11-17.

Hofstede, Geert. "Riding the waves of commerce: A test of trompenaars' 'model' of national culture differences." *International Journal of Intercultural Relations* 20, no.2(1996): 189-198.

Hofstede, Geert. "The cultural relativity of organizational practices and theories." *Journal of International Business Studies* 14, no.2 (1983): 75-89.

Hofstede, Geert. "The cultural relativity of the quality of life concept." *Academy of Management Review* 9, no.3 (1984): 389-398.

Hofstede, Geert. "What is culture? A reply to Baskerville." *Accounting, Organizations and Society* 28, no.7-8 (2003):

811-813.

Hofstede, Geert, and Michael H. Bond. "Hofstede's culture dimensions: An independent validation using Rokeach's value survey." *Journal of Cross-Cultural Psychology* 15, no.4 (1984): 417-433.

Hofstede, Geert, and Michael Minkov. "Long-versus short-term orientation: new perspectives." *Asia Pacific Business Review* 16, no.4 (2010): 493-504.

Hong, Jiewen, and Hannah H. Chang. "'I' follow my heart and 'We' rely on reasons: The impact of self-construal on reliance on feelings versus reasons in decision making." *Journal of Consumer Research* 41, no.6(2015): 1392-1411.

Hossain, Mehdi Tanzeeb. "How cognitive style influences the mental accounting system: role of analytic versus holistic thinking." *Journal of Consumer Research* 45, no.3(2018): 615-632.

Hsee, Christopher K., and Jiao Zhang. "General evaluability theory." *Perspectives on Psychological Science* 5, no.4(2010): 343-355.

Huang, Feifei, Vincent Chi Wong, and Echo Wen Wan. "The influence of product anthropomorphism on comparative judgment." *Journal of Consumer Research* 46, no.5(2020): 936-955.

Huang, Songshan Sam, and John Crotts. "Relationships between Hofstede's cultural dimensions and tourist satisfaction: A cross-country cross-sample examination." *Tourism Management* 72 (2019): 232-241.

Huang, Xun, Zhongqiang Huang, and Robert S. Wyer Jr. "The influence of social crowding on brand attachment." *Journal of*

Consumer Research 44, no.5(2018): 1068 – 1084.

Huang, Yunhui, Jiang Wu, and Wenjie Shi. "The impact of font choice on web pages: Relationship with willingness to pay and tourism motivation." *Tourism Management* 66(2018): 191 – 199.

Huang, Yunhui, Kai H. Lim, Zhijie Lin, and Shunping Han. "Large online product catalog space indicates high store price: Understanding customers' overgeneralization and illogical inference." *Information Systems Research* 30, no.3(2019): 963 – 979.

Huang, Zhongqiang Tak, and Jessica YY Kwong. "Illusion of variety: Lower readability enhances perceived variety." *International Journal of Research in Marketing* 33, no.3(2016): 674 – 687.

Huber, Joel, and John McCann. "The impact of inferential beliefs on product evaluations." *Journal of Marketing Research* 19, no.3 (1982): 324 – 333.

Hughes, Thomas G., and William E. Snell Jr. "Communal and exchange approaches to sexual relations." *Annals of Sex Research* 3, no.2(1990): 149 – 163.

Hui, C. Harry. "Measurement of individualism-collectivism." *Journal of Research in Personality* 22, no.1(1988): 17 – 36.

Hui, C. Harry, and Harry C. Triandis. "Individualism-collectivism: A study of cross-cultural researchers." *Journal of Cross-Cultural Psychology* 17, no.2(1986): 225 – 248.

Hui, C. Harry, and Marcelo J. Villareal. "Individualism-collectivism and psychological needs: Their relationships in two cultures." *Journal of Cross-Cultural Psychology* 20, no.3(1989): 310 – 323.

Hultén, Bertil. "Sensory marketing: the multi-sensory brand-experience concept." *European Business Review* 23, no.3(2011): 256–273.

Hur, Julia D., Minjung Koo, and Wilhelm Hofmann. "When temptations come alive: How anthropomorphism undermines self-control." *Journal of Consumer Research* 42, no.2(2015): 340–358.

IBM. https://www-01.ibm.com/common/ssi/cgi-bin/ssialias? htmlfid=XIE12347USEN, 2014.

Ilicic, Jasmina, and Cynthia M. Webster. "Celebrity co-branding partners as irrelevant brand information in advertisements." *Journal of Business Research* 66, no.7(2013): 941–947.

Imschloss, Monika, and Christina Kuehnl. "Feel the music! Exploring the cross-modal correspondence between music and haptic perceptions of softness." *Journal of Retailing* 95, no.4 (2019): 158–169.

Irmak, Caglar, Lauren G. Block, and Gavan J. Fitzsimons. "The placebo effect in marketing: Sometimes you just have to want it to work." *Journal of Marketing Research* 42, no.4(2005): 406–409.

Jacoby, Jacob, Jerry Olson, and Rafael Haddock. "Price, brand name, and product composition characteristics as determinants of perceived quality." *Journal of Applied Psychology* 55, no.6 (1971): 570–579.

Jahn, Steffen, Hansjoerg Gaus, and Tina Kiessling. "Trust, commitment, and older women: exploring brand attachment differences in the elderly segment." *Psychology & Marketing* 29, no.6(2012): 445-457.

James, David (2005). "Guilty through association: brand association transfer to brand alliances." *Journal of Consumer Marketing* 22, no.1(2005): 14-24.

Jain, Shailendra Pratap, Charles Lindsey, Nidhi Agrawal, and Durairaj Maheswaran. "For better or for worse? Valenced comparative frames and regulatory focus." *Journal of Consumer Research* 34, no.1(2007): 57-65.

Jain, Shalini Sarin, and Joon Sung Lee. "Allegations of sexual misconduct: A view from the observation deck of power distance belief." *Journal of Business Ethics* (2020): 1-20.

Jain, Shalini Sarin, and Shailendra Pratap Jain. "Power distance belief and preference for transparency." *Journal of Business Research* 89(2018): 135-142.

Janiszewski, Chris, and Stijn MJ Van Osselaer. "A connectionist model of brand-quality associations." *Journal of Marketing Research* 37, no.3(2000): 331-350.

Jha, Subhash, M. S. Balaji, Joann Peck, Jared Oakley, and George D. Deitz. "The effects of environmental haptic cues on consumer perceptions of retailer warmth and competence." *Journal of Retailing* 96, no.4(2020): 590-605.

Jia, He, B. Kyu Kim, and Lin Ge. "Speed Up, Size Down: How Animated Movement Speed in Product Videos Influences Size Assessment and Product Evaluation." *Journal of Marketing* 84, no.5(2020): 100-116.

Jia, Jayson S., Baba Shiv, and Sanjay Rao. "The product-agnosia effect: How more visual impressions affect product distinctiveness in comparative choice." *Journal of Consumer Research* 41, no.2 (2014): 342 – 360.

Jia, Jayson S., Uzma Khan, and Ab Litt. "The effect of self-control on the construction of risk perceptions." *Management Science* 61, no.9(2015): 2259 – 2280.

Jiang, Tonglin, Zhansheng Chen, and Constantine Sedikides. "Self-concept clarity lays the foundation for self-continuity: The restorative function of autobiographical memory." *Journal of Personality and Social Psychology* 119, no.4(2020): 945 – 959.

Jiang, Yuwei, Gerald J. Gorn, Maria Galli, and Amitava Chattopadhyay. "Does your company have the right logo? How and why circular-and angular-logo shapes influence brand attribute judgments." *Journal of Consumer Research* 42, no. 5 (2016): 709 – 726.

Jiang, Yuwei, Lingjing Zhan, and Derek D. Rucker. "Power and action orientation: Power as a catalyst for consumer switching behavior." *Journal of Consumer Research* 41, no.1(2014): 183 – 196.

Jiang, Yuwei, Rashmi Adaval, Yael Steinhart, and Robert S. Wyer Jr. "Imagining yourself in the scene: The interactive effects of goal-driven self-imagery and visual perspectives on consumer behavior." *Journal of Consumer Research* 41, no.2(2014): 418 – 435.

John, Deborah Roedder, Barbara Loken, and Christopher Joiner. "The negative impact of extensions: can flagship products be diluted?." *Journal of Marketing* 62, no.1(1998): 19 – 32.

Johnson, Jennifer Wiggins, and Pamela E. Grimm. "Communal and exchange relationship perceptions as separate constructs and their role in motivations to donate." *Journal of Consumer Psychology* 20, no.3(2010): 282 – 294.

Johnson, Palmer O., and Jerzy Neyman. "Tests of certain linear hypotheses and their application to some educational problems." *Statistical Research Memoirs*, 1, (1936): 57 – 93.

Jones, Lynette. "Perception of Force and Weight: Theory and Research." *Psychological Bulletin* 100, no.1(1986): 29 – 42.

Jordan, Jennifer, Niro Sivanathan, and Adam D. Galinsky. "Something to lose and nothing to gain: The role of stress in the interactive effect of power and stability on risk taking." *Administrative Science Quarterly* 56, no.4(2011): 530 – 558.

Joshi, Priyanka D., and Nathanael J. Fast. "Power and reduced temporal discounting." *Psychological Science* 24, no.4(2013): 432 – 438.

Jostmann, Nils B., Daniël Lakens, and Thomas W. Schubert. "Weight as an embodiment of importance." *Psychological Science* 20, no.9 (2009): 1169 – 1174.

Jun, Youjung, Rachel Meng, and Gita Venkataramani Johar. "Perceived social presence reduces fact-checking." *Proceedings of the National Academy of Sciences* 114, no.23(2017): 5976 – 5981.

Jung, Minah, Fausto Gonzalez, and Clayton Critcher. "The vicarious construal effect: Seeing and experiencing the world through different eyes." *Journal of Personality and Social Psychology* 118, no.4(2020): 617 – 638.

Kable, Joseph W. "Valuation, intertemporal choice, and self-control." *Neuroeconomics* (2014): 173 – 192.

Kable, Joseph W., and Paul W. Glimcher. "The neural correlates of subjective value during intertemporal choice." *Nature Neuroscience* 10, no.12(2007): 1625 – 1633.

Kacen, Jacqueline J., and Julie Anne Lee. "The influence of culture on consumer impulsive buying behavior." *Journal of Consumer Psychology* 12, no.2(2002): 163 – 176.

Kappes, Heather Barry, and Carey K. Morewedge. "Mental simulation as substitute for experience." *Social and Personality Psychology Compass* 10, no.7(2016): 405 – 420.

Kardes, Frank R. "Consumer inference: Determinants, consequences, and implications for advertising." *Advertising Exposure, Memory, and Choice* 349, no.7(1993): 163 – 191.

Kardes, Frank R. "When should consumers and managers trust their intuition?." *Journal of Consumer Psychology* 16, no.1(2006): 20 – 24.

Kardes, Frank R., Maria L. Cronley, James J. Kellaris, and Steven S. Posavac. "The role of selective information processing in price-quality inference." *Journal of Consumer Research* 31, no.2 (2004): 368 – 374.

Kardes, Frank R., Steven S. Posavac, and Maria L. Cronley. "Consumer inference: A review of processes, bases, and judgment contexts." *Journal of Consumer Psychology* 14, no.3

(2004): 230 – 256.

Kardes, Frank R., Steven S. Posavac, Maria L. Cronley, and Paul M. Herr. "Consumer inference," in *Handbook of Consumer Psychology*, ed. Curtis P. Haugtvedt, Paul M. Herr, and Frank R. Kardes, Mahwah, NJ: Erlbaum, 165 – 191, 2008.

Kay, Aaron C., and John T. Jost. "Complementary Justice: Effects of 'poor but happy' and 'poor but honest' stereotype exemplars on system justification and implicit activation of the justice motive." *Journal of Personality and Social Psychology* 85, no.5 (2003): 823 – 837.

Kees, Jeremy, Scot Burton, and Andrea Heintz Tangari. "The impact of regulatory focus, temporal orientation, and fit on consumer responses to health-related advertising." *Journal of Advertising* 39, no.1(2010): 19 – 34.

Kell, John. http://fortune.com/2015/08/19/coca-cola-investment-suju-juice/, 2015.

Keller, Kevin Lane. "Conceptualizing, measuring, and managing customer-based brand equity." *Journal of Marketing* 57, no.1 (1993): 1 – 22.

Keller, Kevin Lane. "Brand synthesis: The multidimensionality of brand knowledge." *Journal of Consumer Research* 29, no.4 (2003): 595 – 600.

Keller, Kevin Lane. "Consumer research insights on brands and branding: a JCR curation." *Journal of Consumer Research* 46, no.5(2020): 995 – 1001.

Keller, Punam A. "Regulatory focus and efficacy of health messages."

Journal of Consumer Research 33, no.1(2006): 109-114.

Kelly, E. Lowell. "Consistency of the adult personality." *American Psychologist* 10, no.11(1955): 659-681.

Kervyn, Nicolas, Susan T. Fiske, and Chris Malone. "Brands as intentional agents framework: How perceived intentions and ability can map brand perception." *Journal of Consumer Psychology* 22, no.2(2012): 166-176.

Kiesler, Donald. "The 1982 Interpersonal Circle: A taxonomy for complementarity in human transactions." *Psychological Review* 90, no.3(1983): 185-214.

Kim, Hakkyun, Akshay R. Rao, and Angela Y. Lee. "It's time to vote: The effect of matching message orientation and temporal frame on political persuasion." *Journal of Consumer Research* 35, no.6(2009): 877-889.

Kim, Hakkyun, and Deborah Roedder John. "Consumer response to brand extensions: Construal level as a moderator of the importance of perceived fit." *Journal of Consumer Psychology* 18, no.2(2008): 116-126.

Kim, Hye-Young, and Ann L. McGill. "Minions for the rich? Financial status changes how consumers see products with anthropomorphic features." *Journal of Consumer Research* 45, no.2(2018): 429-450.

Kim, Jarim, and Minjung Sung. "The value of public relations: Different impacts of communal and exchange relationships on perceptions and communicative behavior." *Journal of Public Relations research* 28, no.2(2016): 87-101.

Kim, Jeehye Christine, Brian Park, and David Dubois. "How consumers' political ideology and status-maintenance goals interact to shape their desire for luxury goods." *Journal of Marketing* 82, no.6(2018): 132–149.

Kim, Sara, and Ann L. McGill. "Gaming with Mr. Slot or gaming the slot machine? Power, anthropomorphism, and risk perception." *Journal of Consumer Research* 38, no.1(2011): 94–107.

Kim, Sara, and Aparna A. Labroo. "From inherent value to incentive value: When and why pointless effort enhances consumer preference." *Journal of Consumer Research* 38, no.4(2011): 712–742.

Kim, Sara, Rocky Peng Chen, and Ke Zhang. "Anthropomorphized helpers undermine autonomy and enjoyment in computer games." *Journal of Consumer Research* 43, no.2(2016): 282–302.

Kim, Sara, Ke Zhang, and Daeun Park. "Don't want to look dumb? The role of theories of intelligence and humanlike features in online help seeking." *Psychological Science* 29, no.2(2018): 171–180.

Kim, Tami, Kate Barasz, and Leslie K. John. "Why am I seeing this ad? The effect of ad transparency on ad effectiveness." *Journal of Consumer Research* 45, no.5(2019): 906–932.

Kim, Youngseon, and Yinlong Zhang. "The impact of power-distance belief on consumers' preference for status brands." *Journal of Global Marketing* 27, no.1(2014): 13–29.

King, Ronnel B., and Marianne Jennifer M. Gaerlan. "High self-control predicts more positive emotions, better engagement, and higher achievement in school." *European Journal of Psychology of Education* 29, no.1(2014): 81-100.

Kirmani, Amna. "The self and the brand." *Journal of Consumer Psychology* 19, no.3(2009): 271-275.

Kirsch, Irving. "Conditioning, expectancy, and the placebo effect: Comment on Stewart-Williams and Podd (2004)." *Psychological Bulletin* 130, no.2(2004): 341-343.

Kirsch, Irving. "Response expectancy and the placebo effect." *International Review of Neurobiology* 138(2018): 81-93.

Kivetz, Ran, and Itamar Simonson. "The effects of incomplete information on consumer choice." *Journal of Marketing Research* 37, no.4(2000): 427-448.

Klohnen, Eva, and Shanhong Luo. "Interpersonal attraction and personality: What is attractive-self similarity, ideal similarity, complementarity, or attachment security?." *Journal of Personality and Social Psychology* 85, no.4(2003): 709-722.

Kniazeva, Maria, and Russell W. Belk. "If this brand were a person, or anthropomorphism of brands through packaging stories." *Journal of Global Academy of Marketing* 20, no.3(2010): 231-238.

Koka, Balaji R., and John E. Prescott. "Strategic alliances as social capital: A multidimensional view." *Strategic Management Journal* 23, no.9(2002): 795-816.

Koo, Minyung, Jimmy Wong, and Sharon Shavitt. "Embodied cognition, power and culture." *Advances in Consumer Psychology* 3(2011): 381-382.

Kosslyn, Stephen M., Giorgio Ganis, and William L. Thompson. "Neural foundations of imagery." *Nature Reviews Neuroscience* 2, no.9(2001): 635–642.

Kotler, Philip H. "Marketing management: Analysis, planning, implementation, and Control," 7th edition. Englewood Cliffs, NJ: Prentice-Hall, Inc, 1991.

Krider, Robert E., Priya Raghubir, and Aradhna Krishna. "Pizzas: π or square? Psychophysical biases in area comparisons." *Marketing Science* 20, no.4(2001): 405–425.

Krishna, Aradhna. "An integrative review of sensory marketing: Engaging the senses to affect perception, judgment and behavior." *Journal of Consumer Psychology* 22, no.3(2012): 332–351.

Krishna, Aradhna, and Norbert Schwarz. "Sensory marketing, embodiment, and grounded cognition: A review and introduction." *Journal of Consumer Psychology* 24, no.2(2014): 159–168.

Krishna, Aradhna, Luca Cian, and Nilüfer Z. Aydınoğlu. "Sensory aspects of package design." *Journal of Retailing* 93, no.1(2017): 43–54.

Krishna, Aradhna, Rongrong Zhou, and Shi Zhang. "The effect of self-construal on spatial judgments." *Journal of Consumer Research* 35, no.2(2008): 337–348.

Kruglanski, Arie W., and Edward Orehek. "Partitioning the domain of social inference: Dual mode and systems models and their alternatives." *Annual Review of Psychology.* 58 (2007): 291–316.

Kruglanski, Arie W., and Donna M. Webster. "Motivated closing of the mind: 'Seizing' and 'Freezing.'" *Psychological Review* 103, no.2(1996): 263-283.

Kruschke, John K. "Toward a unified model of attention in associative learning." *Journal of Mathematical Psychology* 45, no.6(2001): 812-863.

Kupor, Daniella, and Kristin Laurin. "Probable cause: The influence of prior probabilities on forecasts and perceptions of magnitude." *Journal of Consumer Research* 46, no.5(2020): 833-852.

Kurt, Didem, J. Jeffrey Inman, and Jennifer J. Argo. "The influence of friends on consumer spending: The role of agency-communion orientation and self-monitoring." *Journal of Marketing Research* 48, no.4(2011): 741-754.

Kwak, Hyokjin, Marina Puzakova, and Joseph F. Rocereto. "Better not smile at the price: The differential role of brand anthropomorphization on perceived price fairness." *Journal of Marketing* 79, no.4(2015): 56-76.

Kwan, Canice MC, Xianchi Dai, and Robert S. Wyer Jr. "Contextual influences on message persuasion: The effect of empty space." *Journal of Consumer Research* 44, no.2(2017): 448-464.

Kwok, Cathy, Cassandra Crone, Yasmina Ardern, and Melissa M. Norberg. "Seeing human when feeling insecure and wanting closeness: A systematic review." *Personality and Individual Differences* 127(2018): 1-9.

Labroo, Aparna A., and Sara Kim. "The 'instrumentality' heuristic: Why metacognitive difficulty is desirable during goal pursuit." *Psychological Science* 20, no.1(2009): 127-134.

Lakoff, George and Mark Johnson. "The metaphorical structure of the human conceptual system." *Cognitive Science* 4 no.2 (1980), 195−208.

Lalwani, Ashok K., and Jessie J. Wang. "How do consumers' cultural backgrounds and values influence their coupon proneness? A multimethod investigation." *Journal of Consumer Research* 45, no.5(2019): 1037−1050.

Lalwani, Ashok K., and Lura Forcum. "Does a dollar get you a dollar's worth of merchandise? The impact of power distance belief on price-quality judgments." *Journal of Consumer Research* 43, no.2(2016): 317−333.

Lalwani, Ashok K., and Sharon Shavitt. "You get what you pay for? Self-construal influences price-quality judgments." *Journal of Consumer Research* 40, no.2(2013): 255−267.

Landau, Mark, Brian Meier, and Lucas Keefer. "A Metaphor-Enriched Social Cognition." *Psychological Bulletin* 136, no.6 (2010): 1045−1067.

Latour, Kathryn A., and John A. Deighton. "Learning to become a taste expert." *Journal of Consumer Research* 46, no.1(2019): 1−19.

Lee, Angela, and Jennifer Aaker. "Bringing the frame into focus: The influence of regulatory fit on processing fluency and persuasion." *Journal of Personality and Social Psychology* 86, no.2(2004): 205−218.

Lee, Hyejin, Ashok K. Lalwani, and Jessie J. Wang. "Price no object!: The impact of power distance belief on consumers' price sensitivity." *Journal of Marketing* 84, no.6(2020): 113-129.

Lee, Julie Anne. "Adapting Triandis's model of subjective culture and social behavior relations to consumer behavior." *Journal of Consumer Psychology* 9, no.2(2000): 117-126.

Lee, Spike, and Norbert Schwarz. "Bidirectionality, mediation, and moderation of metaphorical effects: The embodiment of social suspicion and fishy smells." *Journal of Personality and Social Psychology* 103, no.5(2012): 737-749.

Lee, Tae-Hee, and John Crompton. "Measuring novelty seeking in tourism." *Annals of Tourism Research* 19, no.4(1992): 732-751.

Lee, Wan-chen Jenny, Mitsuru Shimizu, Kevin M. Kniffin, and Brian Wansink. "You taste what you see: Do organic labels bias taste perceptions?." *Food Quality and Preference* 29, no.1(2013): 33-39.

Lemay, Edward, and Margaret Clark. "How the head liberates the heart: Projection of communal responsiveness guides relationship promotion." *Journal of Personality and Social Psychology* 94, no.4(2008): 647-671.

Lempert, Karolina, Eli Johnson, and Elizabeth Phelps. "Emotional arousal predicts intertemporal choice." *Emotion* 16, no.5(2016): 647-656.

Leong, Yuan Chang, Brent L. Hughes, Yiyu Wang, and Jamil Zaki. "Neurocomputational mechanisms underlying motivated seeing." *Nature Human Behaviour* 3, no.9(2019): 962-973.

Leotti, Lauren A., Sheena S. Iyengar, and Kevin N. Ochsner. "Born to choose: The origins and value of the need for control." *Trends in Cognitive Sciences* 14, no.10(2010): 457 – 463.

Lerner, Jennifer S., Ye Li, Piercarlo Valdesolo, and Karim S. Kassam. "Emotion and Decision Making." *Annual Review of Psychology* 66(2015): 799 – 823.

Lerner, Melvin J. "The belief in a just world." in *The Belief in a just World*, 9 – 30. Springer, Boston, MA, 1980.

Leuthesser, Lance, Chiranjeev Kohli, and Rajneesh Suri. "2+2=5? A framework for using co-branding to leverage a brand." *Journal of Brand Management* 11, no.1(2003): 35 – 47.

Levin, Aron M., James C. Davis, and Irwin P. Levin. "Theoretical and empirical linkages between consumers' responses to different branding strategies," in *Advances in Consumer Research*, vol.23, ed. Kim P. Corfman and John G. Lynch, Jr., Provo, UT: Association for Consumer Research, 296 – 300, 1996.

Levin, Irwin P., and Aron M. Levin. "Modeling the role of brand alliances in the assimilation of product evaluations." *Journal of Consumer Psychology* 9, no.1(2000): 43 – 52.

Levin, Irwin P., and Gary J. Gaeth. "How consumers are affected by the framing of attribute information before and after consuming the product." *Journal of Consumer Research* 15, no.3(1988): 374 – 378.

Li, Ren, Sarah Gordon, and Michele J. Gelfand. "Tightness-looseness: A new framework to understand consumer behavior." *Journal of Consumer Psychology* 27, no.3(2017): 377 – 391.

Liberman, Nira, Lorraine Idson, Christopher Camacho, and E.

Higgins. "Promotion and prevention choices between stability and change." *Journal of Personality and Social Psychology* 77, no.6 (1999): 1135 – 1145.

Lichtenstein, Donald R., and Scot Burton. "The relationship between perceived and objective price-quality." *Journal of Marketing Research* 26, no.4(1989): 429 – 443.

Lieven, Theo, Bianca Grohmann, Andreas Herrmann, Jan R. Landwehr, and Miriam van Tilburg. "The effect of brand design on brand gender perceptions and brand preference Theo Lieven, Bianca Grohmann, Andreas Herrmann, Jan R. Landwehr, Miriam van Tilburg." *European Journal of Marketing* 49, no.1/2 (2015): 146 – 169.

Lieven, Theo, Bianca Grohmann, Andreas Herrmann, Jan R. Landwehr, and Miriam Van Tilburg. "The effect of brand gender on brand equity." *Psychology & Marketing* 31, no.5 (2014): 371 – 385.

Lindquist, Jay D., and Carol Kaufman-Scarborough. "The polychronic—monochronic tendency model: PMTS scale development and validation." *Time & Society* 16, no.2 – 3(2007): 253 – 285.

Lisjak, Monika, Angela Y. Lee, and Wendi L. Gardner. "When a threat to the brand is a threat to the self: The importance of brand identification and implicit self-esteem in predicting defensiveness." *Personality and Social Psychology Bulletin* 38, no.9 (2012): 1120 – 1132.

Liu, Yuanyuan, Timothy B. Heath, and Ayse Onculer. "The future ambiguity effect: How narrow payoff ranges increase future payoff appeal." *Management Science* 66, no.8(2020): 3754 – 3770.

Löckenhoff, Corinna, Ted O'Donoghue, and David Dunning. "Age differences in temporal discounting: The role of dispositional affect and anticipated emotions." *Psychology and Aging* 26, no.2 (2011): 274 – 284.

Lockwood, Penelope, Alison L. Chasteen, and Carol Wong. "Age and regulatory focus determine preferences for health-related role models." *Psychology and Aging* 20, no.3(2005): 376 – 389.

Loewenstein, George F. "Frames of mind in intertemporal choice." *Management Science* 34, no.2(1988): 200 – 214.

Loewenstein, George, and Drazen Prelec. "Anomalies in intertemporal choice: Evidence and an interpretation." *The Quarterly Journal of Economics* 107, no.2(1992): 573 – 597.

Loewenstein, George, and Richard H. Thaler. "Anomalies: Intertemporal choice." *Journal of Economic Perspectives* 3, no.4 (1989): 181 – 193.

Loken, Barbara, and Deborah Roedder John. "Diluting brand beliefs: when do brand extensions have a negative impact?." *Journal of Marketing* 57, no.3(1993): 71 – 84.

Lotz, Sebastian, Fabian Christandl, and Detlef Fetchenhauer. "What is fair is good: Evidence of consumers' taste for fairness." *Food Quality and Preference* 30, no.2(2013): 139 – 144.

Luangrath, Andrea Webb, Joann Peck, and Anders Gustafsson. "Should I touch the customer? Rethinking interpersonal touch effects from the perspective of the touch initiator." *Journal of Consumer Research* 47, no.4(2020): 588 – 607.

Lude, Maximilian, and Reinhard Prügl. "Why the family business brand matters: Brand authenticity and the family firm trust inference." *Journal of Business Research* 89(2018): 121-134.

Lumpkin, G. Tom, and Keith H. Brigham. "Long-term orientation and intertemporal choice in family firms." *Entrepreneurship Theory and Practice* 35, no.6(2011): 1149-1169.

Lumpkin, G. Thomas, Keith H. Brigham, and Todd W. Moss. "Long-term orientation: Implications for the entrepreneurial orientation and performance of family businesses." *Entrepreneurship & Regional Development* 22, no.3-4(2010): 241-264.

Luo, Shanhong, and Eva Klohnen. "Assortative mating and marital quality in Newlyweds: A couple-centered approach." *Journal of Personality and Social Psychology* 88, no.2(2005): 304-326.

LVMH. https://www.lvmh.com/news-documents/news/viva-technology-lvmh-opens-luxury-lab/, 2016

Lynch Jr, John G., and Thomas K. Srull. "Memory and attentional factors in consumer choice: Concepts and research methods." *Journal of Consumer Research* 9, no.1(1982): 18-37.

Ma, Zhenfeng, Zhiyong Yang, and Mehdi Mourali. "Consumer adoption of new products: Independent versus interdependent self-perspectives." *Journal of Marketing* 78, no.2(2014): 101-117.

Machado, Joana César, Beatriz Fonseca, and Carla Martins. "Brand logo and brand gender: examining the effects of natural logo designs and color on brand gender perceptions and affect." *Journal of Brand Management* (2020): 1-19.

Machado, Joana César, Leonor Vacas-de-Carvalho, Salim L. Azar, Ana Raquel André, and Barbara Pires dos Santos. "Brand gender and consumer-based brand equity on Facebook: The mediating role of consumer-brand engagement and brand love." *Journal of Business Research* 96(2019): 376–385.

Machiels, Casparus JA, and Nadine Karnal. "See how tasty it is? Effects of symbolic cues on product evaluation and taste." *Food Quality and Preference* 52(2016): 195–202.

MacInnis, Deborah J., and Valerie S. Folkes. "Humanizing brands: When brands seem to be like me, part of me, and in a relationship with me." *Journal of Consumer Psychology* 27, no.3 (2017): 355–374.

Maeng, Ahreum, Robin J. Tanner, and Dilip Soman. "Conservative when crowded: Social crowding and consumer choice." *Journal of Marketing Research* 50, no.6(2013): 739–752.

Maglio, Sam, and Yaacov Trope. "Disembodiment: Abstract construal attenuates the influence of contextual bodily state in judgment." *Journal of Experimental Psychology: General* 141, no.2(2012): 211–216.

Maimaran, Michal, and Ayelet Fishbach. "If it's useful and you know it, do you eat? Preschoolers refrain from instrumental food." *Journal of Consumer Research* 41, no.3(2014): 642–655.

Makens, James. "Effect of brand preference upon consumers perceived taste of turkey meat." *Journal of Applied Psychology* 49, no.4(1965): 261–263.

Malär, Lucia, Harley Krohmer, Wayne D. Hoyer, and Bettina

Nyffenegger. "Emotional brand attachment and brand personality: The relative importance of the actual and the ideal self." *Journal of Marketing* 75, no.4(2011): 35-52.

Mandel, Naomi. "Shifting selves and decision making: The effects of self-construal priming on consumer risk-taking." *Journal of Consumer Research* 30, no.1(2003): 30-40.

Marcora, Samuele. "Perception of effort during exercise is independent of afferent feedback from skeletal muscles, heart, and lungs." *Journal of Applied Physiology* 106, no.6(2009): 2060-2062.

Markus, Hazel, Marie Crane, Stan Bernstein, and Michael Siladi. "Self-schemas and gender." *Journal of Personality and Social Psychology* 42, no.1(1982): 38-50.

Markus, Hazel Rose, and Shinobu Kitayama. "The cultural psychology of personality." *Journal of Cross-Cultural Psychology* 29, no.1(1998): 63-87.

Marketing (UK). "Premium extensions are proving to be the most promising FMCG launches, as manufacturers look to counteract retailers' price cuts." (August 28), 25, 2003.

May, Frank. "The effect of future event markers on intertemporal choice is moderated by the reliance on emotions versus reason to make decisions." *Journal of Consumer Research* 44, no.2 (2017): 313-331.

May, Frank, and Ashwani Monga. "When time has a will of its own, the powerless don't have the will to wait: Anthropomorphism of time can decrease patience." *Journal of Consumer Research* 40, no.5(2014): 924–942.

McAlister, Leigh. "A dynamic attribute satiation model of variety-seeking behavior." *Journal of Consumer Research* 9, no.2 (1982): 141–150.

McCarthy, Michael S., and Donald G. Norris. "Improving competitive position using branded ingredients." *Journal of Product and Brand Management* 8, no.4(1999): 267–285.

McClure, Samuel M., Jian Li, Damon Tomlin, Kim S. Cypert, Latané M. Montague, and P. Read Montague. "Neural correlates of behavioral preference for culturally familiar drinks." *Neuron* 44, no.2(2004): 379–387.

McCracken, Grant. "Culture and consumption: A theoretical account of the structure and movement of the cultural meaning of consumer goods." *Journal of Consumer Research* 13, no.1 (1986): 71–84.

McCracken, Grant. "Who is the celebrity endorser? Cultural foundations of the endorsement process." *Journal of Consumer Research* 16, no.3(1989): 310–321.

McElroy, Todd, and John J. Seta. "Framing effects: An analytic-holistic perspective." *Journal of Experimental Social Psychology* 39, no.6(2003): 610–617.

McSweeney, Brendan. "The essentials of scholarship: A reply to Geert Hofstede." *Human Relations* 55, no.11(2002): 1363–1372.

Mehta, Ravi, and Meng Zhu. "Creating when you have less: The impact of resource scarcity on product use creativity." *Journal of*

Consumer Research 42, no.5(2016): 767-782.

Memili, Esra, Hanqing Chevy Fang, Burcu Koc, Özlem Yildirim-Öktem, and Sevil Sonmez. "Sustainability practices of family firms: The interplay between family ownership and long-term orientation." *Journal of Sustainable Tourism* 26, no.1(2018): 9-28.

Merkin, Rebecca S. "Uncertainty avoidance and facework: A test of the Hofstede model." *International Journal of Intercultural Relations* 30, no.2(2006): 213-228.

Meyvis, Tom, and Chris Janiszewski. "When are broader brands stronger brands? An accessibility perspective on the success of brand extensions." *Journal of Consumer Research* 31, no.2 (2004): 346-357.

Meyvis, Tom, Kelly Goldsmith, and Ravi Dhar. "The importance of the context in brand extension: how pictures and comparisons shift consumers' focus from fit to quality." *Journal of Marketing Research* 49, no.2(2012): 206-217.

Michel, Aaron. http://tech.co/big-brands-partnering-with-startups-2015-11, 2015.

Miele, David B., and Daniel C. Molden. "Naive theories of intelligence and the role of processing fluency in perceived comprehension." *Journal of Experimental Psychology. General* 139, no.3(2010): 535-557.

Mikulincer, Mario, Phillip R. Shaver, and Dana Pereg. "Attachment theory and affect regulation: The dynamics, development, and cognitive consequences of attachment-related strategies."

Motivation and Emotion 27, no.2(2003): 77 – 102.

Miller, Felicia M., and Chris T. Allen. "How does celebrity meaning transfer? Investigating the process of meaning transfer with celebrity affiliates and mature brands." *Journal of Consumer Psychology* 22, no.3(2012): 443 – 452.

Miller, Joan, Hiroko Akiyama, and Shagufa Kapadia. "Cultural variation in communal versus exchange norms: Implications for social support." *Journal of Personality and Social Psychology* 113, no.1(2017): 81 – 94.

Miller, Nancy K. "Representing others: gender and the subjects of autobiography." *Differences: A Journal of Feminist Cultural Studies* 6, no.1(1994): 1 – 28.

Millington, Alison. https://www.marketingweek.com/2015/05/05/adidas-kicks-off-open-source-strategy-as-it-launches-app-with-spotify/, 2015.

Mills, Judson, and Margaret S. Clark. "Communications that should lead to perceived exploitation in communal and exchange relationships." *Journal of Social and Clinical Psychology* 4, no.2 (1986): 225 – 234.

Mills, Judson, and Margaret S. Clark. "Communal and exchange relationships." *Review of Personality and Social Psychology* 3, no.2(1982): 121 – 144.

Minkov, Michael, and Geert Hofstede. "A replication of Hofstede's uncertainty avoidance dimension across nationally representative samples from Europe." *International Journal of Cross Cultural Management* 14, no.2(2014): 161 – 171.

Mishra, Sanjay, Surendra N. Singh, Xiang Fang, and Bingqing Yin. "Impact of diversity, quality and number of brand alliance partners on the perceived quality of a new brand." *Journal of Product & Brand Management*, 26, no.2(2017): 159-176

Miyazaki, Anthony D., Dhruv Grewal, and Ronald C. Goodstein. "The effect of multiple extrinsic cues on quality perceptions: A matter of consistency." *Journal of Consumer Research* 32, no.1 (2005): 146-153.

Moffitt, Terrie E., Louise Arseneault, Daniel Belsky, Nigel Dickson, Robert J. Hancox, HonaLee Harrington, Renate Houts et al. "A gradient of childhood self-control predicts health, wealth, and public safety." *Proceedings of the national Academy of Sciences* 108, no.7(2011): 2693-2698.

Mogilner, Cassie, Jennifer L. Aaker, and Ginger L. Pennington. "Time will tell: The distant appeal of promotion and imminent appeal of prevention." *Journal of Consumer Research* 34, no.5 (2008): 670-681.

Molouki, Sarah, David J. Hardisty, and Eugene M. Caruso. "The sign effect in past and future discounting." *Psychological Science* 30, no.12(2019): 1674-1695.

Monga, Alokparna Basu, and Deborah Roedder John. "Cultural differences in brand extension evaluation: The influence of analytic versus holistic thinking." *Journal of Consumer Research* 33, no.4(2007): 529-536.

Monga, Alokparna Basu, and Deborah Roedder John. "What makes brands elastic? The influence of brand concept and styles of thinking on brand extension evaluation." *Journal of Marketing* 74, no.3(2010): 80−92.

Monga, Alokparna Basu, and Loraine Lau-Gesk. "Blending cobrand personalities: An examination of the complex self." *Journal of Marketing Research* 44, no.3(2007): 389−400.

Monga, Alokparna Basu, and Zeynep Gürhan-Canli. "The influence of mating mind-sets on brand extension evaluation." *Journal of Marketing Research* 49, no.4(2012): 581−593.

Montgomery, Guy, and Irving Kirsch. "Mechanisms of placebo pain reduction: an empirical investigation." *Psychological Science* 7, no.3(1996): 174−176.

Montgomery, Guy H., and Irving Kirsch. "Classical conditioning and the placebo effect." *Pain* 72, no.1−2(1997): 107−113.

Montgomery, Nicole, and Amanda Cowen. "How leader gender influences external audience response to organizational failures." *Journal of Personality and Social Psychology* 118, no.4(2020): 639−660.

Morewedge, Carey K., Young Eun Huh, and Joachim Vosgerau. "Thought for food: Imagined consumption reduces actual consumption." *Science* 330, no.6010(2010): 1530−1533.

Morrin, Maureen, and Srinivasan Ratneshwar. "Does it make sense to use scents to enhance brand memory?." *Journal of Marketing Research* 40, no.1(2003): 10−25.

Mosakowski, Elaine, and P. Christopher Earley. "A selective review of time assumptions in strategy research." *Academy of Management Review* 25, no.4(2000): 796−812.

Motion, Judy, Shirley Leitch, and Roderick J. Brodie. "Equity in corporate co-branding." *European Journal of Marketing* 37, no.7/8(2003): 1080-1094.

Mourey, James A., Jenny G. Olson, and Carolyn Yoon. "Products as pals: Engaging with anthropomorphic products mitigates the effects of social exclusion." *Journal of Consumer Research* 44, no.2(2017): 414-431.

Muller, Dominique, and Fabrizio Butera. "The focusing effect of self-evaluation threat in coaction and social comparison." *Journal of Personality and Social Psychology* 93, no.2(2007): 194-211.

Muraven, Mark. "Building self-control strength: Practicing self-control leads to improved self-control performance." *Journal of Experimental Social Psychology* 46, no.2(2010): 465-468.

Mussweiler, Thomas. "'Seek and ye shall find': Antecedents of assimilation and contrast in social comparison." *European Journal of Social Psychology* 31, no.5(2001): 499-509.

Mussweiler, Thomas. "Comparison Processes in Social Judgment: Mechanisms and Consequences." *Psychological Review* 110, no.3 (2003): 472-489.

Navarrete, Carlos David, and Daniel MT Fessler. "Disease avoidance and ethnocentrism: The effects of disease vulnerability and disgust sensitivity on intergroup attitudes." *Evolution and Human Behavior* 27, no.4(2006): 270-282.

Naylor, Rebecca Walker, Cait Poynor Lamberton, and David A. Norton. "Seeing ourselves in others: Reviewer ambiguity, egocentric anchoring, and persuasion." *Journal of Marketing*

Research 48, no.3(2011): 617 – 631.

Nelson, Michelle R., Frédéric F. Brunel, Magne Supphellen, and Rajesh V. Manchanda. "Effects of culture, gender, and moral obligations on responses to charity advertising across masculine and feminine cultures." *Journal of Consumer Psychology* 16, no.1 (2006): 45 – 56.

Neuberg, Steven L., Douglas T. Kenrick, and Mark Schaller. "Human threat management systems: Self-protection and disease avoidance." *Neuroscience & Biobehavioral Reviews* 35, no. 4 (2011): 1042 – 1051.

Neuberg, Steven L., and Jason Newsom. "Personal need for structure: Individual differences in the desire for simple structure." *Journal of Personality and Social Psychology* 65, no.1 (1993): 113 – 131.

Nevins, Jennifer L., William O. Bearden, and Bruce Money. "Ethical values and long-term orientation." *Journal of Business Ethics* 71, no.3(2007): 261 – 274.

Newman, George E., Margarita Gorlin, and Ravi Dhar. "When going green backfires: How firm intentions shape the evaluation of socially beneficial product enhancements." *Journal of Consumer Research* 41, no.3(2014): 823 – 839.

Niedenthal, Paula M. "Embodying emotion." *Science* 316, no.5827 (2007): 1002 – 1005.

Niedenthal, Paula, Piotr Winkielman, Laurie Mondillon, and Nicolas Vermeulen. "Embodiment of emotion concepts." *Journal of Personality and Social Psychology* 96, no. 6 (2009): 1120 –

1136.

Nisbett, Richard E., Kaiping Peng, Incheol Choi, and Ara Norenzayan. "Culture and systems of thought: Holistic versus analytic cognition." *Psychological Review* 108, no. 2 (2001): 291–310.

Nisbett, Richard E., and Timothy Wilson. "Telling more than we can know: Verbal reports on mental processes." *Psychological Review* 84, no.3(1977): 231–259.

Nisbett, Richard E., and Yuri Miyamoto. "The influence of culture: holistic versus analytic perception." *Trends in Cognitive Sciences* 9, no.10(2005): 467–473.

Nowicki Jr, Stephen, and Marshall P. Duke. "A locus of control scale for noncollege as well as college adults." *Journal of Personality Assessment* 38, no.2(1974): 136–137.

Obeidat, Bader Yousef, Rifat O. Shannak, R. E. M. D. T. Masa'deh, and I. Al-Jarrah. "Toward better understanding for Arabian culture: Implications based on Hofstede's cultural model." *European Journal of Social Sciences* 28, no.4(2012): 512–522.

Oeppen, Jemma, and Ahmad Jamal. "Collaborating for success: managerial perspectives on co-branding strategies in the fashion industry." *Journal of Marketing Management* 30, no. 9–10 (2014): 925–948.

Onozaka, Yuko, and Dawn Thilmany McFadden. "Does local labeling complement or compete with other sustainable labels? A conjoint analysis of direct and joint values for fresh produce claim." *American Journal of Agricultural Economics* 93, no. 3 (2011):

693-706.

Ordabayeva, Nailya, and Daniel Fernandes. "Better or different? How political ideology shapes preferences for differentiation in the social hierarchy." *Journal of Consumer Research* 45, no. 2 (2018): 227-250.

Oyserman, Daphna. "High power, low power, and equality: Culture beyond individualism and collectivism." *Journal of Consumer Psychology* 16, no.4(2006): 352-356.

Oyserman, Daphna, Heather Coon, and Markus Kemmelmeier. "Rethinking individualism and collectivism: Evaluation of theoretical assumptions and meta-analyses." *Psychological Bulletin* 128, no.1(2002): 3-72.

Oyserman, Daphna, and Spike Lee. "Does culture influence what and how we think? Effects of priming individualism and collectivism." *Psychological Bulletin* 134, no.2(2008): 311-342.

Paasovaara, Rami, Harri T. Luomala, Terhi Pohjanheimo, and Mari Sandell. "Understanding consumers' brand-induced food taste perception: A comparison of 'brand familiarity' and 'consumer value-brand symbolism (in) congruity' accounts." *Journal of Consumer Behaviour* 11, no.1(2012): 11-20.

Paharia, Neeru, and Vanitha Swaminathan. "Who is wary of user design? The role of power-distance beliefs in preference for user-designed products." *Journal of Marketing* 83, no.3(2019): 91-107.

Pang, Jun, and Ying Ding. "Blending package shape with the gender dimension of brand image: How and why?." *International*

Journal of Research in Marketing 38, no.1(2021): 216-231.

Park, C. Whan, Andreas B. Eisingerich, and Jason Whan Park. "Attachment-aversion (AA) model of customer-brand relationships." *Journal of Consumer Psychology* 23, no. 2 (2013): 229-248.

Park, C. Whan, Deborah J. MacInnis, Joseph Priester, Andreas B. Eisingerich, and Dawn Iacobucci. "Brand attachment and brand attitude strength: Conceptual and empirical differentiation of two critical brand equity drivers." *Journal of Marketing* 74, no. 6 (2010): 1-17.

Park, C. Whan, Sung Youl Jun, and Allan D. Shocker. "Composite branding alliances: An investigation of extension and feedback effects." *Journal of Marketing Research* 33, no.4(1996): 453-466.

Parker, Philip M., and Nader T. Tavassoli. "Homeostasis and consumer behavior across cultures." *International Journal of Research in Marketing* 17, no.1(2000): 33-53.

Pecher, Diane, René Zeelenberg, and Lawrence W. Barsalou. "Verifying different-modality properties for concepts produces switching costs." *Psychological Science* 14, no.2(2003): 119-124.

Peck, Joann, and Jennifer Wiggins. "It just feels good: Customers' affective response to touch and its influence on persuasion." *Journal of Marketing* 70, no.4(2006): 56-69.

Peck, Joann, and Terry L. Childers. "Individual differences in haptic information processing: The 'need for touch' scale." *Journal of*

Consumer Research 30, no.3(2003): 430 – 442.

Peck, Joann, and Terry L. Childers. "To have and to hold: The influence of haptic information on product judgments." *Journal of Marketing* 67, no.2(2003): 35 – 48.

Pelto, Pertii J. "The differences between 'tight' and 'loose' societies." *Trans-Action* 5, no.5(1968): 37 – 40.

Peng, Ling, Geng Cui, Yuho Chung, and Wanyi Zheng. "The faces of success: Beauty and ugliness premiums in e-commerce platforms." *Journal of Marketing* 84, no.4(2020): 67 – 85.

Pereira, Antonio, Sidarta Ribeiro, Michael Wiest, Leonardo C. Moore, Janaina Pantoja, Shih-Chieh Lin, and Miguel AL Nicolelis. "Processing of tactile information by the hippocampus." *Proceedings of the National Academy of Sciences* 104, no.46 (2007): 18286 – 18291.

Perfecto, Hannah, Kristin Donnelly, and Clayton R. Critcher. "Volume estimation through mental simulation." *Psychological Science* 30, no.1(2019): 80 – 91.

Petit, Olivia, Carlos Velasco, and Charles Spence. "Digital sensory marketing: Integrating new technologies into multisensory online experience." *Journal of Interactive Marketing* 45 (2019): 42 – 61.

Petrova, Petia K., and Robert B. Cialdini. "Fluency of consumption imagery and the backfire effects of imagery appeals." *Journal of Consumer Research* 32, no.3(2005): 442 – 452.

Phillips, Jean, and Stanley Gully. "Role of goal orientation, ability, need for achievement, and locus of control in the self-efficacy and goal-setting process." *Journal of Applied Psychology* 82, no.5 (1997): 792-802.

Pieters, Rik. "Bidirectional dynamics of materialism and loneliness: Not just a vicious cycle." *Journal of Consumer Research* 40, no.4 (2013): 615-631.

Plassmann, Hilke, John O'doherty, Baba Shiv, and Antonio Rangel. "Marketing actions can modulate neural representations of experienced pleasantness." *Proceedings of the National Academy of Sciences* 105, no.3(2008): 1050-1054.

Pocheptsova, Anastasiya, Aparna A. Labroo, and Ravi Dhar. "Making products feel special: When metacognitive difficulty enhances evaluation." *Journal of Marketing Research* 47, no.6 (2010): 1059-1069.

Poelman, Astrid, Jos Mojet, David Lyon, and Samuel Sefa-Dedeh. "The influence of information about organic production and fair trade on preferences for and perception of pineapple." *Food Quality and Preference* 19, no.1(2008): 114-121.

Pornpitakpan, Chanthika. "The persuasiveness of source credibility: A critical review of five decades' evidence." *Journal of Applied Social Psychology* 34, no.2(2004): 243-281.

Pozin, Ilya. https://www.inc.com/ilya-pozin/3-startup-partnerships-you-need-to-know-about.html, 2015.

Preacher, Kristopher J., and Andrew F. Hayes. "Asymptotic and resampling strategies for assessing and comparing indirect effects in multiple mediator models." *Behavior Research Methods* 40, no.3(2008): 879-891.

Prelec, Drazen, and George Loewenstein. "The red and the black: Mental accounting of savings and debt." *Marketing Science* 17, no.1(1998): 4–28.

Prentice, Deborah A., and Dale T. Miller. "Psychological essentialism of human categories." *Current Directions in Psychological Science* 16, no.4(2007): 202–206.

Price, Donald, Damien Finniss, and Fabrizio Benedetti. "A comprehensive review of the placebo effect: Recent advances and current thought." *Annual Review of Psychology* 59(2008): 565–590.

Price, Donald D., Leonard S. Milling, Irving Kirsch, Ann Duff, Guy H. Montgomery, and Sarah S. Nicholls. "An analysis of factors that contribute to the magnitude of placebo analgesia in an experimental paradigm." *Pain* 83, no.2(1999): 147–156.

Priester, Joseph R., and Richard E. Petty. "The influence of spokesperson trustworthiness on message elaboration, attitude strength, and advertising effectiveness." *Journal of Consumer Psychology* 13, no.4(2003): 408–421.

Proffitt, Dennis R., Jeanine Stefanucci, Tom Banton, and William Epstein. "The role of effort in perceiving distance." *Psychological Science* 14, no.2(2003): 106–112.

Proksch, Michael, Ulrich R. Orth, and T. Bettina Cornwell. "Competence enhancement and anticipated emotion as motivational drivers of brand attachment." *Psychology & Marketing* 32, no.9 (2015): 934–949.

Pryor, Kristin. http://tech.co/startup-failure-rates-industry–2016–

01, 2016.

Pullig, Chris, Carolyn J. Simmons, and Richard G. Netemeyer. "Brand dilution: when do new brands hurt existing brands?." *Journal of Marketing* 70, no.2(2006): 52-66.

Pulvermüller, Friedemann. "Brain mechanisms linking language and action." *Nature Reviews Neuroscience* 6, no.7(2005): 576-582.

Pulvermüller, Friedemann, Yury Shtyrov, and Risto Ilmoniemi. "Brain signatures of meaning access in action word recognition." *Journal of Cognitive Neuroscience* 17, no.6(2005): 884-892.

Puzakova, Marina, and Hyokjin Kwak. "Should anthropomorphized brands engage customers? The impact of social crowding on brand preferences." *Journal of Marketing* 81, no.6(2017): 99-115.

Puzakova, Marina, Hyokjin Kwak, and Charles R. Taylor. "The role of geography of self in 'filling in' brand personality traits: Consumer inference of unobservable attributes." *Journal of Advertising* 42, no.1(2013): 16-29.

Puzakova, Marina, Hyokjin Kwak, and Joseph F. Rocereto. "When humanizing brands goes wrong: The detrimental effect of brand anthropomorphization amid product wrongdoings." *Journal of Marketing* 77, no.3(2013): 81-100.

Puzakova, Marina, and Pankaj Aggarwal. "Brands as rivals: Consumer pursuit of distinctiveness and the role of brand anthropomorphism." *Journal of Consumer Research* 45, no.4(2018): 869-888.

Raaijmakers, J. G. W., and R. M. Shiffrin. "Search of associative memory." *Psychological Review* 88(1981): 93-134.

Raghubir, Priya, and Aradhna Krishna. "As the crow flies: Bias in consumers' map-based distance judgments." *Journal of Consumer Research* 23, no.1(1996): 26 – 39.

Raghubir, Priya, and Aradhna Krishna. "Vital dimensions in volume perception: Can the eye fool the stomach?." *Journal of Marketing Research* 36, no.3(1999): 313 – 326.

Raghunathan, Rajagopal, Rebecca Walker Naylor, and Wayne D. Hoyer. "The unhealthy = tasty intuition and its effects on taste inferences, enjoyment, and choice of food products." *Journal of Marketing* 70, no.4(2006): 170 – 184.

Rahnev, Dobromir, Brian Maniscalco, Tashina Graves, Elliott Huang, Floris P. De Lange, and Hakwan Lau. "Attention induces conservative subjective biases in visual perception." *Nature Neuroscience* 14, no.12(2011): 1513 – 1515.

Rangel, Ulrike, and Johannes Keller. "Essentialism goes social: Belief in social determinism as a component of psychological essentialism." *Journal of Personality and Social Psychology* 100, no.6(2011): 1056 – 1078.

Rao, Akshay R., Lu Qu, and Robert W. Ruekert. "Signaling unobservable product quality through a brand ally." *Journal of Marketing Research* 36, no.2(1999): 258 – 268.

Ratcliff, Roger, and Gail McKoon. "A retrieval theory of priming in memory." *Psychological Review* 95, no.3(1988): 385 – 408.

Redden, Joseph P. "Reducing satiation: The role of categorization level." *Journal of Consumer Research* 34, no.5(2008): 624 – 634.

Redden, Joseph P., Kelly L. Haws, and Jinjie Chen. "The ability to choose can increase satiation." *Journal of Personality and Social Psychology* 112, no.2(2017): 186-200.

Read, Daniel, Christopher Y. Olivola, and David J. Hardisty. "The value of nothing: Asymmetric attention to opportunity costs drives intertemporal decision making." *Management Science* 63, no.12 (2017): 4277-4297.

Read, Daniel, Shane Frederick, Burcu Orsel, and Juwaria Rahman. "Four score and seven years from now: The date/delay effect in temporal discounting." *Management Science* 51, no.9 (2005): 1326-1335.

Reeck, Crystal, Daniel Wall, and Eric J. Johnson. "Search predicts and changes patience in intertemporal choice." *Proceedings of the National Academy of Sciences* 114, no.45 (2017): 11890-11895.

Reed II, Americus. "Activating the self-importance of consumer selves: Exploring identity salience effects on judgments." *Journal of Consumer Research* 31, no.2(2004): 286-295.

Reed II, Americus, Mark R. Forehand, Stefano Puntoni, and Luk Warlop. "Identity-based consumer behavior." *International Journal of Research in Marketing* 29, no.4(2012): 310-321.

Reich, Taly, Daniella M. Kupor, and Rosanna K. Smith. "Made by mistake: When mistakes increase product preference." *Journal of Consumer Research* 44, no.5(2018): 1085-1103.

Reimann, Martin, Ulrich F. Lünemann, and Richard B. Chase. "Uncertainty avoidance as a moderator of the relationship between perceived service quality and customer satisfaction." *Journal of*

Service Research 11, no.1(2008): 63–73.

Rescorla, Robert. "Pavlovian conditioning: It's not what you Think it is." *American Psychologist* 43, no.3(1988): 151–160.

Rifkin, Jacqueline R., and Jordan Etkin. "Variety in self-expression undermines self-continuity." *Journal of Consumer Research* 46, no.4(2019): 725–749.

Righetti, Francesca, and Catrin Finkenauer. "If you are able to control yourself, I will trust you: The role of perceived self-control in interpersonal trust." *Journal of Personality and Social Psychology* 100, no.5(2011): 874–886.

Rindfleisch, Aric, James E. Burroughs, and Nancy Wong. "The safety of objects: Materialism, existential insecurity, and brand connection." *Journal of Consumer Research* 36, no.1(2009): 1–16.

Ringler, Christine, Nancy J. Sirianni, Anders Gustafsson, and Joann Peck. "Look but don't touch! The impact of active interpersonal haptic blocking on compensatory touch and purchase behavior." *Journal of Retailing* 95, no.4(2019): 186–203.

Robertson, Christopher J., and James J. Hoffman. "How different are we? An investigation of Confucian values in the United States." *Journal of Managerial Issues* (2000): 34–47.

Roberts, Daniel. http://fortune.com/2015/09/03/sphero-star-wars-droid-toy/, 2015.

Roberts, George. "The nostalgia trend in marketing: Can brands enjoy the same success second time round?" http://www.thedrum.com/opinion/2016/07/15/nostalgia-trend-marketing-can-brands-enjoy-same-success-second-time-round, 2016.

Robinson, Thomas N., Dina LG Borzekowski, Donna M. Matheson, and Helena C. Kraemer. "Effects of fast food branding on young children's taste preferences." *Archives of Pediatrics & Adolescent Medicine* 161, no.8(2007): 792-797.

Roe, Anna Wang, Haidong D. Lu, and Chou P. Hung. "Cortical processing of a brightness illusion." *Proceedings of the National Academy of Sciences* 102, no.10(2005): 3869-3874.

Romero, Marisabel, Adam W. Craig, and Anand Kumar. "Mapping time: How the spatial representation of time influences intertemporal choices." *Journal of Marketing Research* 56, no.4 (2019): 620-636.

Rosenberg, S., C. Nelson, and P. S. Vivekananthan. "A multidimensional approach to the structure of personality impressions." *Journal of Personality and Social Psychology* 9, no.4(1968): 283-294.

Ross Jr, William T., and Elizabeth H. Creyer. "Making inferences about missing information: The effects of existing information." *Journal of Consumer Research* 19, no.1(1992): 14-25.

Roth, Susan, and Lawrence Cohen. "Approach, avoidance, and coping with stress." *American Psychologist* 41, no.7(1986): 813-819.

Rozenkrants, Bella, S. Christian Wheeler, and Baba Shiv. "Self-expression cues in product rating distributions: When people prefer polarizing products." *Journal of Consumer Research* 44, no.4(2017): 759-777.

Rubio, Natalia, Javier Oubiña, and Nieves Villaseñor. "Brand awareness-Brand quality inference and consumer's risk perception in store brands of food products." *Food Quality and Preference* 32 (2014): 289–298.

Rucker, Derek D., and Adam D. Galinsky. "Desire to acquire: Powerlessness and compensatory consumption." *Journal of Consumer Research* 35, no.2(2008): 257–267.

Rucker, Derek D., Adam D. Galinsky, and David Dubois. "Power and consumer behavior: How power shapes who and what consumers value." *Journal of Consumer Psychology* 22, no. 3 (2012): 352–368.

Rucker, Derek D., and Adam D. Galinsky. "The agentic-communal model of power: Implications for consumer behavior." *Current Opinion in Psychology* 10(2016): 1–5.

Rucker, Derek D., Miao Hu, and Adam D. Galinsky. "The experience versus the expectations of power: A recipe for altering the effects of power on behavior." *Journal of Consumer Research* 41, no.2(2014): 381–396.

Ryu, Sungmin, Jeong Eun Park, and Soonhong Min. "Factors of determining long-term orientation in interfirm relationships." *Journal of Business Research* 60, no.12(2007): 1225–1233.

Salerno, Anthony, and Julio Sevilla. "Scarce foods are perceived as having more calories." *Journal of Consumer Psychology* 29, no.3 (2019): 472–482.

Samper, Adriana, and Janet A. Schwartz. "Price inferences for sacred versus secular goods: changing the price of medicine influences perceived health risk." *Journal of Consumer Research* 39, no.6

(2013): 1343 – 1358.

Sarter, Martin, Ben Givens, and John P. Bruno. "The cognitive neuroscience of sustained attention: Where top-down meets bottom-up." *Brain Research Reviews* 35, no.2(2001): 146 – 160.

Schaller, Mark, Carrie Boyd, Jonathan Yohannes, and Meredith O'Brien. "The prejudiced personality revisited: Personal need for structure and formation of erroneous group stereotypes." *Journal of Personality and Social Psychology* 68, no.3(1995): 544 – 555.

Schimmelpfennig, Christian, and James B. Hunt. "Fifty years of celebrity endorser research: Support for a comprehensive celebrity endorsement strategy framework." *Psychology & Marketing* 37, no.3(2020): 488 – 505.

Schneider, David. "Implicit personality theory: A review." *Psychological Bulletin* 79, no.5(1973): 294 – 309.

Schneider, Iris K., Bastiaan T. Rutjens, Nils B. Jostmann, and Daniël Lakens. "Weighty matters: Importance literally feels heavy." *Social Psychological and Personality Science* 2, no.5 (2011): 474 – 478.

Schneider, Iris K., Michal Parzuchowski, Bogdan Wojciszke, Norbert Schwarz, and Sander L. Koole. "Weighty data: Importance information influences estimated weight of digital information storage devices." *Frontiers in Psychology* 5, no.1536(2015): 1 – 7.

Scholer, Abigail, Xi Zou, Kentaro Fujita, Steven Stroessner, and E. Higgins. "When risk seeking becomes a motivational necessity."

Journal of Personality and Social Psychology 99, no.2(2010): 215-231.

Schouten, Alexander P., Loes Janssen, and Maegan Verspaget. "Celebrity vs. influencer endorsements in advertising: the role of identification, credibility, and product-endorser fit." *International Journal of Advertising* 39, no.2(2020): 258-281.

Schuldt, Jonathon P., Dominique Muller, and Norbert Schwarz. "The 'fair trade' effect: Health halos from social ethics claims." *Social Psychological and Personality Science* 3, no.5(2012): 581-589.

Schuldt, Jonathon P., and Mary Hannahan. "When good deeds leave a bad taste. Negative inferences from ethical food claims." *Appetite* 62(2013): 76-83.

Schuldt, Jonathon P., and Norbert Schwarz. "The 'organic' path to obesity? Organic claims influence calorie judgments and exercise recommendations." *Judgment and Decision Making* 5, no.3 (2010): 144-150.

Schwarz, Norbert. "Metacognitive experiences in consumer judgment and decision making." *Journal of Consumer Psychology* 14, no.4 (2004): 332-348.

Schwarz, Norbert. "Feelings-as-information," in *Handbook of Theories of Social Psychology*, vol.1, ed. Paul A. M. Vab Lange, Arie W. Kruglanski and E. Tory Higgins, Los Angelas, CA: Sage, 289-308, 2011.

Schwarz, Norbert, and Gerald Clore. "Mood, misattribution, and judgments of well-being: Informative and directive functions of affective states." *Journal of Personality and Social Psychology* 45, no.3(1983): 513-523.

Schwarz, Norbert, and Gerald L. Clore. "Mood as information: 20 years later." *Psychological Inquiry* 14, no.3-4(2003): 296-303.

Schwartz, Shalom H. "Individualism-collectivism: Critique and proposed refinements." *Journal of Cross-Cultural Psychology* 21, no.2(1990): 139-157.

Schwartz, Shalom, and Wolfgang Bilsky. "Toward a theory of the universal content and structure of values: Extensions and cross-cultural replications." *Journal of Personality and Social Psychology* 58, no.5(1990): 878-891.

Seno, Diana, and Bryan A. Lukas. "The equity effect of product endorsement by celebrities: A conceptual framework from a co-branding perspective." *European Journal of Marketing* 41, no.1-2(2007): 121-134.

Serhal, Rania, Gaëlle Pantin-Sohier, and Joann Peck. "Packaging texture and shape as enhancers for brand positioning: The moderating role of need for touch (NFT): An abstract." in *Academy of Marketing Science Annual Conference*, 281-282. Springer, Cham, 2018.

Sevilla, Julio, Jiao Zhang, and Barbara E. Kahn. "Anticipation of future variety reduces satiation from current experiences." *Journal of Marketing Research* 53, no.6(2016): 954-968.

Sevilla, Julio, and Joseph P. Redden. "Limited availability reduces the rate of satiation." *Journal of Marketing Research* 51, no.2

(2014): 205-217.

Shane, Scott. "Uncertainty avoidance and the preference for innovation championing roles." *Journal of International Business Studies* 26, no.1(1995): 47-68.

Shang, Jen, Americus Reed, and Rachel Croson. "Identity congruency effects on donations." *Journal of Marketing Research* 45, no.3(2008): 351-361.

Shapiro, Stewart, and Mark T. Spence. "Factors affecting encoding, retrieval, and alignment of sensory attributes in a memory-based brand choice task." *Journal of Consumer Research* 28, no.4 (2002): 603-617.

Shavitt, Sharon, and Aaron J. Barnes. "Cross-cultural consumer psychology." *Consumer Psychology Review* 2, no.1(2019): 70-84.

Shen, Hao, and Jaideep Sengupta. "The crossmodal effect of attention on preferences: Facilitation versus impairment." *Journal of Consumer Research* 40, no.5(2014): 885-903.

Shen, Hao, Yuwei Jiang, and Rashmi Adaval. "Contrast and assimilation effects of processing fluency." *Journal of Consumer Research* 36, no.5(2010): 876-889.

Shimp, Terence A., and Thomas J. Madden "Consumer-object relations: A conceptual framework based analogously on Sternberg's triangular theory of love," in *NA-Advances in Consumer Research* vol.15, eds. Micheal J. Houston, Provo, UT: Association for Consumer Research, 163-168, 1988.

Shiv, Baba, Ziv Carmon, and Dan Ariely. "Placebo effects of

marketing actions: Consumers may get what they pay for." *Journal of Marketing Research* 42, no.4(2005): 383 – 393.

Shiv, Baba, Ziv Carmon, and Dan Ariely. "Ruminating about placebo effects of marketing actions." *Journal of Marketing Research* 42, no.4(2005): 410 – 414.

Si, Kao, and Yuwei Jiang. "Bidirectional contrast effects between taste perception and simulation: A simulation-induced adaptation mechanism." *Journal of Consumer Psychology* 27, no.1(2017): 49 – 58.

Simmons, Carolyn J., and John G. Lynch Jr. "Inference effects without inference making? Effects of missing information on discounting and use of presented information." *Journal of Consumer Research* 17, no.4(1991): 477 – 491.

Simon, Carol J., and Mary W. Sullivan. "The measurement and determinants of brand equity: A financial approach." *Marketing Science* 12, no.1(1993): 28 – 52.

Simonson, Itamar, Ziv Carmon, Ravi Dhar, Aimee Drolet, and Stephen M. Nowlis. "Consumer research: In search of identity." *Annual Review of Psychology* 52, no.1(2001): 249 – 275.

Simonin, Bernard L., and Julie A. Ruth. "Is a company known by the company it keeps? Assessing the spillover effects of brand alliances on consumer brand attitudes." *Journal of Marketing Research* 35, no.1(1998): 30 – 42.

Singelis, Theodore M. "The measurement of independent and interdependent self-construals." *Personality and Social Psychology Bulletin* 20, no.5(1994): 580 – 591.

Singelis, Theodore M., Harry C. Triandis, Dharm PS Bhawuk, and Michele J. Gelfand. "Horizontal and vertical dimensions of individualism and collectivism: A theoretical and measurement refinement." *Cross-Cultural Research* 29, no. 3 (1995): 240 – 275.

Singelis, Theodore M., Michael H. Bond, William F. Sharkey, and Chris Siu Yiu Lai. "Unpackaging culture's influence on self-esteem and embarrassability: The role of self-construals." *Journal of Cross-Cultural Psychology* 30, no.3(1999): 315 – 341.

Singelis, Theodore M., and William F. Sharkey. "Culture, self-construal, and embarrassability." *Journal of Cross-Cultural Psychology* 26, no.6(1995): 622 – 644.

Sjödin, Henrik, and Fredrik Törn. "When communication challenges brand associations: a framework for understanding consumer responses to brand image incongruity." *Journal of Consumer Behaviour: An International Research Review* 5, no.1 (2006): 32 – 42.

Smith, Aileen, and Evelyn C. Hume. "Linking culture and ethics: A comparison of accountants' ethical belief systems in the individualism/collectivism and power distance contexts." *Journal of Business Ethics* 62, no.3(2005): 209 – 220.

Smith, Daniel C., and C. Whan Park. "The effects of brand extensions on market share and advertising efficiency." *Journal of Marketing Research* 29, no.3(1992): 296 – 313.

Smith, Maureen, Elaine Wethington, and Ginny Zhan. "Self-concept clarity and preferred coping styles." *Journal of Personality* 64, no.2(1996): 407 - 434.

Smith, Pamela K., and Yaacov Trope. "You focus on the forest when you're in charge of the trees: Power priming and abstract information processing." *Journal of Personality and Social Psychology* 90, no.4(2006): 578 - 596.

Smith, Rosanna K., George E. Newman, and Ravi Dhar. "Closer to the creator: Temporal contagion explains the preference for earlier serial numbers." *Journal of Consumer Research* 42, no.5(2016): 653 - 668.

Soares, Ana Maria, Minoo Farhangmehr, and Aviv Shoham. "Hofstede's dimensions of culture in international marketing studies." *Journal of Business Research* 60, no.3(2007): 277 - 284.

Sokolova, Tatiana, and Aradhna Krishna. "Take it or leave it: How choosing versus rejecting alternatives affects information processing." *Journal of Consumer Research* 43, no.4(2016): 614 - 635.

Song, Hyunjin, and Norbert Schwarz. "If it's difficult to pronounce, it must be risky: Fluency, familiarity, and risk perception." *Psychological Science* 20, no.2(2009): 135 - 138.

Song, Xiaobing, Feifei Huang, and Xiuping Li. "The effect of embarrassment on preferences for brand conspicuousness: The roles of self-esteem and self-brand connection." *Journal of Consumer Psychology* 27, no.1(2017): 69 - 83.

Song, Xiaobing, Jihye Jung, and Yinlong Zhang. "Consumers' preference for user-designed versus designer-designed products: The moderating role of power distance belief." *Journal of*

Marketing Research 58, no.1(2021): 163-181.

Sood, Sanjay, and Kevin Lane Keller. "The effects of brand name structure on brand extension evaluations and parent brand dilution." *Journal of Marketing Research* 49, no.3(2012): 373-382.

Spassova, Gerri, and Angela Y. Lee. "Looking into the future: A match between self-view and temporal distance." *Journal of Consumer Research* 40, no.1(2013): 159-171.

Spears, Nancy, Xiaohua Lin, and John C. Mowen. "Time orientation in the United States, China, and Mexico: Measurement and insights for promotional strategy." *Journal of International Consumer Marketing* 13, no.1(2000): 57-75.

Spector, Paul E., Cary L. Cooper, and Kate Sparks. "An international study of the psychometric properties of the Hofstede Values Survey Module 1994: A comparison of individual and country/province level results." *Applied Psychology* 50, no.2 (2001): 269-281.

Spiggle, Susan, Hang T. Nguyen, and Mary Caravella. "More than fit: Brand extension authenticity." *Journal of Marketing Research* 49, no.6(2012): 967-983.

Spiller, Stephen A., Gavan J. Fitzsimons, John G. Lynch Jr, and Gary H. McClelland. "Spotlights, floodlights, and the magic number zero: Simple effects tests in moderated regression." *Journal of Marketing Research* 50, no.2(2013): 277-288.

Spiller, Stephen A., and Lena Belogolova. "On consumer beliefs about quality and taste." *Journal of Consumer Research* 43, no.6

(2017): 970-991.

Spiller, Stephen A., Nicholas Reinholtz, and Sam J. Maglio. "Judgments based on stocks and flows: Different presentations of the same data can lead to opposing inferences." *Management Science* 66, no.5(2020): 2213-2231.

Sprott, David, Sandor Czellar, and Eric Spangenberg. "The importance of a general measure of brand engagement on market behavior: Development and validation of a scale." *Journal of Marketing Research* 46, no.1(2009): 92-104.

Srivoravilai, Nopporn, T. C. Melewar, Martin J. Liu, and Natalia Yannopoulou. "Value marketing through corporate reputation: An empirical investigation of Thai hospitals." *Journal of Marketing Management* 27, no.3-4(2011): 243-268.

Srull, Thomas, and Robert Wyer. "Person memory and judgment." *Psychological Review* 96, no.1(1989): 58-83.

Steinmetz, Janina, Qian Xu, Ayelet Fishbach, and Ying Zhang. "Being observed magnifies action." *Journal of Personality and Social Psychology* 111, no.6(2016): 852-865.

Stewart-Williams, Steve, and John Podd. "The placebo effect: Dissolving the expectancy versus conditioning debate." *Psychological Bulletin* 130, no.2(2004): 324-340.

Stone, Eric R., Andrew J. Yates, and Allison S. Caruthers. "Risk taking in decision making for others versus the self." *Journal of Applied Social Psychology* 32, no.9(2002): 1797-1824.

Strack, Fritz, Leonard L. Martin, and Sabine Stepper. "Inhibiting and facilitating conditions of the human smile: A nonobtrusive test of the facial feedback hypothesis." *Journal of Personality and Social Psychology* 54, no.5(1988): 768-777.

Streicher, Mathias C., and Zachary Estes. "Multisensory interaction in product choice: Grasping a product affects choice of other seen products." *Journal of Consumer Psychology* 26, no.4 (2016): 558-565.

Streit, Matthew, Kevin Shockley, and Michael A. Riley. "Rotational inertia and multimodal heaviness perception." *Psychonomic Bulletin & Review* 14, no.5(2007): 1001-1006.

Stremersch, Stefan, and Gerard J. Tellis. "Strategic bundling of products and prices: A new synthesis for marketing." *Journal of Marketing* 66, no.1(2002): 55-72.

Strömbäck, Camilla, Thérèse Lind, Kenny Skagerlund, Daniel Västfjäll, and Gustav Tinghög. "Does self-control predict financial behavior and financial well-being?." *Journal of Behavioral and Experimental Finance* 14(2017): 30-38.

Stuppy, Anika, Nicole L. Mead, and Stijn MJ Van Osselaer. "I am, therefore I buy: Low self-esteem and the pursuit of self-verifying consumption." *Journal of Consumer Research* 46, no.5(2020): 956-973.

Su, Lei, Alokparna (Sonia) Basu Monga, and Yuwei Jiang. "How life-role transitions shape consumer responses to brand extensions." *Journal of Marketing Research* 58, no.3 (2021): 579-594.

Su, Lei, Yuwei Jiang, Zhansheng Chen, and C. Nathan DeWall. "Social exclusion and consumer switching behavior: A control restoration mechanism." *Journal of Consumer Research* 44, no.1 (2017): 99 – 117.

Suh, Eunkook. "Culture, identity consistency, and subjective well-being." *Journal of Personality and Social Psychology* 83, no.6 (2002): 1378 – 1391.

Swaminathan, Vanitha, Karen L. Page, and Zeynep Gürhan-Canli. "'My' brand or 'our' brand: The effects of brand relationship dimensions and self-construal on brand evaluations." *Journal of Consumer Research* 34, no.2(2007): 248 – 259.

Swaminathan, Vanitha, Karen M. Stilley, and Rohini Ahluwalia. "When brand personality matters: The moderating role of attachment styles." *Journal of Consumer Research* 35, no.6 (2009): 985 – 1002.

Swaminathan, Vanitha, Zeynep Gürhan-Canli, Umut Kubat, and Ceren Hayran. "How, when, and why do attribute-complementary versus attribute-similar cobrands affect brand evaluations: A concept combination perspective." *Journal of Consumer Research* 42, no.1 (2015): 45 – 58.

Tam, Kim-Pong, Sau-Lai Lee, and Melody Manchi Chao. "Saving Mr. Nature: Anthropomorphism enhances connectedness to and protectiveness toward nature." *Journal of Experimental Social Psychology* 49, no.3(2013): 514 – 521.

Tangney, June P., Roy F. Baumeister, and Angie Luzio Boone. "High self-control predicts good adjustment, less pathology, better grades, and interpersonal success." *Journal of Personality* 72, no.2(2004): 271 – 324.

Taylor, Shelley, Lien Pham, Inna Rivkin, and David Armor. "Harnessing the imagination: Mental simulation, self-regulation, and coping." *American Psychologist* 53, no.4(1998): 429-439.

Thaler, Richard H., and Hersh M. Shefrin. "An economic theory of self-control." *Journal of Political Economy* 89, no.2 (1981): 392-406.

Thompson, Debora V., and Elise Chandon Ince. "When disfluency signals competence: The effect of processing difficulty on perceptions of service agents." *Journal of Marketing Research* 50, no.2(2013): 228-240.

Thomson, Matthew, Deborah J. MacInnis, and C. Whan Park. "The ties that bind: Measuring the strength of consumers' emotional attachments to brands." *Journal of Consumer Psychology* 15, no.1 (2005): 77-91.

Tiedens, Larissa Z., and Alison R. Fragale. "Power moves: Complementarity in dominant and submissive nonverbal behavior." *Journal of Personality and Social Psychology* 84, no.3 (2003): 558-568.

Tiedens, Larissa Z., Miguel M. Unzueta, and Maia J. Young. "An unconscious desire for hierarchy? The motivated perception of dominance complementarity in task partners." *Journal of Personality and Social Psychology* 93, no.3(2007): 402-414.

Torelli, Carlos J. "Individuality or conformity? The effect of independent and interdependent self-concepts on public judgments." *Journal of Consumer Psychology* 16, no.3(2006): 240-248.

Torelli, Carlos J., and María A. Rodas. "Tightness-looseness:

Implications for consumer and branding research." *Journal of Consumer Psychology* 27, no.3(2017): 398 - 404.

Touré-Tillery, Maferima, and Ann L. McGill. "Who or what to believe: Trust and the differential persuasiveness of human and anthropomorphized messengers." *Journal of Marketing* 79, no.4 (2015): 94 - 110.

Triandis, Harry C. "Individualism-collectivism and personality." *Journal of personality* 69, no.6(2001): 907 - 924.

Triandis, Harry C. "The many dimensions of culture." *Academy of Management Perspectives* 18, no.1(2004): 88 - 93.

Triandis, Harry C. "The psychological measurement of cultural syndromes." *American Psychologist* 51, no.4(1996): 407 - 415.

Triandis, Harry. "The self and social behavior in differing cultural contexts." *Psychological Review* 96, no.3(1989): 506 - 520.

Triandis, Harry, Christopher McCusker, and C. Hui. "Multimethod probes of individualism and collectivism." *Journal of Personality and Social Psychology* 59, no.5(1990): 1006 - 1020.

Triandis, Harry C., and Eunkook M. Suh. "Cultural influences on personality." *Annual Review of Psychology* 53, no.1(2002): 133 - 160.

Triandis, Harry, and Michele Gelfand. "Converging measurement of horizontal and vertical individualism and collectivism." *Journal of Personality and Social Psychology* 74, no.1(1998): 118 - 128.

Triandis, Harry, Robert Bontempo, Marcelo Villareal, Masaaki Asai, and Nydia Lucca. "Individualism and collectivism: Cross-cultural perspectives on self-ingroup relationships." *Journal of Personality and Social Psychology* 54, no.2(1988): 323-338.

Trucco, Elisa M., Aidan GC Wright, and Craig R. Colder. "Stability and change of social goals in adolescence." *Journal of Personality* 82, no.5(2014): 379-389.

Trupin, Eric W., "Correlates of ego-level and agency-communion in stage REM dreams of 11-13 year old children." *Journal of Child Psychology and Psychiatry, and Allied Disciplines* 17, no.3(1976): 169-180.

Tsai, Shu-pei. "Utility, cultural symbolism and emotion: A comprehensive model of brand purchase value." *International Journal of Research in Marketing* 22, no.3(2005): 277-291.

Tsui, Anne S., Georges Enderle, and Kaifeng Jiang. "Income inequality in the United States: Reflections on the role of corporations." *Academy of Management Review* 43, no.1(2018): 156-168.

Tu, Lingjiang Lora, Adwait Khare, and Yinlong Zhang. "A short 8-item scale for measuring consumers' local-global identity." *International Journal of Research in Marketing* 29, no.1(2012): 35-42.

Tu, Lingjiang Lora, Jaehwan Kwon, and Huachao Gao. "Express: Heart or mind? The impact of power distance belief on the persuasiveness of cognitive versus affective appeal in education marketing messages." *Journal of Marketing Research* (2021): 00222437211002196.

Tversky, Amos, and Daniel Kahneman. "Judgment under uncertainty: Heuristics and biases." *Science* 185, no.4157(1974): 1124-

1131.

Tversky, Amos, and Daniel Kahneman. "Advances in prospect theory: Cumulative representation of uncertainty." *Journal of Risk and Uncertainty* 5, no.4(1992): 297-323.

Uleman, James S., S. Adil Saribay, and Celia M. Gonzalez. "Spontaneous inferences, implicit impressions, and implicit theories." *Annual Review Psychology*.59(2008): 329-360.

Urminsky, Oleg. "The role of psychological connectedness to the future self in decisions over time." *Current Directions in Psychological Science* 26, no.1(2017): 34-39.

Vaidyanathan, Rajiv and Aggarwal Praveen. "Strategic brand alliances: Implications of ingredient branding for national and private label brands." *The Journal of Product & Brand Management* 9, no.4(2000): 214-228.

Van der Lans, Ralf, Bram Van den Bergh, and Evelien Dieleman. "Partner selection in brand alliances: An empirical investigation of the drivers of brand fit." *Marketing Science* 33, no.4(2014): 551-566.

Van Marrewijk, Marcel. "Concepts and definitions of CSR and corporate sustainability: Between agency and communion." *Journal of Business Ethics* 44, no.2-3(2003): 95-105.

Van Osselaer, Stijn MJ, and Chris Janiszewski. "Two ways of learning brand associations." *Journal of Consumer Research* 28, no.2(2001): 202-223.

Van Rompay, Thomas JL, Marieke L. Fransen, and Bianca GD Borgelink. "Light as a feather: Effects of packaging imagery on sensory product impressions and brand evaluation." *Marketing Letters* 25, no.4(2014): 397-407.

Varadarajan, P. Rajan. "Horizontal cooperative sales promotion: a framework for classification and additional perspectives." *Journal of Marketing* 50, no.2(1986): 61-73.

Vitell, Scott J., Saviour L. Nwachukwu, and James H. Barnes. "The effects of culture on ethical decision-making: An application of Hofstede's typology." *Journal of Business Ethics* 12, no.10 (1993): 753-760.

Völckner, Franziska, and Henrik Sattler. "Drivers of brand extension success." *Journal of Marketing* 70, no.2(2006): 18-34.

Wagner, John A. "Studies of individualism-collectivism: Effects on cooperation in groups." *Academy of Management Journal* 38, no.1(1995): 152-173.

Wagner, John A., and Michael K. Moch. "Individualism-collectivism: Concept and measure." *Group & Organization Studies* 11, no.3 (1986): 280-304.

Walters, Daniel J., and Hal E. Hershfield. "Consumers make different inferences and choices when product uncertainty is attributed to forgetting rather than ignorance." *Journal of Consumer Research* 47, no.1(2020): 56-78.

Wan, Echo Wen, Jiewen Hong, and Brian Sternthal. "The effect of regulatory orientation and decision strategy on brand judgments." *Journal of Consumer Research* 35, no.6(2009): 1026-1038.

Wan, Lisa C., Michael K. Hui, and Robert S. Wyer Jr. "The role of relationship norms in responses to service failures." *Journal of*

Consumer Research 38, no.2(2011): 260-277.

Wang, Chen, Rui Juliet Zhu, and Todd C. Handy. "Experiencing haptic roughness promotes empathy." *Journal of Consumer Psychology* 26, no.3(2016): 350-362.

Wang, Cheng Lu, Noel YM Siu, and Bradley R. Barnes. "The significance of trust and renqing in the long-term orientation of Chinese business-to-business relationships." *Industrial Marketing Management* 37, no.7(2008): 819-824.

Wang, Jessie J., Carlos J. Torelli, and Ashok K. Lalwani. "The interactive effect of power distance belief and consumers' status on preference for national (vs. private-label) brands." *Journal of Business Research* 107(2020): 1-12.

Wang, Jing, and Catherine A. Cole. "The effects of age and expertise on product evaluations: Does the type of information matter?." *Management Science* 62, no.7(2016): 2039-2053.

Wang, Taiyuan, and Pratima Bansal. "Social responsibility in new ventures: profiting from a long-term orientation." *Strategic Management Journal* 33, no.10(2012): 1135-1153.

Wang, Xuehua, Xiaoyu Wang, Xiang Fang, and Qingyun Jiang. "Power distance belief and brand personality evaluations." *Journal of Business Research* 84(2018): 89-99.

Wang, Yajin, and Deborah Roedder John. "Up, up, and away: Upgrading as a response to dissimilar brand users." *Journal of Marketing Research* 56, no.1(2019): 142-157.

Wang, Yajin, and Vladas Griskevicius. "Conspicuous consumption, relationships, and rivals: Women's luxury products as signals to other women." *Journal of Consumer Research* 40, no.5(2014): 834–854.

Wang, Ze, Huifang Mao, Yexin Jessica Li, and Fan Liu. "Smile big or not? Effects of smile intensity on perceptions of warmth and competence." *Journal of Consumer Research* 43, no.5(2017): 787–805.

Wansink, Brian, and Koert Van Ittersum. "Bottoms up! The influence of elongation on pouring and consumption volume." *Journal of Consumer Research* 30, no.3(2003): 455–463.

Washburn, Judith, H., D. Till Brian, and Priluck Randi. "Co-branding: brand equity and trial effects." *Journal of Consumer Marketing* 17, no.7(2000): 591–604.

Washburn, Judith H., Brian D. Till, and Randi Priluck. "Brand alliance and customer-based brand-equity effects," *Psychology & Marketing* 21, no.7(2004): 487–508

Waytz, Adam, Carey Morewedge, Nicholas Epley, George Monteleone, Jia-Hong Gao, and John Cacioppo. "Making sense by making sentient: Effectance motivation increases anthropomorphism." *Journal of Personality and Social Psychology* 99, no.3(2010): 410–435.

Waytz, Adam, John T. Cacioppo, and Nicholas Epley. "Who sees human? The stability and importance of individual differences in anthropomorphism." *Perspectives on Psychological Science* 5, no.3(2010): 219–232.

Waytz, Adam, Nicholas Epley, and John T. Cacioppo. "Social cognition unbound: Insights into anthropomorphism and dehumanization." *Current Directions in Psychological Science* 19, no.1(2010): 58 - 62.

Weisbuch, Max, and Diane Mackie. "False fame, perceptual clarity, or persuasion? Flexible fluency attribution in spokesperson familiarity effects." *Journal of Consumer Psychology* 19, no.1 (2009): 62 - 72.

Wells, Gary L., and Richard E. Petty. "The effects of over head movements on persuasion: Compatibility and incompatibility of responses." *Basic and Applied Social Psychology* 1, no.3(1980): 219 - 230.

Wen, Tao, Tong Qin, and Raymond R. Liu. "The impact of nostalgic emotion on brand trust and brand attachment." *Asia Pacific Journal of Marketing and Logistics* 31, no.4(2019): 1118 - 1137.

West, Patricia M., and Susan M. Broniarczyk. "Integrating multiple opinions: The role of aspiration level on consumer response to critic consensus." *Journal of Consumer Research* 25, no.1 (1998): 38 - 51.

Wetzel, Christopher G., and Chester A. Insko. "The similarity-attraction relationship: Is there an ideal one?." *Journal of Experimental Social Psychology* 18, no.3(1982): 253 - 276.

White, Gregory. "Physical attractiveness and courtship progress." *Journal of Personality and Social Psychology* 39, no.4(1980): 660 - 668.

White, Katherine, and Darren W. Dahl. "Are all out-groups created equal? Consumer identity and dissociative influence." *Journal of*

Consumer Research 34, no.4(2007): 525-536.

White, Katherine, Jennifer J. Argo, and Jaideep Sengupta. "Dissociative versus associative responses to social identity threat: The role of consumer self-construal," *Journal of Consumer Research*, 39, no.4(2012): 704-719.

White, Peter A. "Property transmission: An explanatory account of the role of similarity information in causal inference." *Psychological Bulletin* 135, no.5(2009): 774-793.

Widmaier, Eric P., Hersel Raff, and Kevin T. Strang. "Vander, Sherman, and Luciano's human physiology." New York: MacGraw Hill, 2004.

Widyanti, Ari, and Dewi Regamalela. "The influence of monochronic/polychronic time orientation on temporal demand and subjective mental workload." *Timing & Time Perception* 7, no.3(2019): 243-253.

Wiesenfeld, Batia M., Jean-Nicolas Reyt, Joel Brockner, and Yaacov Trope. "Construal level theory in organizational research." *Annual Review of Organizational Psychology and Organizational Behavior* 4(2017): 367-400.

Wiggins, Jerry S. "Agency and communion as conceptual coordinates for the understanding and measurement of interpersonal behavior," in *Thinking Clearly about Psychology*, ed. William M. Grove and Dante Cicchetti, Minneapolis: University of Minnesota Press, 89-113, 1991.

Wilcox, Keith, Anne L. Roggeveen, and Dhruv Grewal. "Shall I tell you now or later? Assimilation and contrast in the evaluation of experiential products." *Journal of Consumer Research* 38, no.4 (2011): 763 - 773.

Will Crescioni, A., Joyce Ehrlinger, Jessica L. Alquist, Kyle E. Conlon, Roy F. Baumeister, Christopher Schatschneider, and Gareth R. Dutton. "High trait self-control predicts positive health behaviors and success in weight loss." *Journal of Health Psychology* 16, no.5(2011): 750 - 759.

Williamson, Gail, and Margaret S. Clark. "Providing help and desired relationship type as determinants of changes in moods and self-evaluations." *Journal of Personality and Social Psychology* 56, no.5(1989): 722 - 734.

Williamson, Gail M., Margaret S. Clark, Linda J. Pegalis, and Aileen Behan. "Affective consequences of refusing to help in communal and exchange relationships." *Personality and Social Psychology Bulletin* 22, no.1(1996): 34 - 47.

Winterheld, Heike A., and Jeffry A. Simpson. "Seeking security or growth: A regulatory focus perspective on motivations in romantic relationships." *Journal of Personality and Social Psychology* 101, no.5(2011): 935 - 954.

Winterich, Karen Page, Manish Gangwar, and Rajdeep Grewal. "When celebrities count: Power distance beliefs and celebrity endorsements." *Journal of Marketing* 82, no.3(2018): 70 - 86.

Winterich, Karen Page, and Yinlong Zhang. "Accepting inequality deters responsibility: How power distance decreases charitable behavior." *Journal of Consumer Research* 41, no.2(2014): 274 - 293.

Wojciszke, Bogdan and Andrea E. Abele. "The primacy of communion over agency and its reversals in evaluations." *European Journal of Social Psychology* 38, no.7(2008): 1139 – 1147.

Wojciszke, Bogdan, Andrea E. Abele, and Wiesław Baryla. "Two dimensions of interpersonal attitudes: Liking depends on communion, respect depends on agency." *European Journal of Social Psychology* 39, no.6(2009): 973 – 990.

Wong, Vincent Chi, Henry Fock, and Candy KY Ho. "Toward a process-transfer model of the endorser effect." *Journal of Marketing Research* 57, no.3(2020): 565 – 581.

Wu, Ruomeng, Xiaoqi Han, and Frank R. Kardes. "Special fonts: The competing roles of difficulty and uniqueness in consumer inference." *Psychology & Marketing* (2020).

Wyer Jr, Robert S. "Social comprehension and judgment: The role of situation models, narratives, and implicit theories." Psychology Press, 2004.

Wyer Jr, Robert S., and Thomas K. Srull. "Memory and cognition in its social context." Psychology Press, 2014.

Wyer Jr, Robert S., Rashmi Adaval, and Stanley J. Colcombe. "Narrative-based representations of social knowledge: Their construction and use in comprehension, memory, and judgment." in *Advances in Experimental Social Psychology*, vol.34, 131 – 197. Academic Press, 2002.

Xi, Wanyu, Han Gong, and Quansheng Wang. "How hand gestures influence the enjoyment in gamified mobile marketing."

International Journal of Human-Computer Studies 127 (2019): 169 - 180.

Xie, Wenwen, Benjamin Ho, Stephan Meier, and Xinyue Zhou. "Rank reversal aversion inhibits redistribution across societies." *Nature Human Behaviour* 1, no.8(2017): 1 - 5.

Xu, Alison Jing, and Robert S. Wyer Jr. "The effect of mind-sets on consumer decision strategies." *Journal of Consumer Research* 34, no.4(2007): 556 - 566.

Xu, Haiyue Felix, Lisa E. Bolton, and Karen Page Winterich. "How do consumers react to company moral transgressions? The role of power distance belief and empathy for victims." *Journal of Consumer Research* 48, no.1(2021): 77 - 101.

Xu, Jing, Zixi Jiang, and Ravi Dhar. "Mental representation and perceived similarity: How abstract mindset aids choice from large assortments." *Journal of Marketing Research* 50, no.4 (2013): 548 - 559.

Xu, Ping, Claudia González-Vallejo, and Benjamin T. Vincent. "Waiting in intertemporal choice tasks affects discounting and subjective time perception." *Journal of Experimental Psychology: General* 149, no.12(2020): 2289 - 2313.

Yadav, Manjit S., and Kent B. Monroe. "How buyers perceive savings in a bundle price: An examination of a bundle's transaction value." *Journal of Marketing Research* 30, no.3 (1993): 350 - 358.

Yan, Dengfeng. "Numbers are gendered: The role of numerical precision." *Journal of Consumer Research* 43, no. 2 (2016):

303-316.

Yan, Dengfeng, and Anaimalai V. Muthukrishnan. "Killing hope with good intentions: The effects of consolation prizes on preference for lottery promotions." *Journal of Marketing Research* 51, no. 2 (2014): 198-204.

Yan, Dengfeng, and Jaideep Sengupta. "Effects of construal level on the price-quality relationship." *Journal of Consumer Research* 38 (2011): 376-389.

Yan, Li, Hean Tat Keh, and Xiaoyu Wang. "Powering sustainable consumption: The roles of green consumption values and power distance belief." *Journal of Business Ethics* (2019): 1-18.

Yang, Zhiyong, Sijie Sun, Ashok K. Lalwani, and Narayan Janakiraman. "How does consumers' local or global identity influence price-perceived quality associations? The role of perceived quality variance." *Journal of Marketing* 83, no.3(2019): 145-162.

Ybarra, Oscar, Emily Chan, Hyekyung Park, Eugene Burnstein, Benoît Monin, and Christine Stanik. "Life's recurring challenges and the fundamental dimensions: An integration and its implications for cultural differences and similarities." *European Journal of Social Psychology* 38, no.7(2008): 1083-1092.

Yoo, Boonghee, Naveen Donthu, and Tomasz Lenartowicz. "Measuring Hofstede's five dimensions of cultural values at the individual level: Development and validation of CVSCALE." *Journal of International Consumer Marketing* 23, no. 3-4 (2011): 193-210.

Yoon, Eddie, and Steve Hughes. https://hbr.org/2016/02/big-companies-should-collaborate-with-startups, 2016.

Yoon, Yeosun, Gülen Sarial-Abi, and Zeynep Gürhan-Canli. "Effect of regulatory focus on selective information processing." *Journal of Consumer Research* 39, no.1(2012): 93–110.

Yorkston, Eric A., Joseph C. Nunes, and Shashi Matta. "The malleable brand: The role of implicit theories in evaluating brand extensions." *Journal of Marketing* 74, no.1(2010): 80-93.

Zaleskiewicz, Tomasz. "Beyond risk seeking and risk aversion: personality and the dual nature of economic risk taking." *European Journal of Personality* 15, no.1_suppl (2001): S105–S122.

Zane, Daniel M., Robert W. Smith, and Rebecca Walker Reczek. "The meaning of distraction: How metacognitive inferences from distraction during multitasking affect brand evaluations." *Journal of Consumer Research* 46, no.5(2020): 974–994.

Zatorre, Robert J., and Andrea R. Halpern. "Mental concerts: Musical imagery and auditory cortex." *Neuron* 47, no.1(2005): 9–12.

Zauberman, Gal, B. Kyu Kim, Selin A. Malkoc, and James R. Bettman. "Discounting time and time discounting: Subjective time perception and intertemporal preferences." *Journal of Marketing Research* 46, no.4(2009): 543–556.

Zhang, Ke, Yuansi Hou, and Gang Li. "Threat of infectious disease during an outbreak: Influence on tourists' emotional responses to disadvantaged price inequality." *Annals of Tourism Research* 84 (2020): 102993.

Zhang, Ke, Yuansi Hou, Gang Li, and Yunhui Huang. "Tourists and air pollution: How and why air pollution magnifies tourists' suspicion of service providers." *Journal of Travel Research* 59, no.4(2020): 661–673.

Zhang, Kuangjie, Monica Wadhwa, and Amitava Chattopadhyay. "The color of indulgence: How dark color influences indulgent consumption," in *NA - Advances in Consumer Research* vol.44, eds. Page Moreau and Stefano Puntoni, Duluth, MN: *Association for Consumer Research*, 274–278, 2016.

Zhang, Meng, and Xiuping Li (2012). "From physical weight to psychological significance: The contribution of semantic activations." *Journal of Consumer Research* 38, no.6(2012): 1063–1075.

Zhang, Shi, and Sanjay Sood. "'Deep' and 'surface' cues: Brand extension evaluations by children and adults." *Journal of Consumer Research* 29, no.1(2002): 129–141.

Zhang, Yinlong, and Adwait Khare. "The impact of accessible identities on the evaluation of global versus local products." *Journal of Consumer Research* 36, no.3(2009): 524–537.

Zhang, Yinlong, Karen Page Winterich, and Vikas Mittal. "Power distance belief and impulsive buying." *Journal of Marketing Research* 47, no.5(2010): 945–954.

Zhang, Yinlong, and L. J. Shrum. "The influence of self-construal on impulsive consumption." *Journal of Consumer Research* 35, no.5 (2009): 838–850.

Zheng, Frank; Ward, Adrian, and Broniarczyk, Susan, "'Sharing without reading' on social media leads to inflated subjective knowledge" (2017). DIGIT 2017, Proceedings.9.

Zheng, Xiaoying, Ernest Baskin, and Siqing Peng. "Feeling inferior, showing off: The effect of nonmaterial social comparisons on conspicuous consumption." *Journal of Business Research* 90 (2018): 196-205.

Zhong, Chen-Bo and Katie Liljenquist. "Washing away your sins: Threatened morality and physical cleansing." *Science*, 313 no.8 (2006): 1451-1452.

Zhou, Rongrong, and Michel Tuan Pham. "Promotion and prevention across mental accounts: When financial products dictate consumers& investment goals." *Journal of Consumer Research* 31, no.1(2004): 125-135.

Zhu, Meng, Darron M. Billeter, and J. Jeffrey Inman. "The double-edged sword of signaling effectiveness: When salient cues curb postpurchase consumption." *Journal of Marketing Research* 49, no.1(2012): 26-38.

Zhu, Meng, Rajesh Bagchi, and Stefan J. Hock. "The mere deadline effect: Why more time might sabotage goal pursuit." *Journal of Consumer Research* 45, no.5(2019): 1068-1084.